KRAFTWERK

From Düsseldorf to the Future (with Love)

Tim Barr

To the Comely Park Crumblies (with love)

Thanks to Jake Lingwood for his patience above and beyond the call of duty, Jenny Dempsey, Wolfgang Flür, Barbara Uhling-Stollwerck, Klaus Zaepke, Leona Barr, Chris Kempster, Rachel Sheridan, Johnny Davis, Lisa Savage, Paul Wilkinson, Debbie Greenberg, Dorian Lynskey, Ian Calder and *Aktivität*, Neil Jones, Jonathan Miller, Mike Banks, Arthur Baker, Paul Shurey, Rebecca Cresta, Kenny Kingshott, Martin James, François Kevorkian, Leah Riches, Micko Westmoreland, Paul Tysall, Margarete Hay, John Foxx, Rachael Cain, Carl Craig, Chris Raistrick, Afrika Bambaataa, James Hyman, Phil Oakey, Juan Atkins, Derek O'Sullivan, Mark Penman, Simon Edmonds, Paul Mann and Lindsey McLean, Jeff Mills, Emil Schult.

KRAFTWERK

From Düsseldorf to
the Future (with Love)

Tim Barr

EBURY
PRESS

This edition published in Great Britain in 1998

1 3 5 7 9 10 8 6 4 2

Ebury Press
Random House, 20 Vauxhall Bridge Road, London SW1V 2SA

Random House Australia Pty Limited
20 Alfred Street, Milsons Point, Sydney, New South Wales 2061, Australia

Random House New Zealand Limited
18 Poland Road, Glenfield, Auckland 10 New Zealand

Random House South Africa (Pty) Limited
Endulini, 5A Jubilee Road, Parktown 2193, South Africa

Random House UK Limited Reg. No. 954009

A CIP catalogue record for this book is available from the British Library

ISBN 0 09 186490 9

Cover design by Push
Plate Design by Nigel Davies

Front cover photograph © Retna

Typeset by SX Composing DTP, Rayleigh, Essex
Printed and bound in Great Britain by Mackay's of Chatham plc

Papers used by Ebury Press are natural, recyclable products made from wood grown in sustainable forests.

'Machine technology is a type of transformation'

Martin Heidegger

Introduction

Music is a catalyst for change. It's this premise – approached with varying degrees of idealism and cynicism – that's been at the heart of pop culture's relationship with the business of recording since the '50s. And like a barometer of the modern age's increasing scepticism, so this fundamental premise has fallen into disrepute as more and more has been revealed about the operations of the music business itself. We now have a healthy disregard for the manipulative marketing strategies and hyperbole of the record industry (though sometimes, either wittingly or unwittingly, we choose to collude with them when the right artist comes along) and it has become unfashionable to believe in pop music's unerring ability to recalibrate our view of the outside world. That's a shame because the idea that music can cause some kind of shift in our perceptions or somehow alter the way we interact with our sur-roundings does have some basis in fact.

In America during the early years of rock n' roll, pop music had a social impact that far outpaced any overt political initiatives. It became impossible to defend the tenets of segregation, for example, when both black and white audiences thrilled to performances by Little Richard or Chuck Berry despite the institutionalised racism that permeated the culture of the southern states. Within a decade the Civil Rights Movement was tearing down the racial divide's legislative buttressing and it's no accident that much of their grassroots support came from a generation that had grown up listening to radio broadcasts like Alan Freed's *The Moondog Show* or similar programmes by other pioneering DJs such as Mickey Shorr, Georgie Woods, Jack 'The Rapper' Gibson and Gene Nobels which brought black music to the attention of the white population. Soon after, a sea-change in the notion of black identity in the US was coalesced by James Brown's 'Say It Loud, I'm Black & I'm Proud' single.

Elsewhere pop music has played a subtle but equally effective role in crafting what's come to be seen as youth culture's hazily optimistic fusion of individualism, liberalism and communality. The Beatles played wild conceptual games with the format. After all what's more revolutionary than broadcasting a mantra that declares 'all you need is love' to millions of avid viewers in a world where every effort of political, social and commercial will has been directed at suggesting otherwise. The fact that The Beatles – four young working-class lads from Liverpool – enjoyed such conspicuous success in an age when expanding communication networks made it possible for a large proportion of the planet's population to tune into the phenomenon, had an irresistible impact on a wide variety of cultural notions.

The Beatles phenomenon changed the way we dressed, changed the way we perceived ourselves and – more importantly – changed the way we looked at the world around us. To see, or even hear tell of, Lennon driving his psychedelic Rolls Royce around London was to tap into the resonance of a perceptual revolution that opened up a whole new index of possibilities for everyone. How could the world ever be the same again?

After The Beatles, pop culture was no longer content to occupy its traditionally marginal position as a simple adjunct to teen recreation. Having made it on to front-pages around the globe, it had discovered its own wider significance. Lurching unsteadily onto the path which would eventually merge it with every aspect of our daily lives, pop embraced activism (from Lennon's bed-ins to the snotty roar of punk and on to the zenith of rock philanthropy with Live Aid in 1985), avant-garde artistic strategies (think here about the tradition which began with the Velvet Underground and continued with Brian Eno, Pere Ubu and countless others), existential angst (Gram Parsons, bits of The Who and almost the entire Pink Floyd catalogue with varying degrees of success), calculated weirdness (lest we forget about The Residents) and almost every other aspect of our interface with modern life.

The story of Kraftwerk began just as pop culture was beginning to engage with the wider world on equal terms. At first sight, Ralf Hütter and Florian Schneider-Esleben were unlikely recruits to pop's alternative constituency. Both were from comparatively affluent backgrounds, expensively-educated and, indeed, in the midst of formal musical training at a time when pop's enduring mythology – that of raw, untrained talent breaking free from the wrong side of the tracks – was already well-established. Instead of guitars, the pair played organ and flute and though they hung out at concerts, the type of events they preferred were usually sternly avant-garde classical recitals; famously they once claimed to have attended a concert by the radical German composer Karlheinz Stockhausen (who at the time was professor of composition at the College of Music in Cologne, just half-an-hour's drive from Hütter and Schneider-Esleben's base in Düsseldorf) while under the influence of LSD.

Despite their seeming lack of counter-cultural credentials, Hütter and Schneider (who shortened his name in the interests of brevity sometime between Kraftwerk's second LP and the release of their third, *Ralf & Florian*, in 1973) have been responsible for some of the most hugely influential pop records of the late twentieth century. Though other artists have outsold them many times over, Kraftwerk's modest output has provoked a paradigm shift in modern music that has been unequalled since The Beatles. And because pop culture is now an integral part of mainstream culture, they've had an equally significant impact on the way we interact with the world that surrounds us. Without Kraftwerk, the experience of urban youth in the '90s would be radically different. There would be no contemporary dance music as we know it; and thus none of the clubs which provide our gateway into a world of synthetic melodies and machine beats every weekend; our approach to technology (for the sake of argument, let's include motorways, trains, nuclear power, robots, space stations, calculators and computers here) would be subtly but radically reshaped and the whole fabric of futurism – both utopian and dystopian – in contemporary media would be irrevocably altered.

The fact is that – as with The Beatles – you don't have to have ever listened to a single Kraftwerk record for their music to have affected you. If you've ever danced to house, techno, electro or rap, listened to records by artists as varied as David Bowie, Simple Minds, Cabaret Voltaire, Front 242, Depeche Mode, Human League and The Blue Nile (or any one of a million others), read contemporary sci-fi, bought yourself an electronic drum kit (especially a Roland Octapad) wondered why nobody talks about the UK/US domination of pop music anymore or found yourself being able to make some kind of sense out of the babble of neon, electricity, circuit boards and future shock that make up modern life then, somehow, somewhere, Kraftwerk have become the ghost in your machine.

So how did it happen? Despite a professional career which has spanned more than three decades, less is known about Kraftwerk than any other successful group in the history of pop. Their infrequent brushes with the music press have been elliptical affairs, revealing almost nothing of the group's hermetic existence. In stark contrast to the sprawling, brutally revealing confessions offered by many other major artists (part amateur psychoanalysis, part ruthless self-romanticisation) in the name of promotion, Kraftwerk's engagements with journalists have been characterised by a polite, but purposeful, rejection of any enquiries about their private lives or individual motives. Maybe they're still the most compelling and mysterious force in modern music precisely because of this fact.

What is clear is that Kraftwerk have refined and redefined the processes of pop from a starting point that few other major artists have shared. The most obvious point is one of nationality. When Hütter and Schneider first joined forces, pop music was wholly dominated by Britain and America. The language of rock and pop was, almost without exception, English and the acts who inspired a million kids to dream themselves into pop stardom belonged to a transatlantic cabal whereby Elvis, Buddy Holly and Chuck Berry begat The Who, The Beatles and The Stones who, in turn, inspired the next generation of US bands such as The Byrds, Love and The Doors who then inspired the next wave of British acts and so on. Back then, pop music was a closed shop characterised by influences shuttling back and forward across the ocean between the UK and the US and though those influences undeniably seeped into mainland Europe, that particular traffic was all one way. The possibility that, one day, a German group would launch an album into the Top Ten on both sides of the Atlantic without translating their songs into Anglo-American may have occurred but only in the provinces of drug-dazed fantasy – it certainly wasn't a consideration that ever bubbled up in the currents of the pop music mainstream. The idea that the same group would eventually go on to reorder the course of modern music was, frankly, unthinkable.

Another obvious point is that, in a period where the mythology of pop revolved around intuitive, almost primal, creative urges, Kraftwerk were very obviously a cerebral entity. The concepts and artistic strategies that they articulated through the medium of pop were informed by a wide variety of outside factors which, in the late '60s and early '70s, would have been viewed with a great deal of suspicion by the mainstream music scene. Formally trained musicians, especially those with a comprehensive understanding of the avant-garde and a heavily theoretical approach, weren't exactly over-running the charts at the time.

More importantly, thanks to Hütter and Schneider, Kraftwerk were the first successful group to be able to challenge many of the music industry's most deep-rooted conventions. Their independent thinking has driven them to follow their own artistic instincts regardless of the consequences. It didn't ever matter if they had hits or not because, come what may, they've always been more interested in creative fulfilment and the idea of Kraftwerk not just as a group but as a total artistic concept. This has led them to step outside the relentless music business cycle that stipulates a sequence of recording/promotion/album release/tour whenever they want and take the time to experiment for as long as they please. This ability to slip in and out of the industry process at will has set them apart from almost every other pop group before or since and contributed a great deal to the mystique which surrounds them.

During the '70s, Kraftwerk's desire for an increasing level of control over their own affairs led to an even greater degree of independence from the machinery of the music business. At that time, the normal practice (as it remains today for the majority of acts signed to large record companies) was for the record company to arrange and pay for all recording sessions relating to the work of a contracted artist. Not only did this mean that the company's A&R (Artist and Repertoire) department effectively had a much greater involvement in the creative process – it was standard procedure for an A&R man to first choose the studio and then drop by at his convenience during the recording to check on progress, make suggestions and generally look after the company's interest – but it also meant that the record company retained ownership of the actual master recording.

This is a subtle point but an important one. It wasn't uncommon for a group to make the definitive recording of one of their songs only to fall out of favour with their record company and have the track shelved. The group would still be able to use the song, which would usually have been owned jointly by the writers (in this case the group themselves) and the song's publishers according to the terms of their publishing contract but, if they ever wanted to release it, the song would have to be re-recorded. For a group like Kraftwerk, whose inimitable recording techniques are as much a part of their compositions as the actual notes and melodies, this situation could have potentially disastrous consequences.

The nature of record company contracts is, naturally, that they're weighted in favour of the company as the party which is making the most significant financial investment. When push comes to shove, as it frequently does in the music business, the record company is always in the driving seat. For Hütter and Schneider, this would have been an uncomfortable situation. Sons of professional parents (a doctor and an architect respectively) and products of the more avant-garde climate of the Düsseldorf Conservatory, they were used to being in control of their own destiny.

As soon as they were in a position to renegotiate their record contract – which, in Europe, fortuitously happened to be just after the phenomenal success of the fourth Kraftwerk LP, *Autobahn* – Hütter and Schneider (with possibly a little help from their newly acquired American manager Ira Blacker) worked out what was, at that time, a revolutionary deal. Kraftwerk would effectively take over their own A&R duties and license their master recordings, together with completed sleeve artwork, to the record company (in this case EMI) for manufacturing, distribution and marketing, thereby reducing any outside interference to a minimum. Since their Kling Klang studio was, by that stage, relatively well-equipped, they were self-sufficient as far as recording was concerned (a sensible but still radical state of affairs for the time) and could therefore please themselves how and when they recorded. It was a strangely business-like strategy for a pop group during the '70s, though it was also years ahead of its time and, in a way, oddly subversive. But it left Kraftwerk free to focus on shaping their music without outside intervention.

It's this kind of original thinking that has helped deepen the mystery behind the group. Kraftwerk have achieved and sustained a level of autonomy within the music industry that's almost unparalleled. Free from the mediation of record companies and other outside agencies, the group's vision of how the music should sound and be presented has arrived into the world intact. The purity of this process and their obvious artistic leanings have led to them being described as 'the last great modernist group of the twentieth century' but they're also much more than that.

During the first two decades of their career, it was often an overlooked fact that Kraftwerk's music contains some overtly political aspects. Though the pristine surfaces and voluptuously modern production values of classic albums like *The Man Machine* and *Computer World* may be immediately seductive, they conceal themes which run deeper than the everyday pop conceits of cars and girls (though both of those subjects are certainly close to Kraftwerk's heart) in lyrics which are as minimal and elegant as Japanese *haiku*.

This, after all, was a group born out of an intellectual, sophisticated background in one of Germany's most cosmopolitan cities. They had been exposed to many of the contemporary artistic climate's most radical theories and would have had more than a nodding acquaintance with the burgeoning counter-culture movement which in Europe had adopted a much more revolutionary tendency than it's American counterpart. Hütter, Schneider and percussionist Karl Bartos were all heavily influenced by Karlheinz Stockhausen (Kraftwerk's concept of *elektronisch Volksmusik* – literally 'electronic people's music' – was borrowed and updated from Stockhausen's theories) while Emil Schult, who was behind many of the group's conceptual and artistic ideas, had been a star pupil of Germany's other major artistic figure during the post-war period, Joseph Beuys. It's hardly surprising then that Kraftwerk were willing to engage with wider theoretical issues.

According to one insider, by the time the classic Kraftwerk line-up of Hütter, Bartos, Flür and Schneider had emerged in the early '70s, the atmosphere around the group wasn't dissimilar to that which existed around the Velvet Underground and Andy Warhol's Factory. Painters, writers, performance artists, musicians and designers (Düsseldorf is the fashion capital of Germany) were all part of the loose circle which orbited the band. This was during an immensely exciting period of psychological change in Germany as the first post-war generations struggled to imprint their own identity on mainstream culture. Around Düsseldorf in particular these changes were also manifested physically – as the national economy moved into its upswing, money funnelled into the city from its surrounding industrial areas banks and financial centres, promoting an unprecedented building programme which transformed the character of the city completely between the late '60s and Germany's eventual post-reunification slump.

Artistic, political and philosophical debate was therefore a common feature of the group's daily experience. For Kraftwerk's inner circle, it was an unremarkable and perfectly normal part of their working routine to discuss fairly sophisticated concepts over dinner before heading to Kling Klang for an evening's work on their music. The fact that they moved so far ahead of other groups in terms of conceptuals, musical structures and imagery was partly the result of the creative hothouse which they found themselves at the centre of (though the mythology of the band might suggest that these circumstances were all part of a carefully calculated masterplan) and which they enjoyed being involved in.

Kraftwerk's most obvious political and, at least in terms of pop music, revolutionary act was to make a virtue out of their nationality rather than concealing it under an Anglo-American veneer as most people, specifically the music industry, might have expected. The decision had its roots in a confluence of wider factors, though it's easy to forget that, given the general psyche of post-war Germany, how brave a move it was. Any activity which could be construed in terms of nationalism in any way was still seen as profoundly disturbing and contentious in the context of what was, after all, still fairly recent history. But for Hütter and Schneider, artistically literate and well-versed in the ways of the avant-garde, this was a sign that they were heading in the right direction. Controversy and outrage have attended the birth of every major artistic development over the last century – from impressionism through Dada and surrealism to abstract expressionism – and certainly some of Kraftwerk's musical heroes at the time, Stockhausen, John Cage, Morton Feldman and Pierre Henry, had attracted their fair share of it. However, a much more fundamental reason existed for the decision not to ape the majority of European groups who adopted pseudo-Anglo-American personalities to get ahead in pop. By using their own language and celebrating their national identity, Kraftwerk were articulating the mood of Germany's post-war generation – it was time to reclaim German culture from the dark shadows of recent history and move forward.

The music journalist Simon Witter (who later became one of the first European journalists to investigate the house music phenomenon during his time as a correspondent for *i-D*) raised a related, but equally significant point, regarding the concept behind Kraftwerk's recording of 'Autobahn' in 1974. For most of those in the generation immediately before Kraftwerk's, their declaration on 'Autobahn' that 'the road is a grey ribbon' was a wildly romantic and somewhat contentious response to one of the most visible reminders of a past most would have preferred to forget. It was bad enough that the autobahn network was a product of Hitler and the Third Reich but, in a country with a strong cultural tradition of being 'at one with nature' (a tradition that was strongly apparent in the work of Der Blaue Reiter and the German Expressionist movement), the general consensus was that the roads simply perpetuated an act of vandalism on the otherwise beautiful German countryside. As usual, for Kraftwerk, recording a song that celebrated the autobahn wasn't quite as apolitical and innocuous an act as it may have seemed.

Again, the sub-text has a generational context. By appropriating the autobahn as a symbol of modern Germany and therefore as something to be praised, Kraftwerk were voicing a current of feeling that was prevalent in the younger generation pertaining not only to a willingness to forget the past but also a willingness to actively embrace the future.

It's this ability to address wider issues in a subtle and new way which has separated Kraftwerk from the more insular concerns of everyday pop. *Autobahn* was also the point when they began to outstrip – both creatively and commercially – the other German groups with whom they've been regularly associated. Though Tangerine Dream had reached the UK Top Ten with their *Phaedra* album in 1973, they lacked Kraftwerk's incisive facility for alchemising with perfect pop hooks and precision-tooled imagery and couldn't sustain their new-found mass appeal much beyond 1975's *Rubycon*. Similarly, Neu!, Düsseldorf's other major musical force ran out of steam in the same year with perhaps their best ever LP *Neu! 75* sadly just missing the upsurge of punk which might just have proved their salvation. Another group of German innovators, Hamburg's Faust, ground to a halt in 1974 when Virgin, their record company, rejected their proposed fifth LP though they had inadvertently stumbled on to something of a parallel course to Kraftwerk when they synthesized a compelling blend of electronics and Tamla Motown on their *Faust So Far* album a couple of years before.

The most significant challenge to Kraftwerk's status as Germany's most intriguing group during the '70s came from Düsseldorf's neighbouring city, Cologne. Formed in 1968, Can originally emerged from the same collision of contemporary pop and the more formal environs of the serious avant-garde that inspired Hütter and Schneider's project. The brainchild of two musicians – Holger Czukay and Irmin Schmidt – who had studied under Stockhausen, Can were the intersection of a number of disparate influences and it was the perpetual state of artistic flux at that intersection, as the band's grab-bag of influences and creative urges battled it out, which made their records so absorbing.

Czukay and Schmidt recruited guitarist Michael Karoli and jazz drummer Jaki Liebezeit, originally setting up operations under the name Inner Space. But it was with the addition of a black American artist, Malcolm Mooney that the first classic Can line-up was established. The group's music was developed out of long improvisational sessions which gave their sound a frequently anarchic twist, especially given Mooney's eccentric vocal style. On the band's exceptional debut album, 1969's *Monster Movie*, Liebezeit's metronomic drumming underpinned an astonishing hybrid of weird, freeform eclecticism and unrelenting strangeness. At the centre of it all was a curiously unsettling magic which established Can as a force to be reckoned with.

Freedom to improvise and experiment was crucial for Can and, like Kraftwerk, they were quick to set up their own studio, first in a castle outside Cologne called Schloss Norvenich and then subsequently in a disused cinema in Weilerswist. With the creative space they needed, and engineer Conny Plank at the controls, they turned out an astonishing double-album, *Tago Mago*, in 1971. With Damo Suzuki replacing Mooney (he'd returned to the States on the advice of his psychiatrist) the overall sound was tighter, though still determinedly abstract, while the album's ambitious but inspired range was reflected in a rapidly growing cult following.

The albums which followed, 1972's *Ege Bamyasi* and 1973's ground-breaking *Future Days*, expanded things even more. But sometimes the stars can shine too bright and though 1974's *Soon Over Babaluma* was a masterpiece it was their last truly great record. Having hit their creative peak, it became increasingly obvious that Can were, by now, playing on borrowed time. Too anarchic and strange to ever break into the mainstream, even if they'd wanted to, their constituency became a more-or-less static audience of musical misfits and bargain bin explorers, but the impact they had on the more experimental currents of European rock was profound.

With Can's nearest rivals Amon Düül II having reached a stage of creative exhaustion by the time of their 1973 *Live In London* set, it was clear that Kraftwerk were now moving ahead of their contemporaries on the German scene. But the commercial success of *Autobahn* had also introduced the group to a wider audience throughout Europe and the USA. For many of those who bought the album during its considerable stay in the US album charts, *Autobahn* was their first taste of modern music which had developed from a tradition that was outside the normal mainstream of pop.

This was where Kraftwerk's career began to diverge noticeably from pop's regular narrative. In small isolated pockets in cities around the world – New York, Sheffield, Geneva, Detroit, Manchester, Brussels,

London, Milan and Chicago – their bleak, industrial symphonies struck a chord with pop's disaffected constituency. Art students, outsiders, the terminally unhip (at least in terms of 1974's fashion dichotomy of denim and army surplus or no-questions-asked bovver boy chic), weirdos, romantics – anyone, basically, who imagineered themselves beyond the turgid dullness of grinding guitars, bluesy wails and what passed for rock n' roll raunch in the mid-'70s – bought into the Kraftwerk aesthetic in a big way.

For many of those in the margins and backwaters of pop, *Autobahn* was a direct challenge to the dominance of guitar-based rock in the central currents of the music scene. It was the opening salvo in a series of assaults on rock throughout the '70s. (It's perhaps no coincidence that in 1974, the year in which *Autobahn* locked itself into the US charts for no less than twenty-two weeks, the sound which would eventually launch dance music's first serious attempt on rock's pre-eminence – disco – was beginning to permeate New York's underground club scene.) It was by accident rather than by design that Kraftwerk tapped into a groundswell of disaffection for the excesses of rock (most noticeably manifested by punk) but the results were effectively the same.

In London during 1975, those who would be key players on the punk scene (and there were very few of them despite what history has made of it since) were already coming together. A contingent of art students, a few misfits and a couple of opportunists, what they had in common was a desire to reshape just a little bit of the world in their own favour. As the scene evolved along a time-line which roughly equated to the months between the formation of the legendary London SS and the group members' subsequent emergence in The Clash and Generation X, a loose manifesto was blueprinted, partly from the rhetoric of the Sex Pistols camp, but mostly just a common articulation of shared frustrations. The central themes of this manifesto were a rejection of rock's bloated establishment, a snotty, nose-thumbing irreverence towards anyone connected to it and a rigorous do-it-yourself ethic (which was inevitable really since this sweeping manifesto dismissed just about everyone else).

Punk was also about exclusion. If you liked Yes, Led Zeppelin, Deep Purple or pretty much any other act who reeked of rock's flatulent trappings, then no matter how hard you tried, you'd never really be part of the revolution and neither (not in a million years) would those groups themselves. There were a few pre-1975 acts, however, that punk did pledge allegiance to – The Stooges, MC5, The Velvet Underground, David Bowie and, significantly, Kraftwerk – who were to have a profound impact on the sounds which emerged from punk's aftermath.

Punk opened doors and broadened the horizons for a number of previously marginal musical developments. Though the first wave of punk groups were still tied to the guitar, bass, drums template of rock, those who came after expanded on the original rejection of heavy rock or seized the opportunity to do so and explored a wide range of musical avenues. Howard Devoto's first post-Buzzcocks group, Magazine, offered an interesting median point between the two developments. Clearly influenced by Kraftwerk and Neu!, the band's sound was dominated by lush keyboards with John McGeogh's heavily textural guitar parts slipping gears in and out of their proto-*motorik* rhythms.

The groups that followed, expecially those from Britain's industrial and commercial centres such as Sheffield and Liverpool, extended punk's rejection of guitar rock to a rejection of the guitar itself. In 1977 a Sheffield duo, Ian Craig Marsh and Martyn Ware, formed a group called Dead Daughters. Expanding to a four-piece they first changed their name (appropriately enough) to The Future before finally settling on The Human League. Within two years, they released their first LP which included a notice on the sleeve proudly announcing that no guitars whatsoever had been involved in the recording. It was the ultimate punk rock statement but it also demonstrated just how deeply the Kraftwerk aesthetic had hit home.

While these developments were taking place in the UK, across the Atlantic some interesting and significant twists were occurring in Kraftwerk's inexorable progress towards the future. By 1977, disco was moving into its peak period and, all of a sudden, it seemed like the entire city of New York was pulsing to a brand new beat. The most potent symbol of disco's upswing was Studio 54, an *arriviste* club in the centre of Manhattan which courted hedonism and controversy in equal measures. Opened in April 1977 by Ian Schrager and Steve Rubell, a couple of entrepreneurial promoters from upstate New York, Studio 54 quickly became notorious both for the scale of its ambition and the number of celebrities it attracted. On any given night you might find Warhol or Bianca Jagger hanging out beside the dancefloor or maybe fashion designers like Halston or Calvin Klein eyeing up the dress-to-impress crowd.

That summer, the dancefloor of Studio 54 – and those of other

Manhattan clubs such as New York, New York (where a young French DJ, François Kevorkian was in charge of the turntables), Maurice Brahms' Infinity down on Lower Broadway and Hurrah – echoed to the icy crystalline strains of Kraftwerk's 'Trans-Europe Express' which, though it didn't exactly trouble the charts, had a huge impact among the dance fraternity. The track's blend of cool European sophistication and hypnotic groove could have been purpose-built for the coke-fuelled glitterati at 'the 54' (as Chic so archly name-checked it in that most celebrated of disco hits 'Good Times') but it was also a big record in more underground clubs like The Loft where Hütter and Schneider saw for themselves how the dance scene was interpreting their music. Within a few months, it seemed like every other disco record on release had taken notes from the heavily phased hi-hat sound on 'Trans-Europe Express' while the rest were borrowing the Morse code percussion of 'Metal On Metal' as the basis for their extended breakdown sections.

But while those who danced the night away at Studio 54 found Kraftwerk fascinating, they were mostly affluent, white and not quite the type who'd be inclined to start a full-scale musical revolution on the basis of a few great records. That honour would fall to a group of black kids in the projects of New York, Chicago and Detroit.

Although its popularity on the dancefloor was undeniable, in terms of the general musical climate in 1977, *Trans-Europe Express* still sounded like it had dropped intact out of the future. It was so far in advance of anything else that its real impact took years to filter back into the scene by way of a complex nexus of block parties, backstreet clubs and bedroom studios. All through the late '70s and early '80s, new musical prototypes were being assembled from Kraftwerk's blueprint and, as those prototypes were developed, modern pop culture began to form itself out of these fragmentary sounds and ideas.

The decade which followed the release of Kraftwerk's sixth album, *The Man Machine*, in 1978 was characterised by a curious mix of halting, unfulfilled sub-genres and sequences of genuine innovation. In England, the burgeoning post-punk movement threw up bands such as ABC, Scritti Politti and A Certain Ratio who were interested in exploring the perimeters of pop but, as the mainstream gathered steam to satisfy its disconcerting desire for the ultimately hollow excesses of stadium rock, this alternative seam slowly dried up. Before that happened, however, there were some startling and perceptive glimpses of how the future might turn out.

In May 1979, the Tubeway Army single 'Are Friends Electric?' spliced Kraftwerk with Philip K. Dick and punk's sense of bitter dislocation to create the first overhelmingly synthetic Number One (neither of the other two big synth hits of this era – Jean Michel Jarre's 'Oxygene' and Space's 'Magic Fly' – had reached the top of the charts and, by this stage, Kraftwerk hadn't even breached the Top Ten). It was the beginning of an all-out assault on the charts by synth-dominated bands which culminated in Kraftwerk's first (and only) chart-topping single with 'The Model' in December, 1981.

While acts such as OMD, Soft Cell and Visage were scoring hits by versioning their own customised riffs on the Kraftwerk theme, there were some even more subtle and intriguing developments taking place. In 1980, John Foxx, the former lead singer with Ultravox!, released his first solo album. Set against an icy backdrop of sparse synthetic rhythms and abstract melodies, the songs on *Metamatic* were strange, dislocated tales of alienation, dystopian futurism and preternatural sci-fi that sometimes touched base with, say, Kraftwerk's *Radio-Activity* (Foxx had been a confirmed Kraftwerk fan ever since he'd been introduced to their music by Caroline Coon, one-time girlfriend of Jimi Hendrix and sometime manager of The Clash) but more often seemed to inhabit some weird extra-terrestrial discotheque. It was the first obvious signalling of the way in which Kraftwerk's aesthetic would be extrapolated into the future as the decade progressed.

Elsewhere in England, an embryonic synth outfit called Fashion had recruited singer/guitarist Dave Harris to replace their recently ousted vocalist. An acutely talented and perceptive songwriter, Harris's background was in the Birmingham soul and funk scene where he'd carved out a modest, if unspectacular, reputation for himself. But faced with the raw, untapped potential of his new band-mates, Harris (newly rechristened with a contraction of his Christian name and the addition of an extra consonant as the more glamorous and, significantly, Teutonic-sounding De Harriss) rose to the challenge and drilled them into an astonishing super-funk collision between Kraftwerk and Sly Stone.

On the strength of a passing encounter with the Gina X Performance single 'No GDM', Harriss then set about enlisting the talents of German producer Zeus B. Held to help realise his vision. Held was a classically-trained musician who'd given up playing the piano in order to follow a career in production. Significantly, this career switch had been inspired by the work of Conny Plank on releases by Kraftwerk and Can.

The resulting album, *Fabrique*, was a dizzyingly accomplished fusion of funk rhythms and heavily-sequenced electronics. Despite the fact that the album's singles 'Move On' and 'Street Player-Mechanik' (tracks that the group had constructed from a handful of vocoderised catch-phrases and a pulsing *motorik* groove) enjoyed considerable success in clubs, chart action didn't follow and Harriss split from the band to work with former Pink Floyd keyboard player Rick Wright on the less radical electronic soundscapes of Zee. 'He only wanted to work with me because I had a Fairlight,' complained Wright later, clearly unimpressed by the fact that Harriss had anticipated techno's marriage of black street-funk and Kraftwerk's electronic futurism by several years.

But undoubtedly Harriss was heading in the right direction. By the time 'Move On' announced his prescient mix of tough dancefloor grooves and robot funk, another synthesis was already beginning to leak from the South Bronx. Rap had announced itself late in '79 with 'Rapper's Delight' by a trio of Jersey unknowns put together by label boss Sylvia Robinson under the name The Sugarhill Gang. Though it was a watered-down take on the sound that was really being forged in the projects of New York City, the record became a huge international hit. Inspired by the success, if not the actual content of 'Rapper's Delight', other record labels and artists moved to cash-in on the upswing. However, it wasn't until 1982 that the most striking talents from the original South Bronx scene managed to score hits for themselves.

The most significant record in the early evolution of the new genre was Grandmaster Flash's breathtaking 'The Adventures Of Grandmaster Flash On The Wheels Of Steel' a wild cut n' paste epic that prefigured a huge shift in the way that future rap acts would approach the process of making music. But it was 1982's 'The Message' – a raw, synthetic update of the tradition successfully mined by the likes of James Brown, The Last Poets and Gil Scott Heron – that gave Flash his first big international hit. Harnessed to a protean electro beat and an achingly hard synthetic feel, 'The Message' became one of the cornerstones of the new sound emerging from black America.

The tough, electronic surfaces of 'The Message' were, in part, a response to a record that revolutionised the music issuing out of New York, and many other American cities, over the next few years. 'Planet

Rock' was a studio construct put together by Afrika Bambaataa, Arthur Baker and programmer John Robie. Bambaataa was an iconoclastic Bronx DJ, famed for his wildly eclectic sets while Baker was an ambitious young record producer from Boston who'd been seduced by the rap sound. Both Baker and Bambaataa were ardent Kraftwerk fans and, in an era when the idea of assembling a track from borrowed riffs was commonplace, they hatched a plan to cross-match the beat from Kraftwerk's 'Numbers' with the melody-line from 'Trans-Europe Express' to create their own record. The result was 'Planet Rock' a groundbreaking collage of dense electronic grooves and melodies that ushered in a whole new era of dance music.

At first, 'Planet Rock' was simply classified as a rap record alongside other releases emerging from the underground scene in New York. But when an obscure soul/dance outfit called Shock released a single called 'Electrophonic Funk' it provided the new genre with a name – electro. Other loosely-disguised versions of Kraftwerk's 'Trans-Europe Express' blueprint followed, such as The Egyptian Lover's 'Egypt, Egypt' or Warp 9's 'Light Years Away' though another early electro hit, Man Parrish's 'Hip Hop Be Bop', did break with this tradition by forging a slick hybrid of rhythms lifted from the *Trans-Europe Express* LP with melodies that were clearly inspired by those on *The Man Machine* album.

While electro redefined the direction that hip hop would take, other developments were taking place further west. In Chicago, kids from the projects in Cabrini Green and elsewhere were fashioning their own new sound from fragments of disco, stripped down Philly soul and Kraftwerk.

The story of house music really began in 1977 when a young New York DJ called Frankie Knuckles arrived in Chicago to help launch a new club called The Warehouse. With him he brought many of the techniques he'd learnt from working in Manhattan nightclubs; beat-mixing (splicing records together to create a continuous mix), programming (the order in which the records are played to ensure maximum impact) and a useful awareness of how a club's atmosphere and ambience could be controlled and manipulated through sound. In a city where most clubs were still soundtracked by jukeboxes, he caused a sensation.

By the time Knuckles left The Warehouse in 1983, the club's name was already being used to describe the heady fusion of electronic Euro-disco (tracks from Kraftwerk to Moroder and beyond), soul and anthemic dancefloor hits (a legacy of Knuckles' years at The Continental Baths in

New York alongside the revered Larry Levan) that were being played there. But as Knuckles set up operations at a new club, The Power Plant, on Chicago's north-side, another brilliantly-inspired DJ arrived back in town from a stay in California. Ron Hardy was a mercurial figure with a strongly self-destructive streak and a taste for tougher, moodier and weirder sounds. At The Music Box on Chicago's south-side, he'd play odd disco moments like 'Disco Circus' by Martin Circus alongside Ministry's proto-industrial workouts, 'Planet Rock' and Kraftwerk sewing them all into a dense, heavily repetitive, narcotic loop. It was a rawer, gutsier alternative to Knuckles and The Power Plant, heavily drug-influenced and, if anything, even more radical than anything that had been witnessed at The Warehouse.

The friendly, but intensely competitive, rivalry between Knuckles at The Power Plant and Hardy at The Music Box created a whole new sound as each tried to outdo the other, evolving the music at a break-neck pace. And among the baggy-panted, alternative-looking kids on the packed dancefloors in both clubs were a bunch of other wannabe DJs and record producers like Jesse Saunders, Vince Lawrence, Marshall Jefferson and Herb Jones who appropriated the sound of these clubs as a template for their own DJ sets and, eventually, the first seminal house records.

As in London during the mid-'70s – when a relatively small number of like-minded people alchemised punk out of their disaffected, anti-rock, outsider status – to be house in Chicago during the mid-'80s was also to be part of an alternative constituency. A significant percentage of the scene's prime movers were black, gay and from a predominantly working class background. Others such as Rachael Cain (who later recorded as Screamin' Rachael for the Trax label) had already experimented on the fringes of the American punk movement. House kids embraced Kraftwerk, not only because their music seemed to stem from a tradition that was outside the guitar-oriented tradition of white UK/US rock but because many of the group's most powerful themes – modernity, depersonalisation, a hovering ambivalence between nostalgia and futurism – mapped directly on to many of their own concerns.

Further across the American mid-west, in Detroit, a parallel development was taking place. The Motor City had never succumbed to disco, preferring instead the rougher, home-grown sound of George Clinton's spaced-out funk. Clinton's numerous projects – Parliament, Funkadelic, Bootsy's Rubber Band and The Brides Of Funkenstein –

provided both an inspirational rhythmic base (Clinton's bass-player, Bootsy Collins had been the key member of James Brown's band during the classic 'Get Up (I Feel Like Being A) Sex Machine'/'Get Up, Get Into It And Get Involved'/'Talkin' Loud & Sayin' Nothing' period) and a neat line in psychedelic futurism.

Many compelling analyses have already been written about black America's enduring fascination for science fiction and futurism. The basic riff in much of this writing on what's been called Afro-futurism focuses on a simple equation: since the heritage of black Americans has effectively been erased as a consequence of the events surrounding the slave trade, there is nothing for them to look back on (pre-Civil Rights history has a vastly different resonance for black Americans obviously) *ergo* they prefer to look forward. This extremely simplified version of the argument is convincingly supported by a number of manifestations, not the least of which is the continuing popularity of Gene Roddenberry's *Star Trek* series and its associated spin-offs amongst young black Americans (think here about how each episode is formulated around an armature of tension between life-forms from different planets, or even galaxies, which is always resolved by the *denouement* into at least some kind of mutual understanding or inter-species tolerance). In the writings of one of America's most compelling science fiction authors, Samuel R. Delaney, many of these same connections and resonances are made explicit, but George Clinton was one of the first to set them to music.

In Detroit, dominated by Ford's auto-assembly robots and huge industrial plants which transmuted raw metal into fully-completed cars, Kraftwerk slotted perfectly into a whole network of associations but they also tapped into a rapidly coalescing youth culture that was fusing Afro-futurism with a smart, preppy kind of cosmopolitanism. GQ was a favoured read, smart and achingly well-designed films such as *American Gigolo* (sharp European style, strongly aspirational glamour) or *Blade Runner* (dystopian sci-fi, heavy gadget count) were key influences. Into this dropped Kraftwerk with their futuristic themes and sound, exotic European style and pristine industrial sheen. They could almost have been custom-built to hit Detroit in the biggest possible way.

In fact it was a black-owned radio station in Detroit, WLBS, that gave the band's *Computer World* LP its first US airplay. The station's enthusiastic support prompted Kraftwerk's new American record company Warner Bros. to step up the promotional campaign for the release. Then both 'Numbers' and 'Pocket Calculator' became huge local hits as a result of their heavy rotation on another influential Detroit radio show hosted by the mysterious Electrifying Mojo, this time on the rival WJLB station. The impact this had on the city's music scene was almost incalculable.

For Juan Atkins, a Parliament-obsessed bass player living in the Detroit suburb of Belleville, Kraftwerk were the catalyst for a whole new music. Atkins had been playing bass in a funk band when he discovered a synthesizer in a local music store. Impressed by its sonic possibilities, he traded in his bass guitar and spent a whole summer recording strange electronic mantras by dubbing between two cassette recorders. Using only the synthesizer – a Korg MS20 – to create all the music, including the drum parts, each track was painstakingly crafted to replicate the sound of UFO's, spaceships and other planets. It was weird, individual music that didn't sound like anything else, until the day Atkins heard Kraftwerk drifting out of a transistor radio. The similarities between his own painstakingly-recorded experiments with the synthesizer and the new sound tumbling out of the radio convinced him that he was already a Kraftwerk fan.

During his first semester at community college, Atkins played his tapes to Rick Davis, a Vietnam veteran with a taste for Tangerine Dream and vintage synths. Together the pair formed Cybotron, scoring a significant electro hit with 'Clear' (a track which adapted the melody from Kraftwerk's 'Hall Of Mirrors' and the beat from 'Trans-Europe Express') and recording an album, Enter, for the California-based Fantasy label in 1983. Atkins took care of the rhythms and grooves, sometimes clearly referencing Kraftwerk tunes such as 'Computer World' (on the track 'Industrial Lies'), sometimes combining their feel with his grittier funk tendencies. But the cracks are evident between the computerised funk that Atkins contributed and the portentous, obviously rock-oriented leanings of Davis on the album's least successful cuts. When Davis enlisted a local music store salesman, John Howesley to play guitar, Cybotron's days were numbered. For Atkins this was a retrograde step which didn't square with his vision of where the group should be going. Soon afterwards he quit and settled down – with a handful of Kraftwerk albums and some George Clinton licks – to change the future of music.

Atkins was techno's first real visionary. Although some of the tracks on Cybotron's Enter album, such as 'Cosmic Cars' or 'Cosmic

Raindance', are clearly the prototype for the records which followed under his new Model 500 alias, his subsequent solo releases were the first to create something entirely new from the synthesis of Kraftwerk and Clinton. 'No UFOs', recorded during some downtime in Cybotron's studio and later released in 1985 as the first Model 500 single, was the official beginning of Detroit techno's future history but others were already beginning to align themselves with Atkins' vision long before that record spilled out into the world.

Two kids who shared a class at school with Atkins' younger brother were fascinated by the strange electronic sounds they'd hear on cassettes smuggled out of the house by their class-mate. Soon Derrick May and Kevin Saunderson were spending all their free time hanging out in the studio with Juan Atkins. May got a job in a video arcade to get the money for a synthesizer of his own, Saunderson delivered pizzas. Impressed by their enthusiasm, Atkins taught them everything he could about music-making and studio-craft and together the trio forged a new philosophy to go with the new music.

Detroit's party scene was also building towards the same point. Atkins and May set up as a DJ team under the name Deep Space and played wherever they could, choosing only records that fitted with their progressive outlook. On the city's dancefloors, Kraftwerk's 'Numbers' and 'Home Computer' were the biggest records imaginable and Deep Space were happy to oblige with sounds that fitted within similar parameters. On the radio Electrifying Mojo and another wildly inspired DJ known only as The Wizard mapped on to an equally forward-thinking sound by playing the most futuristic music they could lay hands on. It was a time of feverish experimentation. Groups of High School students laid on sophisticated theme parties, hiring Deep Space or perhaps their nearest rivals, Direct Drive, to provide the music. One group of students got so successful with their party promotions they made enough money to go into a studio and make a record to be played exclusively at their own parties. The track that resulted, 'Charivari', was named after a hip clothing store in New York, it was also the name that the party organisers used as a banner for their own organisation but, fearing reprisals from the store's owners, they changed the artist title at the last minute to A Number Of Names. The rare copies still in existence offer the best indication of how Detroit sounded during this exceptional period. More than anything, 'Charivari' sounds like the work of a black Kraftwerk.

By 1986, the pioneering trio of Atkins, Saunderson and May had been joined by other DJs and would-be producers – Thomas Barnett, James Pennington, Art Forrest, Eddie Fowlkes and Darryl Wynn – who contributed and collaborated (in various combinations) on many of the early techno classics. And the scene now had its own club, The Music Institute, where Detroit's take on Kraftwerk was spun far out into the future. The club's reputation soon spread and the queues around the block were joined by visiting artists (Depeche Mode were amongst the earliest visitors), camera crews and journalists eager to check Saunderson and May on the turntables spinning a mix that often included unreleased tracks by members of techno's inner circle.

During these years, Detroit had come to inhabit a different space from either house music (though many of those involved in the city's music scene were frequent visitors to Chicago clubs like The Music Box and The Power Plant) or techno's most immediate predecessor, electro. But when records by Atkins, May and Saunderson began filtering into Europe on labels with strangely futuristic names like Metroplex and Transmat they were perceived, at first, as some kind of mutant strain of both.

Together house and techno revolutionised the international music scene and, as a consequence, redefined the sound of the modern world. Conspiracy theorists may like to juggle with the fact that the pharmacology which fuelled the irresistible rise of these Kraftwerk-inspired dance trends was actually of German origin but the end result, however, is still the same. The fabric of modern music has irrevocably shifted towards Kraftwerk's original vision and, in many ways, the developments of the last decade are a vindication of their radical pop blueprint.

Significantly the strategies of electronic dance have also looped back into the group's own music. In 1991, Kraftwerk released their own unique version of a greatest hits album, *The Mix*, featuring updated versions of tracks such as 'Autobahn', 'Trans-Europe Express' and 'Pocket Calculator' reconstructed around beats that were clearly informed by house and techno. This wasn't a new departure for the group. They'd watched the developments in New York, Chicago and Detroit with interest and, during the early '80s, had commissioned François Kevorkian's sharp electro-styled remix of 'Tour De France' while 12" versions of the 1987 single 'The Telephone Call' included a 'Housephone' variant. Both Ralf Hütter and Florian Schneider have since maintained a keen interest in the dance scene, often displaying a surprising depth of knowledge about underground artists and record releases which only the most committed dance fans would be aware of, while Wolfgang Flür has gone on to work with Mouse On Mars, a well-respected Cologne techno outfit.

It's appropriate, therefore, that when Hütter and Schneider decided to relaunch Kraftwerk as a live force after a four year absence from the stage, they chose to do so at Tribal Gathering, the UK's largest dance music festival. The response to that appearance was spectacular (a remarkable feat taking into consideration the fact that the group hadn't released a record since 1991) and confirmed that Kraftwerk's reputation is at last beginning to match up to their achievements.

In the three decades since Ralf Hütter and Florian Schneider first met, Kraftwerk have rewritten the rules of pop music. What's so extraordinary about this is the fact that they've done it without ever conforming to the expectations of the mainstream music world. Perpetual outsiders, they have never been interested in success (artistic or otherwise) on any terms other than their own. And the reality is that it's by following their own individual instincts which has enabled them to accomplish the biggest revolution in contemporary music since The Beatles.

Hütter and Schneider's unconventional approach has also made them the most uniquely subversive force in modern pop music. The Sex Pistols may have had a neat line in polemic but, ultimately, they were a far more conventional proposition than Kraftwerk. Their would-be revolution was still founded on rock guitar riffs, a strict adherence to pop mythology and a heavy reliance on a normal band format. By contrast, it has often seemed that the only thing Kraftwerk have in common with the traditions of pop is the fact that they make pop music. Over the years, they've often played subtle subversive games with the parameters of what it means to be a pop group: posing as robots, suggesting that the group is a machine and that individual members are merely cogs within it, their insistence on using terms such as 'sound workers' rather than musicians, referring to their Kling Klang studio as 'a laboratory' and so on. But their subversion isn't only artistic. The revolutionary record deal that they conceived for themselves back in the '70s has altered the way the music industry views its contractual obligations to artists. In so many subtle ways – and some not so subtle – Kraftwerk have changed pop music irrevocably.

Emil Schult has pointed out that this is just one indicator of Kraftwerk's approach to their career as a complete artistic work. While other groups have been content to treat each of their album releases or live shows as separate, self-contained entities which together form a body of work, Hütter and Schneider's attitude is to treat everything they do as Kraftwerk – record releases, touring, sleeve design, image, even the rare interviews they grant – as part of the same piece. The total work of art in this case *is* Kraftwerk. This approach has, of course, placed certain restrictions on the group's activities but it has also enabled them to create the most cohesive and consistent identity in pop history.

There is no doubt that Schult himself has played a significant part in this. The strategy obviously bears traces of the influence Joseph Beuys had on his former pupil and, consequently, Kraftwerk themselves. Famously, Beuys once constructed a chronology of the events in his life (originally completed in 1964 but continually revised and updated until his death) which transmuted many of his experiences into the kind of entries normally found in a gallery catalogue. Effectively the explicit aim of this idiosyncratic autobiography was to suggest that his entire life was one complete work of art. Beuys was also keenly interested in ways of managing his interaction with the outside world in order to shape and control his own public persona in keeping with this idea.

The concept of retaining control over the outside world's perceptions of the group's activities and interests has become increasingly important throughout Kraftwerk's career. Partly, just as with Beuys, this is an artistic strategy aimed at preserving the purity of the group's creative vision. But it's also a crucial means of maintaining the privacy of the group's founder members, Hütter and Schneider, who feel uncomfortable (and probably rightly so) about the ruthless exegesis of personal and private details which goes on in the name of pop journalism. Little is known about the group – less in fact than almost any other phenomenon in pop – beyond what they have been prepared to reveal in the few elliptical interviews they have conducted over the years. The pursuit of Kraftwerk, therefore, is the pursuit of an enigma. They are the last truly great mystery of modern music.

What we do have, of course, are fleeting glimpses gained through their infrequent live appearances and, these days at least, their equally infrequent record releases. The few promotional videos they have made – filmed so far apart that viewing them now feels like watching a sequence of time-lapse photography – offer little in the way of clues outside the occasional sightings of four men who once looked nothing like conventional pop stars until the world eventually caught up and recognised in their sharp, automaton look the ideal image for the modern pop group.

For some, the mystery at the centre of the Kraftwerk phenomenon is an enduring part of the group's appeal. For others, eager to understand how four musicians from Germany altered the course of modern music, it's a baffling and often frustrating part of their identity. This book is an attempt to answer at least some of the questions about Kraftwerk and the events which have made them the most innovative and influential force in pop. It's not a definitive account but it's unlikely that even Ralf Hütter and Florian Schneider, accustomed as they are to moulding and shaping Kraftwerk's public image according to their own artistic inclinations, would provide that. Instead it's just one particular spin on the narrative of a pop group who changed the world in which we live.

At the time of writing, Kraftwerk are expected to deliver a new album (though even some of the group's most committed fans are sceptical that anything will materialise). There is nothing new about this – rumours about a forthcoming release have surfaced at frequent intervals every year since 1991's *The Mix* – but reports that Ralf Hütter has already presented a tape of five new tracks to EMI Germany seem to make the speculation just a little more plausible. Who knows what effect the modern soundtrack that Kraftwerk inspired – rap, electro, house, techno, drum n' bass – will have had on the development of their own music? The truth is that anything is possible because Kraftwerk's story isn't yet fully played out.

Derrick May once suggested that Kraftwerk's records are like postcards from the future. In a way that's true. When the group's *Computer World* album was released in 1981, for instance, IBM hadn't yet developed the PC, the Internet was still the stuff of science fiction and the idea of a central database keeping tabs on us all had more to do with Orwell's Big Brother than reality. All these things have come to pass and yet, conceptually and musically, *Computer World* still sounds like a record that's come to us from some time years ahead of now.

Computer World also prefigured many of the musical developments which took us through the '80s and '90s. But, in some ways, Kraftwerk's records are also like postcards to the future, floating out ideas and possibilities, hopes and dreams. And, somehow, the future seems to have paid attention. Driving to work along the autobahn in a car built by robots, listening to radio broadcasts beamed down from a satellite, stopping at traffic signals controlled by computer and wondering whether to go to a house club or a techno club this weekend, that's something worth remembering.

1

History is a funny thing. When you're in the middle of it you're either too busy, too drunk or, in this case, too cold to pay much attention. It's just after one on the morning of Sunday 25th May, 1997. In a large tract of leafy English countryside somewhere between Luton and Harpenden, the temperature is falling like a stone. In the centre of a vast circle of giant-sized tents, isolated groups of people huddle around makeshift fires made from scraps of paper, twigs and plastic water bottles, desperately trying to keep warm. Oblivious to everything that's going on around them, they focus intently on the tiny flames, chat desultorily and try to ignore the stench of burning plastic coiling through the night-time air. But these people aren't campers or travellers, they're clubbers and they've paid £35 each to attend the largest dance music festival ever held in England. Now they've seen what they came to see, done what they came to do, they sit, quietly exhausted and unfazed by the dense tangle of electronic beats and basslines leaking from the tents around them.

This is Tribal Gathering '97, the culmination of years spent working towards this moment for its promoters Universe, the UK's last surviving outdoor dance party organisers. Universe boss Paul Shurey is in a euphoric mood. Though acts such as Orbital, Carl Craig and Speedy J are playing live sets in some of the huge marquees which surround the party site, in his head he's replaying the events of the last hour or so, free – at least for a while – from the million-and-one minor difficulties which spring up from minute to minute in the running of something as big as this. 'Incredible,' he murmurs to no one in particular, though a substantial proportion of the 30,000 club-kids who've travelled from all over the UK and Europe to attend might have agreed with him.

Ralf Hütter and Florian Schneider are in a similarly buoyant mood. They have just performed live in front of one of the biggest audiences of their career and are already describing the experience as 'the best show we have ever played' to David Phillips, another member of the Universe team.

For Phillips, who'd previously organised gigs for Public Enemy and Nirvana during the decade he'd spent working as a promoter with the Mean Fiddler organisation (Universe's partners for Tribal Gathering '97) it was a dream come true. 'I've been a Kraftwerk fan since I was a kid,' he explains, 'and personally I think they're the most important band that ever happened. They've had a fantastic influence on the way dance music has developed so it was always a dream of mine to bring them together with all the artists they've inspired.'

Shortly before Phillips joined Universe in 1993 to help promote that summer's Big Love rave he had been working with Mark Kauffman, the son of a Rio diamond polisher, on an ambitious event to be held at Lydd Airport in Kent under the name Experience. The proposed line-up for Experience included Orbital, Dee-Lite, Beastie Boys and, thanks to Phillips, Kraftwerk. Phillips had already made tentative approaches through the group's UK agency Wasted Talent but it was a meeting with Scumeck Sabottka – one of Germany's biggest promoters and the man who loosely fits the bill as the nearest thing Kraftwerk have to a manager in the conventional sense – that took him one step closer to making his dream come true.

'Initially, the signs weren't very encouraging,' remembers Phillips. 'For a start, it's very difficult to get access to Kraftwerk. There's also the fact that they won't play anywhere that they haven't seen and approved personally. But we made arrangements to fly Ralf and Florian over from Düsseldorf to look at the site. They came over and we discussed our plans for the event, explained exactly what we were aiming to do and showed them how it would all be laid out.'

Though the Experience team got to the stage of preparing contracts, they were unable to secure a licence for the event and it was subsequently cancelled. But Phillips didn't give up on the idea. A year later, at Tribal Gathering in Munich (Universe had temporarily moved their big events abroad due to the increasing difficulty of obtaining entertainment licences for them in England) he introduced Paul Shurey to Scumeck Sabottka and the idea of a Kraftwerk appearance at a future Universe event was discussed. The chances of pulling it off, however, seemed slim.

'When we first spoke to Scumeck you couldn't have got a more blank response,' recalls Shurey. 'But we're not faint-hearted so we kept exploring other avenues and eventually, after a lot of persistence, we got a dialogue started with the band.'

By the summer of 1995, with England's licensing boards beginning to relax a little in the wake of a rapidly declining moral panic about large-scale raves, Universe were holding Tribal Gathering at Otmoor Park in Oxfordshire and already planning another event for the following year.

Initial proposals for the 1996 line-up of Tribal Gathering did include Kraftwerk but by the autumn of 1995 Hütter and Schneider had decided to focus on recording and felt that preparations for a one-off live appearance would be an unnecessary distraction. Dismayed, but not entirely despondent, Universe offered to fly them over to see the event for themselves with a view to perhaps playing the following year instead.

Shurey and Phillips were optimistic that the highly-charged atmosphere and sheer scale of Tribal in action might be more persuasive than any number of discussions. But their strategy almost backfired when, at the last minute, magistrates in Oxfordshire refused a Public Entertainment Licence for the event on the grounds that it would cause severe traffic congestion in the area immediately surrounding the site (this despite the fact that a proposed open-air concert by The Who had been granted a licence just a few days previously for a site in central London, where traffic management would obviously be a much more significant problem). Following an unsuccessful four-day appeal against this decision at Thame Magistrates Court, Universe – who had already sold around 25,000 tickets for the event – launched another appeal, this time at Crown Court level. With time running out fast, however, the only real option was to frantically scour the countryside for an alternative site and worry about the appeal, which could potentially take months to sort out, at a later date.

Eventually the team reached an eleventh-hour agreement with the promoters of Fiesta '96 to join forces at Luton Hoo estate in Bedfordshire and hold a combined event there within a few weeks of the original Otmoor Park date. Shurey and Phillips breathed a sigh of relief. A forced cancellation would have caused them enormous financial losses. It could also have cost them any chance they might have had of persuading Kraftwerk to play at a future Tribal Gathering.

When it did take place, just three weeks later, Tribal Gathering '96 was a huge success. Despite the logistical problems of shifting such a large production to another site within such a short space of time, the event was one of the smoothest running Universe promotions so far. Though a few acts, most notably Underworld, were unable to play at the rescheduled event due to other commitments, almost all of the original line-up – including The Chemical Brothers, Leftfield and Laurent Garnier – remained intact. Even the dismal weather failed to dampen the general euphoria. But only a handful of the 25,000 people in attendance realised that among them were representatives of the group who had inspired, in one way or another, almost everything that was happening around them. Kraftwerk had taken up Paul Shurey's offer and come to check out Tribal Gathering for themselves.

What they saw that day made an obvious impact. 'In the beginning, everyone connected with the band was being very negative about the prospect of them playing at Tribal,' explains Shurey. ' They weren't at all convinced that they even wanted to do a live show. But after we flew them over for the 1996 event, they began to seriously entertain the idea. That's when we started to get very excited. I'd been a big fan of Kraftwerk since *Trans-Europe Express* and it was their music that drew me to house and techno in the first place. None of us would be doing what we do now if it wasn't for them. They inspired the whole dance music movement. So it was a very big thing for us to even start believing it would happen.'

As ever with the Kraftwerk organisation, negotiations were delicate and painstaking. Another member of the Universe team, Ian Jenkinson, later confessed that 'they were really hard to get hold of, they'd always be cycling in the Pyrenees or something.'[1] But discussions had progressed far enough that by January 1997, Ralf Hütter and Scumeck Sabottka had flown in from Düsseldorf to look over the Luton Hoo site once more and confirmed that Kraftwerk would, after all, perform live at Tribal Gathering '97 but, as Jenkinson, pointed out 'only on the condition that they had total control over every aspect of the event. They're a law unto themselves: they're very, very serious about what they do. Everything has to be bang on the button. And so that meant creating a dedicated space, them bringing their own fourteen-strong road crew and us basically building their studio in the middle of a field!'[2]

When the news leaked out, early reactions ranged from disbelief to astonishment. 'The jury was still out as to whether Kraftwerk would fit with our audience,' says Shurey, 'but we seriously believed that, given the fact that they had influenced almost the whole dance scene, it would work brilliantly. Nobody had ever brought them together with the artists they'd inspired in the context of a dance music event before and we were thrilled that we were going to be the ones who did that for the first time. If they turned up to play, we were very confident that they would get a terrific reaction from our audience. I never thought, for a minute, that it would be anything other than the perfect audience for their music.'

By the time work began on the site, six weeks before the event itself, the excitement was palpable. It seemed like every national magazine and newspaper – whether they were dance-related or not – was carrying a special feature about Kraftwerk. The group themselves were, of course, not giving interviews but the prospect of their appearance at Tribal generated more column inches than any other music event that summer. The scale of coverage was unprecedented but it was even more astonishing in view of the fact that it was all for a group that hadn't released any new material since 1986.

One major theme of Universe's publicity for the event was that Kraftwerk's appearance at Tribal Gathering would be their first live performance anywhere in the world for over a decade. This wasn't the case. It wasn't even their first live show in England for ten years. Kraftwerk had opened the bill for an anti-nuclear benefit, headlined by U2, at Manchester's G-Mex in June 1992. The gig, which also featured Public Enemy and Big Audio Dynamite, was part of a series of protests promoted by Greenpeace against the building of a second nuclear facility at Sellafield (originally known as Windscale, the Sellafield atomic power station in Cumbria had been the focus for much anti-nuclear feeling following several well-publicised accidents and growing fears about the high incidence of cancer among locals in the surrounding area).

Prior to the Greenpeace show, Kraftwerk had also played a secret warm-up gig in, of all places, the student union bar at Leicester Polytechnic. 'It was unbelievable,' explains Phonogram's Simon Blackmore who spent most of the gig standing next to another keen Kraftwerk fan, Erasure's Vince Clarke. 'The place only held about 200 people and even then it wasn't full – you could wander about quite comfortably. Most of the students didn't give a toss who was playing, they were just there to get drunk, so there weren't actually that many people there who even realised what was going on. They played quite a long set, including a great version of "Tour De France" and, of course, "Radioactivity" but I remember that they came on really late because Germany were playing in the World Cup qualifiers and the match went to extra time. They wouldn't come on until the game was over . . .'

A year earlier, Kraftwerk had also played several dates in the UK (including two at London's Brixton Academy) as part of a world tour in support of *The Mix* album, their typically individual and inspired version of a greatest hits collection. That tour finished in Budapest in late '91, having never got any further than Europe. The group's subsequent shows in America and Japan were mysteriously cancelled for reasons which were never officially confirmed, though speculation as to the cause varies from Schneider's hatred of touring to Hütter's supposed unwillingness to co-operate with a directive from the American Musician's Union requiring all acts using computers and sequencing in their live shows to provide a detailed breakdown of what was actually being performed and what was being controlled by computer. Given the group's notorious reticence about such matters, this is as convincing a suggestion as any other but, as with many of the mysteries surrounding the band, it's probable that the truth is much simpler. Touring a large-scale production is an expensive and risky business. Without a hit record in the charts any major tour is a significant gamble, especially in America where the huge distances that need to be covered can accelerate costs significantly. For two men in their mid-40s who preferred to live their daily lives in a very orderly fashion, the disruption of touring and the financial gamble it required may just have seemed like a headache they could get by without.

Media coverage of the concerts at the beginning of the '90s (there were a handful of Italian shows in 1990 which previewed *The Mix* tour set and some further gigs during 1993 in Holland, Belgium, Germany and Austria which revisited almost exactly the same set with the sole addition of the first ever live performances of 'The Man Machine') was nothing out of the ordinary. So why did Kraftwerk's appearance at Tribal arouse such excitement? Partly it was down to exceptionally good PR on the part of Phuture Trax who handled the Universe organisation's press campaign for the event. A lot of it was also due to the internal mechanisms of the media and the simple fact that Kraftwerk's combination of eccentricity, perfect pop and incalculable intellectual otherness made for a great story. But most of all it was due to the huge shift in perceptions of the group as their impact on dance music became increasingly evident.

The vocabulary of contemporary dance music is entirely Kraftwerk's. It's their sonic language that now pours out of our television screens and radios, the sound systems in trendy underground clubs and naff town centre discotheques; it is their manicured noise that's lovingly reshaped and refabricated on records as diverse as Aux 88's 'Break It Down', Sash's 'Encore Une Fois' and Daft Punk's *Homework* and it's the result of their sheer delight in the structures and surfaces of electronic tone that drifts out into the ether from fairground PAs and supermarket speakers. But this realisation didn't become overt until the summer of 1995 when dance music finally broke through the barriers to become contemporary pop music. It was at that point that dance music stopped being alternative music culture and assumed mainstream status.

It took ten years for the music that Kraftwerk inspired to make that leap. The transformation really began much earlier in a variety of locations, first with the synth-pop-meets-dance stylings of early '80s clubs like Blitz and the Beat Route in London, then slightly later in Chicago niteries such as the Warehouse and the Music Box where DJs Frankie Knuckles and Ron Hardy cut together disco, Philly soul and Kraftwerk's machine aesthetic to create house music; in New York where the themes of 'Trans-Europe Express' and 'Metal On Metal' were mutated and twisted into rap and electro and in Detroit where Kraftwerk's original vision was first distilled and then gently alchemised with funk to create techno.

When these developments converged in the acid house scene of the late '80s, the sound had already warped into the future. It was too new, too fresh for anyone to worry about where it came from or where it was going, despite even Derrick May's assertion that Detroit techno was simply '. . . like George Clinton and Kraftwerk stuck in an elevator.'[3] In all the colour and immediacy and narcotic euphoria of acid house, few people worried about making such connections explicit. And, in the beginning anyway, the scene was so tiny that it wouldn't have made any difference if they had. As the scene evolved and expanded, fragmented and refracted throughout the early '90s trace elements were hard to pick out. The novelty of it all tended to obscure everything but the moment and the moment wasn't history but the future. It was a time for looking forward and not back. That, at least, was how it felt in the vortex of a peak-time dancefloor and significantly how it also seemed to most of those commentating on the phenomenon for the few publications who weren't afraid to embrace the subject. The artists at the centre of it all hadn't forgotten their primary influence in the slightest.

On a European tour in 1991, the Detroit group Underground Resistance met Hütter and Schneider for the first time. It was a significant meeting since, in terms of influence, ideology and their determination to play the music industry by their own maverick rules, Underground Resistance's approach closely resembles that of Kraftwerk. (Though another Detroit techno artist, Carl Craig, confided to *The Face* in May 1997 that: 'My feeling now is that Underground Resistance have taken over the position that Kraftwerk held ten years ago. Even though some people might have considered Kraftwerk to be a pop band, they were the epitome of the underground for us in Detroit. They helped to develop a lot of minds to think beyond what is today. I love them because they were visionaries. But now UR are just as important. There's that same sense of mystique and anticipation about their releases that there used to be around Kraftwerk records.')

Underground Resistance are part of Detroit's so-called second wave of techno producers, following the original pioneering trail of Juan Atkins, Derrick May and Kevin Saunderson. Formed in 1988 by Mike Banks and Jeff Mills they were the first group to actively politicise the content of techno – in the way that Public Enemy did with rap – and use their records as a means of challenging mainstream attitudes (as Kraftwerk did on *Autobahn*). Many of the group's working methods bear a striking similarity to those of Kraftwerk. Banks and Mills would often discuss conceptuals and theories before working on their music, for example, and they enforced a strict media blackout so that, effectively, their only lines of communication were through their record releases. This meant that, by 1991, although Underground Resistance had become one of the most highly-regarded forces in modern music for those who had heard their music, very few people outside of techno's inner circle were even aware of them. Even fewer were aware of the group's history: Mike Banks had previously played guitar in one of George Clinton's numerous spin-off projects before forming the group Members Of The House who were featured on Virgin's definitive *Techno – The New Dance Sound Of Detroit* compilation (the album which introduced techno to Europe), Jeff Mills was one of Detroit's most inspired DJs and had made a profound impact on the city's musical direction with his radio shows on WJLB as The Wizard.

The two groups met in East Berlin on a Saturday afternoon towards the end of October. Kraftwerk were in the middle of the German leg of their 1991 world tour. On arriving at the venue, however, as Hütter later explained to the *Rheinische Post* journalist Philipp Roser, they discovered that 'the concert hall was too dusty for the highly sensitive electronic machines'[4] and decided to cancel the show (it was postponed and played at another venue four weeks later).

'They were very aware of who we were and what we did,' explains Mike Banks. 'They seemed very happy to see us. They're really cool people, quite funny, very much for peace.'

Later that night, Ralf and Florian went to hear Jeff Mills DJ at the Tresor club which is situated in a former bank vault not far from the war-time headquarters of the Luftwaffe. 'After his set, Jeff asked them where all those funky grooves in Kraftwerk's music came from. It turns out they were big soul fans. They said they very much respected James Brown and his music . . .'

Mike Banks and Ralf Hütter have remained on good terms ever since. 'Ralf is a very sensitive person,' he considers. 'I wish there were more people like him. He's very forward-thinking but he has a spiritual side too and that appeals to me. And, obviously he's a very private person. In fact, Ralf is the original Invisible One!' (Due to his notorious dislike of personal publicity, Banks guards his own privacy fiercely, refusing to be photographed and, for the most part, interviewed. His identity is concealed from all but the most trusted insiders and he often goes to great lengths to keep it that way. There are many tales of music journalists who have tried to penetrate the Underground Resistance operation by visiting the group's Submerge distribution headquarters in Detroit and setting up a conversation with the person they think is most likely to be Mike Banks in the hope of getting enough quotes to put together an article. Since few people know what he looks like and everybody around the organisation is primed to play along, in almost all cases, the journalist ends up conducting an interview with the wrong person. This elusiveness has earned him the epithet 'The Invisible One'.)

In a rare brush with the outside world, Mike Banks agreed to help co-ordinate the Detroit stage at Tribal Gathering which featured performances from Juan Atkins, Aux 88, Carl Craig, Kevin Saunderson, former Music Institute DJ Darryl Wynn, Jeff Mills and Alan Oldham, another one-time member of the Underground Resistance organisation. 'Getting Kraftwerk was instrumental in getting all the Detroit guys to play,' explains Paul Shurey. 'But we had to promise that we'd close the Detroit tent for two hours while Kraftwerk were onstage so that they could all get to see them. That was one of the main conditions they stipulated!'

Kraftwerk arrived on the Tribal Gathering site three days before the event itself with a fleet of trucks carrying the equipment from their Kling Klang studio. 'There were artics as far as the eye could see,' remembers David Phillips, 'it was like Bon Jovi were coming to play at Tribal!' The Universe team had already been on-site since the beginning of April, starting off with a group of around two dozen which grew steadily as personnel from the various tent, fencing and staging companies were added. By the time Kraftwerk arrived, the site was already bustling with additional crews from SSE and Spot Co, who were taking care of the event's sound and lighting.

Ralf Hütter and Scumek Sabottka had investigated the site some months earlier and there were already detailed plans for Kraftwerk's stage arrangement so the setting-up work progressed quickly. 'We were effectively building their studio onstage,' recalls Shurey. 'We had to keep backstage security very tight – it was probably the most sterile backstage environment I've ever experienced. But there was still a tremendous feeling of excitement around the whole stage area.'

Sound-checks and rehearsals followed until, on the day before the event, Kraftwerk were ready to do a full run-through. 'That's when the reality sank in,' says Shurey. 'That's when I realised that Kraftwerk – who'd started the whole thing off – were actually going to play at Tribal Gathering. There were only about twenty or thirty of us watching the run-through. They played the whole set and it was great. It made the hairs stand up on the back of my neck.'

While it seemed like everyone else was fitting their plans for Tribal Gathering around Kraftwerk's set, Ralf Hütter and Florian Schneider were checking out the running order for reasons of their own. 'They wanted to see Laurent Garnier and Jeff Mills especially,' noted Ian Jenkinson, pointing out that Kraftwerk had 'kept a closer eye on the scene than people might think.'[5]

This is confirmed by The Bowling Green's Micko Westmoreland who met up with the band in June 1993 at the Ars Electronica festival in Linz, Austria. 'They're a lot more informed than you'd think, they definitely have a good overview on what's going on in the dance scene.'

In fact, Ralf and Florian have a number of close friends who are heavily involved in the dance scene. During the recording sessions for *The Mix*, Ralf had invited Jens Lissat (co-owner of the German trance label No Respect and a well-known DJ and producer on the Frankfurt, Berlin, Cologne club scene) into Kling Klang to give his opinion on the work in progress while Florian's contacts on the underground techno scene include Berlin's Basic Channel amongst others.

In many ways, therefore, playing at Tribal Gathering was a logical step for Kraftwerk. Having created the framework for modern dance music it seemed only fitting that one day they'd be welcomed back as conquering heroes by those whom they'd inspired and sparked into action. What they didn't anticipate, however, was the strength of the response from the audience at Luton Hoo.

By the time Kraftwerk were due onstage at around ten on the Saturday evening, Tribal Gathering's Trans-Europe tent was packed. Most of the people closest to the stage had picked their spots hours earlier, swaying gently to Andy Weatherall's Two Lone Swordsmen sound system, but intent enough on maintaining the best possible vantage point for Kraftwerk's set that they'd taken it in turns to watch each other's spaces while their friends made rapid dashes to the beer tent or the toilets. Several thousand others, unable even to squeeze into the tent, milled around outside trying to find positions that would allow them just a glimpse of the stage.

As the first few bars of 'Numbers' twisted the night air into Kraftwerk's mechanical universe, the tent crew took emergency measures, hastily dismantling the sides of the marquee to open up the sight-lines for those still stuck outside. Ralf Hütter, who before the gig had mentioned his apprehensions about how this audience – radically different from any that Kraftwerk had ever played to before – would take to their music, must have been astonished as the canvas dropped away from the sides of the huge tent to reveal an enthusiastic crowd of more than 12,000 dancing in unison to the track's driving *motorik* beat.

To a crowd accustomed to nothing more visually exciting than a DJ spinning records on a couple of turntables, Kraftwerk's stage set looked breathtaking. Two giant video screens on either side of the stage pumped out graphics and visuals in time with the music – archive footage of the Tour De France for 'Tour De France' (much of it already seen in the promo video for the single), trains and railway stations for 'Trans-Europe Express' and suitable El Lissitzky-inspired graphics for 'The Man Machine' – while behind the group themselves were four more screens, the usual banks of fluorescent strip lights and, of course, the entire contents of Kling Klang.

The group's line-up – Ralf Hütter, Henning Schmitz, Fritz Hilpert and Florian Schneider – was identical to the one which appeared during Kraftwerk's 1993 concerts though Florian's distinctive features were remarkably altered by his shaven head. Fritz Hilpert was originally one of the group's sound engineers, he'd been drafted in to replace Wolfgang Flür who had parted company with Kraftwerk during the late '80s. Schmitz was another engineer who had been recruited during *The Mix* tour after Portuguese musician Fernando Abrantes proved to be an unsuitable replacement for Karl Bartos who quit the group in 1990, shortly before the lengthy recording sessions for *The Mix* drew to a close.

While this wasn't the line-up that had recorded the group's most classic albums, the crowd didn't seem to care. As 'Numbers' segued into 'Computer World', the atmosphere was electric, more like an old skool rave than a concert, with people on all sides grinning and bobbing in time to the music. Canadian techno producer Richie Hawtin seemed torn between standing still and getting a reasonable picture on his miniature Sony video camera or forgetting about the video altogether in favour of dancing. In the end, he reached an unhappy compromise, filming brief sections of the performance and then grooving frantically for another few minutes before the thought that he should really be recording all of this for posterity prompted him to hoist up the camera once more.

Onstage, the group – facing the audience head-on in a flat, four abreast formation behind their synthesizers instead of their famous v-shaped set-up designed by Wolfgang Flür – showed no discernible signs of surprise. In fact, they displayed few emotions at all, but those close enough to the stage could deduce from the not-quite-deadpan expressions that Kraftwerk weren't, after all, robots. They looked nervous.

It's easy to figure out why they might have been at least a little apprehensive during the early stages of this performance. After all, Kraftwerk had never done a show under circumstances quite like these. Media interest in the Tribal Gathering appearance was intense and, with their reputation at a career peak, the stakes were high. If it went wrong, the damage could be incalculable. Added to this was the fact that they'd broken with their long-standing tradition of playing a smaller, warm-up gig before any important concert (as they'd done before the anti-Sellafield 2 benefit at G-Mex). The performance was also being broadcast by BBC Radio One as part of their coverage of the whole event. Together with Ralf's anxieties about whether the crowd at Tribal would enjoy Kraftwerk's music or not, all these factors cranked up the pressure enormously.

But they needn't have worried. The crowd at Tribal was probably one of the most partisan audiences the group had ever played to. For most of those inside the Trans-Europe tent that night, Kraftwerk weren't just a particularly favoured group, they were the originators, the creative force whose innovations had inspired a whole new music, and more importantly, a whole new youth culture. To be in the audience at Tribal that night to see Kraftwerk was as much about a celebration of that culture as it was about the gig itself. Because of this, the show had a resonance far greater than that of any normal concert. Like Shea Stadium, Woodstock, the Screen On The Green or Spike Island, it was a meta-gig with meaning and significance beyond the sum of the rhythms and melodies which were being generated onstage. And for some, the moment Kraftwerk stepped onstage at Tribal signalled the high-water mark of dance culture's progress from the backstreets of New York, Chicago and Detroit through acid house and rave to become mainstream youth culture.

The first half of the set Kraftwerk played was more or less a straight re-run of their 1993 shows (with the exception of 'Computer Love' which was left out at Tribal) – 'Numbers', 'Computer World', 'Home Computer', 'The Man Machine', 'Tour De France' and an updated version of 'Autobahn' – but there were also a few surprises. 'Sellafield 2', originally written for Greenpeace's anti-nuclear campaign, preceded 'Radioactivity' while the video screens pulsed with relevant statistics. Then, following a beefed-up variation on the 'Trans-Europe Express'/'Abzug'/'Metal On Metal' theme, the stage curtains closed as the Tribal crowd whooped and hollered and wondered if it was all over.

It wasn't of course. It's a common Kraftwerk ploy to play games with their audiences towards the end of their live shows by retreating behind the stage curtains, only to re-emerge just when the crowd is starting to believe they won't. This time they reappeared with their hand-held mini-keyboards to play 'Pocket Calculator' by now clearly enjoying themselves (with Florian in particular throwing some neat dancefloor shapes) and obviously aware that the Tribal crowd were loving every gorgeous, iridescent beat, every dizzyingly inspired synth riff.

And then the curtains closed again. Or rather they didn't. Some obstruction, or just a simple mechanical failure, meant that the motorised drapes came to an abrupt halt halfway through the course of their travel. While Ralf desperately ad-libbed on his mini-keyboard, a member of the stage crew clambered onto the lighting gantry and shinned precariously up the curtain rail to solve the problem. It was a moment somewhere between farce and high drama (especially considering the fearless roadie had to execute the repair perching on a slim piece of tubular steel thirty or forty feet above the ground) but it did have a strangely positive effect. Sometimes a show can be too perfect, creating an intangible psychic distance between those onstage and those in the crowd, an us-and-them gap that dance culture's intrinsic democracy finds hard to stomach. The curtain foul-up was a pointed reminder that, after all, Kraftwerk were just like everyone else – hey, things go wrong for them too. It was a dumb moment but it made a connection all the same.

When the troublesome curtains eventually opened again to the opening strains of 'The Robots' the crowd were euphoric. It felt as though every nuance of modern dance culture was focused in the gorgeous electronic syncopations which fluttered somewhere between the track's dense riffing bass and the beautifully elegant synthetic melodies that floated out into the night sky over Luton Hoo. From the perspective of the '90s, 'The Robots' is the closest thing Kraftwerk have to a signature tune, encapsulating almost all the themes which have threaded through their later career – technology, modernity, the inter-section between man and machine, depersonalisation, short-circuited emotions, futurism and so on – laced through with hard funk and their inimitable brand of high camp humour. So it was a perfect moment when the onstage screens dropped down to reveal the deconstructed skeletal robots which have become the group's trademark since the release of *The Mix* in 1991, dancing and gyrating to the beat of 'Robotronik' while their human counterparts punched out their heavily-sequenced groove.

Inevitably, the curtains tried to close again and didn't. As the crowd roared their appreciation, a member of the road crew tried to salvage some privacy by pulling them closed at stage level while his intrepid associate clambered back up the rigging again.

And then, just when it seemed like it might actually be all over, the curtains opened again to reveal all four members of Kraftwerk dressed in brand new one-piece uniforms that looked like they'd been borrowed from Disney's proto-cyber epic *Tron*. Black with a fluorescent yellow grid pattern, the new outfits were matched by yellow-framed dark glasses to provide a very super-cool futurist look, midway between a cycling team and a bobsleigh crew. But the biggest surprise was the music itself. At first, the unfamiliar combination of swelling synth chords and acidic counterpoints seemed like a revamped introduction to a familiar song, but when the groove dropped into a kinetic bass riff and accelerated to lightning fast speed, it became obvious that something else was happening. It was clearly still in its embryonic stages but for the first time in more than a decade, Kraftwerk had unveiled a new track.

Significantly, though the pristine surfaces and jitterbug syncopations of the introduction were identifiably Kraftwerk, most of this new workout also bore unmistakable traces of hard dancefloor techno (disappointingly, however, if anything it sounded closer to Frankfurt trance than the cool Detroit-inflected shapes of Underground Resistance or Basic Channel). A pointer to the content of a new Kraftwerk album? Nobody was sure, although some suggested that it could be the group's contribution to the soundtrack of a forthcoming Wim Wenders film, *The End Of Violence*. What mattered more than anything else was that, after all this time, a new Kraftwerk track had tumbled out into the world and, as the final echoes drifted out into the ether, the crowd's reaction was deafeningly positive.

The set closed with a spectacular version of 'Music Non Stop' – screens flashing 'Boing, Boom, Tschak' in sync with the droll human beatbox vocal of the intro – which was relatively short in comparison to some of the heavily extended versions that the group played during their 1991 tour. In the customary Kraftwerk tradition, towards the end of the track, Florian Schneider left the stage, followed at intervals by Fritz Hilpert and then Henning Schmitz, leaving Ralf alone with the music and the lights and the crowd, before finally he too disappeared into the wings.

Most of the crowd at Tribal had never seen anything like it. The magnificence of the stage set, the purity of the sound and the quality of the music itself would have been enough to ensure a fantastic response, but it also felt like something even more special had occurred. Kraftwerk had come out of retirement (or so it seemed) to align themselves with the scene they had inspired and in a way, it felt like history had just happened – as if, suddenly, dance culture had realised how far it had come since the days of empty warehouses and tiny sweatboxes. It was a realisation that crept up and shouted out loud: 'Hey! If Kraftwerk take us seriously, then we must be serious!' The cheering that followed threatened to outstrip the volume of the sound system.

Backstage, the mood mirrored the fantastically euphoric atmosphere out-front. Ralf and Florian were visibly elated, beaming happily at the small gathering of well-wishers who had come to offer their congratulations. In an uncharacteristic demonstration of his feelings, Ralf even gave one of the female members of the Universe team a hug.

As the crowd began filtering out of the Trans-Europe tent, heading off to hear Randall play or catch the beginning of Carl Craig's live set, the night air was thick with conversational fragments about Kraftwerk's astounding set. One recurring theme came from those who'd been close to the front of the stage. Some enterprising fan down there had persuaded his girlfriend to give him a blow job while Kraftwerk were playing. Obviously, they reckoned, it was some weird kind of wish fulfilment thing. ' "Oral sex and Kraftwerk?" Couldn't get any better than that, mate . . .'

Oblivious to this phenomenon, Ralf and Florian, were by this time making their way to the backstage area behind the Detroit tent. Carl Craig had just gone onstage and was busy blowing 5000 minds with a fusion of techno and live jazz when they walked up the backstage access ramp. After chatting for a while to Mike Banks and Jeff Mills, they decided to watch some of Carl's set from the side of the stage before disappearing back into the rapidly cooling night air.

Kraftwerk's experience at Tribal Gathering was so exceptional that they promptly decided to organise another show, this time a little closer to home. A concert was hastily arranged for October as part of Multimediale 5 at the ZKM (Centre For Art & Media Technology) in Karlsruhe. In keeping with the group's tradition of performing a smaller warm-up gig for such events, they also arranged to play at the Posthof in the Austrian town of Linz, two days before the Karlsruhe date.

David Phillips was invited out to the show in Karlsruhe. 'I went out to dinner with them,' he remembers. 'It was all a bit dream-like, I almost had to pinch myself occasionally. But there is quite a gap between them personally and the way they're perceived. Because they haven't done many interviews and all that's been available are photographs, the thing about their image has been built up in a certain way. They're just very forward-thinking people who make fantastic pop music. They're intellectuals, but they're not sort of scary serious, in fact they've got a great sense of humour in my experience. I think the important thing is that the music speaks for them. That's what makes it so special.'

The point Phillips makes about the public perception of Kraftwerk was one which Florian Schneider also brought up in conversation with Micko Westmoreland. 'I'd been to see Kraftwerk play at the Ars Electronica festival in Linz and I met up with Florian the next day,' he explains. 'We were going to see the Balanescu Quartet later that night but, since it was a nice sunny day we went down to the Danube for a couple of hours and chatted. One of the things he said was that there was almost too much legacy attached to the band. They just followed what they were interested in and the whole thing built up around that.'

The shows in Linz and Karlsruhe followed a similar format to the Tribal Gathering shows with the addition of an updated version of 'Airwaves' (from the *Radio-Activity* LP) and two more new songs, both obviously in the very early stages of development. A further two new tracks were played at the soundcheck for the Karlsruhe gig but weren't included in the concert. By the time of these shows, the new song which the group had debuted at Tribal had already undergone a number of changes, a normal part of the evolutionary process that Kraftwerk employ in their song-writing.

The troublesome curtain problems that Kraftwerk experienced at Tribal resurfaced in both Linz and Karlsruhe, together with a number of other technical problems that affected the video screens and the group's robots. For the opening night of the ZKM, a former army munitions complex which was being converted into a multi-media centre for the Karlsruhe area, Kraftwerk also used a quadraphonic speaker system to create multi-dimensional sound effects. However, the bare concrete structure of the ZKM caused a lot of acoustic problems, including heavy feedback. 'All the same,' says David Phillips, 'it was still an amazing show.' (Maybe it was just coincidence, maybe it was the same couple going one better or maybe it says something about Kraftwerk's inspired brand of seductive electronic futurism but in a odd postscript to the events at Tribal Gathering, the story quickly circulated that, close to the front of the stage in Karlsruhe, a couple had been spotted having full sex during the group's set.)

Whatever effect Tribal Gathering and the subsequent concerts in Austria and Germany had on their audiences, the results were surprising, even by Kraftwerk's standards. Within a few months, the group had announced a 1998 world tour, beginning with three dates at the Akasaka Blitz in Tokyo before heading to America for their first live performances there since 1981.

2

Germany's artistic life in the late '60s was dominated by two men, Karlheinz Stockhausen and Joseph Beuys, both of whom had a significant effect on the development of Kraftwerk. Born in Cologne in 1928, Stockhausen grew up in the North Rhine-Westphalia area around Düsseldorf, the region's capital. At sixteen, he was drafted into the army and spent the last year of the Second World War as a stretcher-bearer before enrolling in the classical academy at Bergisch Gladbach. After a year there he moved on to study piano and composition in Cologne and subsequently spent time in Paris studying under the radical French composer Olivier Messiaen.

Initially, Stockhausen was interested in serialism, a method of composition which had been pioneered by Arnold Schoenberg during the 1920s. A heavily structured and theoretical approach to the art of music, serialism used a fixed sequence of all 12 notes of the chromatic scale to create melody and harmony. Taken to its strictest form, no note in the sequence could be played out of order (i.e. until the other 11 notes had been played). Stockhausen was particularly influenced by two of Schoenberg's pupils, Alban Berg and Anton Von Webern and by 1951 he was already refining Webern's exploration of serialism in *Kreuzspiel* (*Crossplay*) where other elements such as rhythm, dynamics and tone colour were also used in strict sequence.

Stockhausen's interest in pushing the boundaries of composition and tone soon led him to electronics. His first major work in this area was 1955's *Gesang der Jünglinge*, which has been described as 'the first undisputed masterpiece of electronic music' but by the '60s, compositions such as *Mikrophonie I* (for two microphones, two filters, two potentiometers and six players) or *Kurzwellen* (four instrumentalists with short wave receivers and a sound projectionist) were pushing the envelope even further.

As Stockhausen pursued these aims, his growing reputation as an innovator was fuelled by the controversy surrounding his radical ideas. The extremism of his theories made good copy, not only for specialist musical publications but for the wider media too which helped to establish him as the pre-eminent musical presence in post-war Europe. Significantly, he maintained a base in Cologne (just twenty miles from Düsseldorf) first as the founder and artistic director of a prestigious New Music course and then as professor of composition at the College of Music which clearly intensified his immense influence on the musical climate of the North Rhine-Westphalia region, so a great deal of his thinking found its way into the music of bands like Can (Holger Czukay and Irmin Schmidt studied directly under him at Cologne) and Kraftwerk.

What Stockhausen wanted to do was not only create a new language for music but to encourage new ways of listening to it. As his theories were developed and refined he became increasingly interested in the mechanics of individual timbres and their impact on the overall form of a musical piece. His concept of music as a sequence of sound events, each precisely shaped and sculpted in order to create a number of surfaces from which the complete piece was assembled had a huge impact on the way Kraftwerk eventually approached their music. Even as late as the '80s, Ralf Hütter still explained the group's working methods in terms that were clearly Stockhausen-inspired: 'We aim to create a total sound – not to make music in the traditional sense with complex harmony. A minimalistic approach is more important for us. We spend a month on the sound and five minutes on the chord changes!'[1] Similarly, a few years later, when David Toop asked him if Kraftwerk were ever 'seduced by sound so much that form gets lost?' Hütter confirmed they were but pointed out that, far from being their main problem, it was actually their aim 'because form we don't care for too much.'[2] Both answers were text book Stockhausen.

In the visual arts, Stockhausen had an equally radical contemporary. Joseph Beuys was a charismatic free-thinker who grew up around Krefeld, just 12 miles north of Düsseldorf. As the only son of an upper middle-class family, he was well schooled in both art and science, eventually deciding to pursue a career in medicine. When war broke out in 1940, the nineteen-year-old Beuys volunteered for the Luftwaffe in order to escape the draft and trained as an aircraft radio operator before becoming a combat pilot. His experiences during the war subsequently filtered into his controversial artistic career (he often liked to explain his recurring use of felt and fat as sculptural materials, for example, as being the result of a plane crash he'd had in Russia during the war when the wreckage of his plane was found by nomadic Tartars who, as a way of keeping him warm and healing his wounds, rubbed him with fat and wrapped him in felt).

After the war Beuys gave up his plans for a medical career and instead enrolled at the Academy of Art in Düsseldorf to study sculpture, though he also continued to maintain a keen interest in science, philosophy, literature and the occult. These subjects were referenced in much of his subsequent artistic output which was catalysed in the early '60s by the experimentalism of the Fluxus group (with whom Ralf Hütter was also involved). At the time, Düsseldorf was becoming one of Germany's most important centres for contemporary art and Beuys was exposed to a number of radical artistic strategies but the importance of the Fluxus group's fusion of everyday life with visual and performance art and literature had a lasting effect. Beuys became increasingly interested in the intersection between art and society and in 1967 he set up the first of several activist groups, the German Student Party (though it wasn't exclusive to students in the conventional sense; Beuys believed that every human being is a student since, in a broad sense, life is the pursuit of knowledge).

By this time, Beuys was teaching at the Academy of Art in Düsseldorf (the GSP grew out of the public debates that Beuys regularly held in his class there) and, like Stockhausen, gaining worldwide notoriety for the radical nature of his art. One of his star pupils at the time was Emil Schult.

Born in Dessau, Schult grew up in the Lower Rhine area of Germany. His childhood, he says, was 'preoccupied with all sorts of little projects in art and science' (there's a striking similarity here with biographical details about the early life of Beuys himself), but by the time he was studying at the Düsseldorf Academy he was also interested in music and spent his free time either investigating Düsseldorf's exceptional collection of contemporary art at Schloss Jägerhof or practising his electric violin. He became involved in the city's burgeoning music scene and began to learn guitar too, inspired by the instrument's ability to 'create extreme electric sounds.' But it was his extraordinary talent for visual and conceptual art which was to have a profound effect on Kraftwerk when he eventually began to work with them during the 1970s and the influence of Beuys on many of their most inspired manipulations of image and theory can be traced directly to Schult's experiences at the Düsseldorf Academy.

In 1968, the year that Beuys changed the name of the German Student Party to the less prosaic but equally controversial Fluxus Zone West, Ralf Hütter met Florian Schneider-Esleben on a jazz improvisation course at the Düsseldorf Conservatory where both were studying (Ralf played electric organ, Florian played flute).

Ralf Hütter was born in Krefeld on 20th August, 1946. He's reticent about revealing any details about his childhood other than pointing out that it was unremarkable but close friends have suggested that – though he has a sister with whom he gets on well (apparently her daughter has a very similar nature to Ralf's) – as the only son of a successful father, he was both indulged and put under pressure to achieve the high standards demanded by his family background. The same sources point out that this is a significant factor in his friendship with Florian Schneider.

Schneider was born on 7th April, 1947 near Lake Constance on the River Rhine. His father, Paul Schneider was one of Germany's most celebrated architects and many of his buildings can still be seen around the Düsseldorf area including the headquarters of the Mannesmann steel corporation which overlooks the very same power station (*kraftwerk*) that inspired the group's name. Florian has two sisters but it's been suggested that, as the family's only son, he too felt the pressure of meeting the exacting standards expected of him.

A remarkably candid insight into Hütter and Schneider's family relationships is offered by Ralf's observation that 'we were born after the war . . . it's not much of an incentive to respect our fathers.'[3] Yet it's clear that Paul Schneider at least, took an active interest in his son's musical career. Through his contacts at Mannesmann, Schneider sorted out the rental of the company-owned property at 9 Bergerallee which became Kraftwerk's home base from the early '70s until the lease ran out in 1981.

Florian was already playing flute in a jazz group with various musicians (some of whom went on to become members of Amon Düül II) when he and Ralf decided to work together. By the summer of 1968, they had set up under the name Organisation and were playing at parties in art galleries, universities and performance 'happenings' around the North Rhine-Westphalia area. Inspired by the Fluxus group, a fairly extensive circuit had built up for more avant-garde musical events which, although outside the traditional pop-oriented club and dancehall scene, provided the group with plenty of opportunities to play. Can also played on this circuit including one legendary gig for the opening of an exhibition by the French sculptor Armand at the Düsseldorf Kunsthalle, when vocalist Malcolm Mooney caused a scandal by auctioning off the artist's work to members of the public for a fraction of their value. The gig effectively ended Can's career on the art gallery circuit.

Despite their name, which was both a reference to Stockhausen's strict serialism and a sly Derrida-esque pun on the nature of Ralf's instrument, Organisation had a typically fluid line-up, based around the nucleus of Hütter and Schneider. Their music focused on a heavily improvisational, sometimes chaotic, methodology which referenced jazz, high-brow avant-garde theory and the broad seam of sonic experimentalism that Aphex Twin or Squarepusher would mine more than two decades later. Though it wasn't Hütter and Schneider's only musical project at this time, it was certainly the main focus of their activities and, thanks to the generous intervention of Conny Plank, the only one to make it on to record.

A one-time jazz musician and radio sound engineer, Plank was a crucial figure in the German rock scene of the late '60s and early '70s. A keen fan of British and American pop, he was nevertheless keen to establish an independent German sound. Initially financing his activities through his day job, he set up a production company called Rainbow Productions to help record and find deals for the increasing number of groups springing up around the Cologne, Düsseldorf, Essen and Dortmund area of the Ruhrgebeit (it was Plank who later masterminded the setting up of Can's Inner Space studio). Late in 1969, Plank invited Organisation to his studio on the outskirts of Cologne with a view to recording some of their more structured musical experiments.

Though Organisation's line-up was still relatively fluid, the personnel who made it along to the recording sessions consisted of Ralf Hütter (electric organ), Basil Hammoudi (voice, musical box, glocken-spiel, conga, gong), Florian Schneider (electric flute, alto flute, electroviolin, tambourine, bell, triangle), Butch Hauf (bass, skaky tube, small bells, plastic hammer) and Fred Monicks (drums, bongos, maracas, cowbell and tambourine). The resulting LP, *Tone Float*, was as far as it's possible to get from Kraftwerk's later adventures in perfect pop but it offers some interesting glimpses into the kind of impulses that were occupying Hütter and Schneider at the time.

Produced by Plank and the band themselves, *Tone Float* was a curious amalgam of diverse musical strategies; a groove snatched from

Stockhausen here, a beat group bassline there and a riff lifted straight from the vocabulary of psychedelic rock emerging somewhere in between. On the 20 minute title track, Hütter's electric organ vamps even sound suspiciously like Ray Manzarek's jamming on some of The Doors' most drug-hazed and formless releases. Despite the confusion, the extended percussion solos and the lack of any discernible tune, tracks such as 'Silver Forest' do offer some interesting electronic moments but, on the whole, *Tone Float* succumbs to the worst excesses of experimental rock.

It's an impressive tribute to Plank's powers of persuasion that he managed to get this masterpiece of self-indulgence released by RCA in the UK (it was therefore available in Germany only as an import, presumably saving a lot of blushes on Hütter and Schneider's part). Unsurprisingly, however, the album didn't sell and within a few months of its release in 1970 the band broke up.

Though the sleeve artwork for the Organisation album was as reprehensible as the music it contained, it did possess one notable feature. The back cover included the image of a traffic cone, the symbol which Kraftwerk adopted as something of a trademark throughout their early career. In the context of the poorly-executed Expressionist pastiches of the *Tone Float* cover, however, it looks remarkably forlorn and out of place.

Undeterred by this creatively and commercially unsuccessful debut, Hütter and Schneider resolved to continue working with each other. Their experiences with Organisation may have been useful in determining their strict control over future musical ventures, since they'd learnt a significant lesson about the value of creating music by committee, but it would take some time before the improvisational twists and avant-garde quirks of their music were edited out in favour of the machine pop symphonies of their most influential records.

Soon after the break-up of Organisation, Hütter and Schneider rented some space in a building not far from Düsseldorf's main railway station. Initially, the plan was not to create their own studio but simply to have a regular place in which to work and rehearse (always a major problem for most bands). They did install some soundproofing but this was designed to prevent complaints from the neighbouring apartment blocks rather than creating the correct acoustic environment for recording.

'We started off Kling Klang studio in 1970, which really marked the beginning of Kraftwerk,' recalled Ralf Hütter some years later. 'The studio was, in fact, just an empty room in a workshop premises that was part of an industrial area in Düsseldorf. We fitted sound insulation material into the sixty square-metre room, and we now use other adjoining rooms where we make instruments. When we first moved in, we started recording with stereo tape machines and cassette recorders in preparation for our first record.'[4] (In fact, Hütter seems to be deliberately playing up Kling Klang's industrial associations here – the studio is actually in the centre of the city's red-light district.)

By the summer of 1970, Hütter and Schneider had already worked up some new material and recruited drummer Andreas Hohmann to help with the rhythmic structure of their music. Kraftwerk were to have numerous problems with their drummers during their early years, both in terms of their playing style (during this period Hütter and Schneider became increasingly frustrated with the extravagant technique of their drummers, some of whom had come from a jazz background) and their reluctance to get involved with the group's growing interest in technology.

'We used several acoustic drummers as we turned our attention to more rhythmic music,' remembers Hütter, 'and soon found that amplifying drums was desirable for us but not readily accepted by the players.'[5]

The drummer who would have been ideally suited to the group at this time was working in Cologne with Can. Jaki Liebezeit's precise, metronomic drumming provided exactly the minimal repetitive feel that the duo were after. Instead, according to one source, they were constantly frustrated by the tendency of their drummers to overplay in a style that they considered wholly inappropriate for their music. Unsurprisingly this created a lot of tension both during rehearsals and recording since the fashion in mainstream rock at the time was for drummers to show off their mastery of the kit by playing more rather than less. This was the complete antithesis of the style Hütter and Schneider were chasing, a fact that was no doubt bewildering to many of the drummers they recruited.

Work on the first Kraftwerk LP began in July, 1970. By this time, Hütter and Schneider had moved into the house at 9 Bergerallee which would be home, design studio and workshop for the various members of Kraftwerk over the next eleven years. Bergerallee is situated not far from the local government offices, just a couple of minutes walk from the River Rhine. Almost immediately opposite, on the other side of the river, sits Düsseldorf's main power station, the *kraftwerk* from which the band took their name. In keeping with the group's later image, it is conspicuously well-designed in a style that looks back towards classicism and forwards to the future, the power station of electronic sci-fi dreams.

At the time Hütter and Schneider chose their new name, Düsseldorf was being extensively rebuilt. Much has already been made of Kraftwerk's interest in many of the concepts originally connected with Marinetti and the Italian Futurist movement during the '20s – speed, dynamism, modernity – and there's no doubt that it has become an overwhelmingly powerful theme in their work. The scaffolding and heavy machinery on the numerous building sites around the city would obviously have echoed those particular riffs but it would have touched other resonances too. The rebuilding work was eradicating the last traces of the damage suffered by the city during the war and for anyone of Hütter and Schneider's generation, struggling to establish an individual German identity in the post-war climate, it would have been a potent symbol of the need to move forward and leave the past (i.e. the war and all it related to) behind. At the centre of all this was the power station, providing the electricity that drove the machinery, that lit the building sites and offices where new deals were being done every day to erect even more new buildings. And from the windows of the house at Bergerallee the pair could look out at the power station – both the heartbeat of the city and the engine of its reconstruction – driving the city into the future. Their new name, it must have seemed, was staring them in the face.

There are no details of how much material Kraftwerk actually recorded in their newly-acquired premises (the studio wasn't christened Kling Klang until work began on *Trans-Europe Express* in 1976) and how much was done during the final sessions at Conny Plank's studio but given the fact that the group was still heavily reliant on conventional instrumentation and that their own equipment at the time was limited to Ralf's Farfisa Professional electric piano, a Revox tape machine, a cassette recorder, a vibraphone and, of course Florian's flute, it seems likely that most of the work took place in Cologne.

According to John Foxx, who worked with him some years later, Conny Plank was an easy producer to get along with. 'He wasn't dictatorial at all,' explains Foxx, 'a lot of the time he'd just listen to what was going on with the music. His forte was mixing and it was just awe-inspiring to watch him do that. He'd place instruments in the soundfield that were quite close but create the illusion that they were far away at the same time. It was quite psychedelic. A lot of his techniques were based round old echo boxes like the Roland Space Echo but he also liked to layer textures and harmonies to get effects that were very complex by very simple means. I thought he was a genius.'

The production treatments on most of the first Kraftwerk album are trademark Conny Plank techniques – the subtle, trippy echoes of 'Megaherz' or the heavily effected coda of 'Ruckzuck' – but there were also some unexpected influences at work too. It's possible to trace the dynamics of Detroit garage bands like The Stooges and MC5 (alongside the obvious Stockhausen references) in the spiralling groove of 'Stratovarius' for example.

'Conny once told me that Iggy and The Stooges were a formative influence on Kraftwerk,' recalls Foxx. 'They were very interested in Stockhausen but also in the Detroit stuff. Of course they realised they couldn't be rockers so they made a kind of Marcel Duchamp version of rock n' roll for themselves . . .'

Ralf later admitted that 'I always liked what the Stooges were doing: they dared. With electronics, you can hide yourself behind the machines or you can expose yourself. There are various ways of exhibiting oneself. We are perhaps also interested in Iggy because of the Fluxus happenings in which I was involved as a student – action action baby! With electronic instruments you can be alone, all alone onstage, like Iggy: you don't even have a guitar to hide yourself. To some, physical discoveries of rock music can correspond to some fundamental and terrible psychological discoveries, like reading a book that changes the vision of the world you had before. After that, you never walk quite the same way . . . Iggy Pop, for instance, was a drummer and he stopped to go even further. He became a singer.'[6]

In contrast with the more traditional free-form improvisational nature of the Organisation sessions, the Kraftwerk album marked a distinct progression towards a more structured style of experimentation. The group's use of electronics throughout – particularly on 'Vom Himmel Hoch' – was also a step forward. But the album still has a curiously schizophrenic feel, touching at times on the cosmic rock of their German contemporaries or settling into weird Stockhausen-inspired jams at others, often in the space of the same track.

Hütter and Schneider's problems with the rhythmic base of their music continued when Andreas Hohmann decided to leave the band during the recording sessions for the album, subsequently disappearing from the music scene altogether.

'Nobody wanted to play with us because we were going to do all kinds of strange things,' noted Hütter. 'We were just doing feedbacks and overtones and sounds and rhythms. No drummer wanted to play or stay with us because they all wanted to play drum kits and we had these electronic things.'[7]

Hohmann's replacement was a young drummer called Klaus Dinger who was already making a name for himself around Düsseldorf. With him onboard, Kraftwerk returned to the studio to recommence work on the recording sessions for the album.

When the album was completed in the autumn of 1970, Kraftwerk returned to the live circuit. 'We must have played almost every youth club, factory and university between here and Dortmund,' observed Hütter, drily. 'When our friends were doing their so-called bourgeois jobs, getting their cars and money and everything, we had nothing. I had an old grey Volkswagen and a trailer with some synthesizers in it and we went from city to city playing.'[8]

On its release, late in 1970, *Kraftwerk* was a modest success, selling well enough for Philips to take up the group's contractual option for another album. But though the album offered a few glimpses of what lay ahead – notably Hütter's stark, minimalist sleeve design which featured the trademark traffic cone and, on the inner sleeve, an electrical generator – there was little indication of the elegantly structured compositional and conceptual style which would come to characterise the group's best work. The reasons for this were partly explained by Ralf during a revealing interview with the Cologne-based *Musik Express* magazine.

'It is a very simple thing,' he pointed out when asked about the success of the album. 'We have our own studio in Düsseldorf that we can use for our own productions. And through an identification of all the direct or indirect participants with the music we were able to transfer the maximum statement to the LP. Groups who reproduce their personality musically are always bought. Additionally, our music is in a phase that isn't finished yet. Through this circumstance of imperfection we enable the listener to have his own reflections. The music of Kraftwerk requires only a minimum of concept. We produce the music within a musical frame, in which contrary points are always present and must be present. An example of that: high – low, forward – back, above – below, in front – behind. You can trace this scheme well with the number 'Ruckzuck'. The number is nothing but a chase in which the electric flute of Florian Schneider-Esleben sets the pace. Florian increases up to the point where nothing else is possible, to the total dissolution of existing musical forms.'[9]

To expand their sonic horizons and flesh out the group's sound for live work, Hütter and Schneider recruited bass player Eberhardt Krahnemann and Michael Rother, a young guitarist from the Düsseldorf music scene. At the time he was approached to join Kraftwerk, Rother was playing in a local group called The Spirits Of Sound along with Wolfgang Flür. The group had initially done cover versions of songs by artists such as The Mamas And The Papas but had progressed to playing their own, fairly experimental, material in the clubs around Düsseldorf and had built up a reasonable following. Rother's defection to Kraftwerk, however, was a critical blow from which the band didn't recover.

'When Michael was taken, I was unhappy with the situation because we couldn't find another guitarist,' remembers Flür. 'He was such an important person and a very good friend and we really didn't want to replace him, so we quit The Spirits Of Sound. But for a long time afterwards I blamed Kraftwerk for the break-up of our band.'

The new five-piece Kraftwerk didn't last long. Eberhardt Krahnemann left after just one session, astonishingly followed by Ralf Hütter, leaving the trio of Schneider, Rother and Dinger to carry on as Kraftwerk.

'This departure is incomprehensible for many,' explained Ralf, 'but for me it is very natural. You may compare my break with the group with that of an erotic relationship to a woman that cools down with time. If you have reached such a point it is nonsensical to try and continue. But it's not that I've isolated myself completely from the group, I am still in rather good contact with Kraftwerk, which is mirrored in sessions, personal conversations and other things.'[10]

While Hütter concentrated on his architecture studies, the new Kraftwerk line-up set about dissolving the more organised structures that had begun to emerge on the album with a heavily improvisational sound. At concerts during this time, the trio would sometimes stretch tracks to more than twice their usual length, leaving few discernible traces of the original. The resulting sound bore many of the elements which would eventually surface in the psychedelic proto-punk of Neu!, the band that Rother and Dinger subsequently went on to form.

'With Kraftwerk we smashed up the structures . . .' recalls Michael Rother. 'It was very heavy music that we were playing. It is hard for me to explain what the music was like. Perhaps chaotic is the word that I am looking for – punk is like Sunday School after this!'[11]

A bootleg recording exists of the group playing live in Cologne around this time. Kraftwerk collector John Shilcock describes the performance as 'very noisy with lots of acoustic drums being bashed and cymbals being crashed and even electric guitars . . . like one great long improvised heavy metal session.'[12] While there are recognisable elements of Kraftwerk's 'Ruckzuck' and 'Von Himmel Hoch' on this recording, there are also similarities with early Neu! tracks such as 'Hallogallo' and 'Negativland' in places.

Though no material from this line-up was ever officially released, the group did go into the studio to record an album with Conny Plank. 'We didn't finish it,' says Rother, 'it was the difference between being live and being in the studio. It was a bit sterile.'[13] According to him, around twenty to thirty minutes of music were recorded at these sessions, comprising of three or four tracks, but he points out that 'the music was not like anything that got released by Kraftwerk.'[14]

In May 1971, the trio appeared on a German television show, *The Beatclub*, performing a lengthy, and densely repetitive, piece called 'Rückstoss Gondolero' on a stage set decorated with Kraftwerk's trademark traffic cones. Powered by Dinger's vigorous drumming, the track did feature some electronic treatments from Florian Schneider (dressed uncharacteristically in a white T-shirt and dungarees) but, again, the band's sound had more in common with Neu! than Kraftwerk.

With no visible success to show for their efforts during the six months they'd been together and an increasing sense of their different musical aims, Rother and Dinger began to get restless.

'At the time, it was very hard for us,' remembers Rother. 'The music was very depressing, we had no roadies. We just turned up in a small bus, the three of us with all our equipment, doing it all ourselves. We did one big festival, with Family, I think. They had a dozen or so roadies and we played before them. These roadies were already taking our equipment off stage when we were still playing. We couldn't argue! Of course, Family jumped on stage with everything perfect and we packed our gear and were gone . . . it was very interesting, but a hard time and very exhausting. We used to argue after a time. It was inevitable in these conditions, so we split and Hütter rejoined Schneider.'[15]

In August 1971, Rother and Dinger formed Neu!, recruiting Conny Plank to record their debut album for Bruno Wendel and Gunter Korber's Brain label in just four nights at Windrose Studio in Hamburg a few months later. A masterpiece of fuzz guitars, heavy phasing and Plank's distinctively psychedelic production, *Neu!* was a viscerally absorbing classic that went on to become a surprise hit, selling 35,000 copies in West Germany alone (for the live gigs that followed the album's release, Rother and Dinger enlisted the services of Eberhardt Krahnemann who had, by that time, resurfaced as a member of Guru Guru).

Hütter and Schneider, meanwhile, began preparations for Kraftwerk's second LP. Now without a drummer – and perhaps wary of involving other musicians given the events of the previous months – the pair hit on the idea of using rhythms from one of the pre-programmed units which were then beginning to appear as a means of providing accompaniment for home organists (the unit they acquired was probably an Echolette Drummer One or something fairly similar, since there were only a limited number of models on the market at the time). 'By changing the basic sounds with tape echo and filtering we made the rhythm tracks for our second album,' explained Ralf. 'Our instrumental sounds came from home-made oscillators and an old Hammond organ that gave us varied tonal harmonies with its drawbars.'[16]

Without the problem of having to record conventional instrumentation, Hütter and Schneider were able to do much of the preparation work for *Kraftwerk 2* in their own studio. The actual recording began on 26th September 1971 at Ralf Arnie's Star Musik Studio in Hamburg with, once again, Conny Plank at the controls. The absence of any other musicians left Hütter and Schneider free to experiment with a variety of instruments. On 'Wellenlänge', for example, Ralf played bass guitar against a background of taped treatments and ambient atmospherics while Florian picked out abstract melodic figures. Amplified breathing sounds were used for the disturbingly minimal 'Atem' (predating the intro of 'Tour De France' by more than a decade) while Florian's guitar playing on 'Strom' fluctuated somewhere between Morricone and The Stooges.

They emerged a week later, on 1st October 1971 with a completed album that undeniably bore the traces of either severe drug ingestion or intense, defiantly extremist experimentation or perhaps both.

Unsettling, achingly minimal, tracks like 'Spule 4' were hardly compositions at all, just drifting atmospheres randomly punctured by Florian's elliptical guitar phrases or a monotone bass pulse and wrapped up in Conny Plank's stoned echo games. The final cut, 'Harmonika' was a dense, wheezing harmonium extemporisation that sounded like it had been thrown together at the last minute to fill a gap, it certainly didn't fit with the spaced-out abstraction elsewhere on the album.

Only 'Klingklang' the seventeen-minute opening track made any concessions to the paying public with its pretty melodic figures and embryonic machine groove. Even then, it seemed as though Hütter and Schneider were deliberately subverting expectations by messing around with the tape speed to create queasy pitch-shifting effects that sabotaged the soothing mantra-like prettiness of the track. But there were definite hints in sections of 'Klingklang' of the sound that would emerge from the group in years to come. The track was of some historical significance in other ways too. Along with Sly Stone's 'Family Affair' (released almost simultaneously with the *Kraftwerk 2* LP late in 1971) it was the first time a drum machine had ever been used on a pop record.

History aside, overall, *Kraftwerk 2* sounded like Hütter and Schneider were back on their Stockhausen kick in a big way. Not even Conny Plank's gloriously empathic production could disguise the fact that – 'Klingklang' excepted – the new release wasn't much of a progression from the group's previous album. What it did demonstrate, however, was the fact that the pair were still clearly testing the boundaries of their new two-man group format.

Six months before, talking about the first Kraftwerk album, Ralf had dismissed the idea that commercial status was in any way important to the group. 'The success doesn't matter,' he explained. 'What matters is that a communication with the listener will be realised through the music and that the listener feels appealed.'[17]

It was obvious that commercial considerations had played little part in the recording sessions for *Kraftwerk 2* and so it must have come as little surprise that, when the LP reached the shops, it failed to match the success of its predecessor. But the opportunity to stretch out and experiment to such radical extremes undoubtedly had an enormous impact on Kraftwerk's future development. Sooner or later they would begin collating their definitive sound from the most successful fragments of these early experiments.

Despite the desultory nature of the *Kraftwerk 2* recordings, Hütter and Schneider did play some gigs during the closing months of 1971. 'I remember we played a dance party in some arts centre in Düsseldorf in '71,' notes Hütter, '. . . I had this old little drum machine. At a certain moment we had it going with some echo loops and some feedback and we just left the stage and joined the dancers. It kept going for an hour or so.'[18]

What's striking about this anecdote is not only the fact that, simply from an artistic point of view, the idea of leaving a drum machine running while you join the crowd on the dancefloor is a fantastic strategy but also how shockingly *modern* it sounds in the context of contemporary dance culture. Dancing to drum loops in 1971? If, as it is according to Jeff Mills, the definition of techno is 'something you can't imagine' then Kraftwerk were playing with the shapes of pure techno long before they ever dreamt of *Computer World*. There's a significant resonance too, with the implicitly democratic force of dance culture's eventual breakdown of the invisible barrier between stage and audience.

Partly this was due to the influence of their hometown. Kraftwerk were always enthusiastic visitors to clubs and discotheques. 'Düsseldorf is a very big amusement area,' asserts Hütter, 'there are clubs for everyone. You could track it down to a different shoe style from one club to another and appropriate music in each context. It's a cinematic thing – there are hundreds of them, all with no live music, always records and tapes and never anywhere which features people on stage. For us it has become a public living room . . . we go out to the discotheque all the time and dance.'[19]

It would be some time, however, before the group channelled these kind of recreational pursuits into their music. As 1971 drew to a close, Kraftwerk were still overshadowed by a number of other German bands, particularly Can and Tangerine Dream who were, at that time, achieving considerable success on both commercial and critical levels. Can's 1971 double album, *Tago Mago*, was an extraordinary release which referenced many of the points Kraftwerk had encircled on their first two LPs and a whole lot more besides. Tangerine Dream, meanwhile, had just released *Alpha Centauri*, the record which began their particular love affair with the synthesizer (in this case a borrowed VCS3) and which would eventually propel them towards their first purely synthesized release, *Phaedra*, just two years later. Observers at the time considered both groups to be streets ahead of Kraftwerk. Despite this, there was no enmity on Hütter and Schneider's part – they even jammed with Can on occasional visits to the group's studio at Schloss Norvenich.

There was little doubt though that, sooner or later, Kraftwerk were going to have to pull out something special if they were ever going to become a viable commercial proposition. While their contemporaries in other cities were gaining ground, they still seemed to be playing the same art gallery openings, youth clubs and universities that they always had. Something had to give. Tangerine Dream's Edgar Froese had an experience that offers a significant insight into the mood of some members of the German underground scene around this time.

'There was a gig somewhere in the south of Germany,' remembers Froese, 'where we walked on stage with the usual line-up and were playing some crazy free music with rock instruments and all of a sudden we realised that if you do that for years you end up nowhere with nowhere to go. Even though we were doing crazy things, the sound was pretty normal. We felt we had to make an absolute break, so after the gig we decided to sell everything we had in the way of normal instruments and do something completely new.'[20]

At some point, Kraftwerk were going to experience a similar epiphany but the seeds were already beginning to be sewn in the rare flashes of prescience which had given birth to the hypnotic electronic mantra of tracks such as 'Klingklang' and 'Von Himmel Hoch' from the LPs with which they'd ushered in the decade. Within a few years, Kraftwerk would have developed a talent for looking into the future. If, however, as 1971 drew to a close, they could have seen what the end of the decade held in store for them, they would have been amazed.

The hiatus which temporarily severed the creative relationship between Ralf Hütter and Florian Schneider for six months during the spring and summer of 1971 was destined never to recur. Their association has since become one of the longest-standing and most intriguing partnerships in the history of contemporary pop. Some years later, Ralf Hütter was asked if they would ever consider splitting up.

'We already tried, but it didn't work,' he pointed out. 'Our understanding is too stimulating: we discovered lots of things because we were together and loneliness could never have taken us where we are now. It's a necessary duality . . . kling and klang!'[21]

In the final days of 1971, Hütter and Schneider settled down for a period of well-earned rest. Over the past three years, they'd recorded three albums, played numerous gigs and negotiated themselves into a visible position within the German music scene that would provide them with at least some kind of platform for their own personal musical vision. While 1972 would be a busy year for many of their contemporaries (Neu! were preparing to release two LPs over the next twelve months) for Kraftwerk it proved to be a period of relative inactivity. There would still be sporadic live appearances of course and time spent upgrading their studio, but with Hütter requiring an increasing amount of time for his architectural studies, Kraftwerk's assault on the future would have to be put, temporarily, on hold.

3

The thrill of the new is an integral part of pop culture's charm. But as the '70s got properly underway the risks of exploration suddenly seemed too great for a record industry which had got fat on the profits of exploiting the unknown and was now attempting to conduct itself in a more adult and business-like manner. Almost overnight, record companies stopped talking in terms of artists and music and began talking in terms of product and units. The new terminology was brutally utilitarian but it also offered a keen insight into the psyche of what was, after all, a relatively new business.

The most visible effect of this transformation was that pop music entered into a period of consolidation rather than innovation. With The Beatles and Jimi Hendrix out of the picture, fresh takes on the pop phenomenon were hard to come by and the record industry actively encouraged a more conservative set of value judgments about the artists on their labels. Musicianship rather than the ability to conjure up new ideas became the dominant theme of pop's new conservatism. Distinct divisions were formed between album-oriented rock music, which was seen as a serious artistic endeavour and the supposedly lightweight, disposable format of pop. There were a few exceptional artists who managed to bridge the chasm between these two opposing spheres but they were in the minority, most mined their own specific seam and paid little attention to developments outside it.

For those who found this a bewildering state of affairs, Kraut-rock – as the new German movement was being tagged – was a welcome diversion from the dull musical diet on offer elsewhere. The modest commercial success of Can and Tangerine Dream and to a lesser extent groups such as Ash Ra Tempel and Neu! was enough to suggest that there was a reasonable market for strange, oblique, often challenging music which operated outside the mainstream consensus. The anarchic, free-wheeling nature of the German groups clearly connected with the ever-present constituency of pop's disaffected.

In some ways, what set the German scene apart was the fact that it was plugged in to a tradition of avant-garde art that, outside of the Velvet Underground, most British and American groups simply weren't exposed to. By 1972, the network of happenings, exhibitions and performance artworks across Germany was an established part of the cultural fabric. Much of it had been inspired by the recent activities of the Fluxus group but it was also part of a wider willingness to engage with the theories and practices of the avant-garde which was evidenced by the status of both Stockhausen and Beuys in their home country. Germany had a long and significant history of avant-garde art, stretching back through the work of John Heartfield, Käthe Kollwitz, Max Ernst and Kurt Schwitters, Ludwig Kirchner and groups such as Die Brücke and Der Blaue Reiter and, of course, the Bauhaus, each of which mapped on to specific developments in the social, political and intellectual climate of the country. Like these, the upswing in avant-garde activity during the late '60s and early '70s keyed in to a particular prevailing mood.

A central concern for the post-war generation of Hütter and Schneider was the crisis of identity in German culture that had been precipitated by the events of the war. The avant-garde offered a way of breaking with the past and establishing a new cultural identity.

'There was really no German culture after the war,' explains Hütter. 'Everyone was rebuilding their homes and getting their little Volkswagens. In the clubs when we first started playing, you never heard a German record, you switched on the radio and all you heard was Anglo-American music, you went to the cinema and all the films were Italian and French. That's okay but we needed our own cultural identity.'[1]

Such concerns, of course, were completely alien to the British and American bands who dominated the music scene. But this predominant theme among young Germans helped to create a climate which was more than receptive to the activities of the avant-garde and exposed many of those in the post-war generation to artistic ideas which they would otherwise have been unaware of. For many of the groups on the German scene, this translated into a rejection of British and American music in favour of something more identifiably individual.

'We had to turn the camera and to take a picture of ourselves,' says Hütter, 'to expose ourselves to the media because the post-war German generation remained in the shadow: those who are older than us had Elvis or The Beatles for idols . . . those are not bad options, but if we completely forget our identity, it becomes quickly empty and not consistent. There's a whole generation in Germany, between thirty and fifty, who has lost its own identity and who never even had any.'[2]

With the benefit of hindsight it's easy to see that similar themes would eventually manifest themselves in the rhetoric of punk (which thanks to Jamie Reid and Malcolm McLaren also had strong links with the avant-garde) some years later; perhaps it was some kind of intuitive understanding of this fact that made Kraftwerk one of the few established groups to survive the onslaught of punk with their reputation not only undamaged but enhanced.

This cultural drive helped establish a framework of experimentation and debate which had an obvious impact on Kraftwerk's musical direction. This was already apparent in the heavily experimental nature of the records they'd produced so far but it would emerge in a much more specific way in the recordings that Hütter and Schneider were about to embark on.

Little is known about Kraftwerk's activities during 1972. It's unlikely that they didn't record at all so the absence of any official release suggests that either they were unhappy with the results or they were simply using these sessions as a way of experimenting in private until the material was sufficiently developed to warrant a new release. This would help to explain the dramatic shift in the group's music which occurred between the release of *Kraftwerk 2* in late '71 and their third LP in the autumn of 1973.

Kraftwerk's first major engagement during 1973 was at a festival of German rock music in Boulogne-Billancourt near Paris. Sponsored by the French magazine *Actuel*, their appearance there served to highlight the fact that Kraftwerk were by now beginning to assert their individuality. Whatever they had been doing over the preceding months, reports from the concert suggested that they were now a more focused and polished live act than their contemporaries on the domestic scene. As they'd done during the concerts in late '71, Hütter and Schneider played without any additional musicians, using their rhythm unit to provide the required accompaniment.

'We were the first ones to use the drum machine on stage,' Hütter pointed out, 'especially for the concert in Boulogne-Billancourt. . . . back then, no drummer accepted to use the machine. They were deprived from the physical side of drumming. That cerebral, automatic and hallucinating rhythm used to fascinate us. But we still keep a possibility to exit from it and to manually improvise over the robotic background.'[3]

Soon after their return from France, Hütter and Schneider struck up a friendship with the artist Emil Schult who was involved in the local music scene at the time. When Hütter and Schneider first met him, Schult was playing guitar and electric violin with various groups around the Düsseldorf music scene. Intrigued by his ideas and artistic theories they invited him to Kling Klang and he soon became a regular member of Kraftwerk's circle, eventually moving into the house at 9 Bergerallee.

Though Schult's talents as a painter far outweighed his skill as a musician, he did contribute to the group's various musical activities and appeared with them, playing guitar and violin, at various concerts and festivals around Germany during the following months. It was clear, however, that Schult recognised the potential of the chemistry between Hütter and Schneider. In the long hours they spent chatting about music, art and politics over strong coffee in the cafes around Düsseldorf, he encouraged them to think about the possibilities of Kraftwerk in new ways.

Not all the ideas which came up during these sessions were Schult's, of course. Many of them were already latent in Hütter and Schneider's approach to their music. But Schult had an active part in helping them to express many of these concepts more clearly. 'He is our medium,'[4] noted Ralf.

Schult's impact on the group had an immediate effect on the album they began recording in May 1973. Though he was untrained as a musician, he had an instinctive ear for melody. The simple but effective phrases he picked out during the improvised sessions and concerts which he was involved in were largely a result of his limited facility on the guitar and violin but they intrigued both Hütter and Schneider who began exploring ways of simplifying their own melodic ideas. As a painter, Schult describes his work as 'research into precise and maximum expression' and it was this theme which became a crucial part of Hütter and Schneider's subsequent musical endeavours.

Schult also encouraged them to think about ways of including the post-war generation's concerns about cultural identity into their music. Notions about what it was to be German, about what could be salvaged from the nation's cultural tradition in view of the war and so on were already an important part of Hütter and Schneider's intellectual discourse but hadn't yet become part of their music. Conversations with Schult and the wider circle of artists, fashion designers and other musicians who were, by now, orbiting the group brought these issues into focus. Inspired by this, the pair now began investigating ways of forging an explicitly German sound, one which would link the bright new future they imagined for themselves with more traditional cultural themes.

'Coming from Germany, historical myths are all the more prevalent and stronger,' explained Hütter. 'It's the country of Beethoven, Mozart, the untouchables.'[5]

With Conny Plank at the controls again, Kraftwerk's third and most convincing album yet was recorded between their own studio in Düsseldorf, Studio 70 in Munich and two studios in Cologne – Comet and Rhenus – where Plank had sorted out a deal to utilise studio down-time (those periods when the studio isn't otherwise occupied) in return for a substantial discount.

The tracks which surfaced from these sessions were the strongest that Kraftwerk had so far recorded and marked a quantum leap forward from the tentative experimentation of their previous releases. Significantly, the melodies on many of the new compositions bore obvious links with both German classical and folk music traditions.

Hütter and Schneider had also invested in their first synthesizers – a Mini-Moog and an Arp Odyssey respectively. Along with Ralf's Hammond and Farfisa organs, these new instruments increased the group's tonal palette enormously. On 'Kristallo' they juxtaposed a classically-inspired harpsichord theme against a heavily synthetic and extraordinarily funky bassline (they'd obviously been paying close attention to the bass parts played by Bootsy Collins on their favourite James Brown records) and a mechanical 4/4 rhythm. The track's coda was an equally intriguing piece of synthetic classicism which evidently had been influenced by Beethoven.

Similarly, 'Tanzmusik' (literally 'dance music') took familiar themes from German folk music and placed them in the context of Kraftwerk's driving drum box rhythm. The track's most immediate predecessor was 'Klingklang' from their previous LP, but this time they eschewed the calculated weirdness of tape manipulations in favour of creating a more straight-forward pop-oriented dynamic.

The similarities between 'Tanzmusik' and 'Klingklang' were echoed in 'Tongebirge' which developed the opening theme of 'Ruckzuck' (a harmonised flute which had been added towards the end of the Kraftwerk recording sessions as a means of creating a hookline for the track). But the track which would close the album, 'Ananas Symphonie', prefigured something else altogether. For the first time, Kraftwerk had used a simple vocal phrase (in this case, the track title) to add a new kind of texture to their music. By treating the vocal synthetically through a borrowed vocoder, Kraftwerk had stumbled on a technique which was to be of crucial importance to them in the future.

Overall, the new recordings were more focused and less self-indulgent than anything they'd done previously. Though they were still a long way from creating fully-fledged pop music, the stronger melodic emphasis helped to make the experimental strategies of 'Tongebirge' and 'Heimatklänge' accessible to a wider audience.

During the final stages of recording the new LP, Hütter and Schneider recruited Wolfgang Flür, a drummer who was already well-known on the local music scene. Flür's musical career had begun in 1963 when he formed The Beathovens with some school friends. Heavily influenced by The Beatles, the group played cover versions of songs like 'Please Please Me' and 'Love Me Do' at local fetes and school parties, eventually graduating to professional gigs in the dancehalls and clubs around Düsseldorf. By 1967, The Beathovens were popular enough around the local scene to be invited to play as the support act when The Who and John's Children (featuring Marc Bolan) appeared at the Düsseldorf sports arena.

'The music scene in Düsseldorf wasn't any different than in other cities,' notes Flür. 'It was common to play in bands in those years just for the attention of girls! We wanted to be loved and to be stars. The most we knew about bands was what we read in the music papers. We also listened to the AM station on the mono radio and, every Saturday, Radio Luxembourg would play the English Top 20 in the afternoon. I remember being amazed by one particular hit – the guy was stammering and I couldn't believe it. "My g-g-g-generation . . . " Unbelievable! It was amazing to me that this guy was making money and he couldn't speak properly!'

After five years, The Beathovens went their separate ways and Flür played in a series of bands with names which perfectly expressed the nature of the times – Fruit, Anyway, Liberty – before joining forces with guitarist Michael Rother to form The Spirits Of Sound. They began by playing cover versions of chart songs, picking up gigs on the mainstream club circuit that was entirely alien to more experimental groups like Kraftwerk and Can. But soon they were adding their own material too, original songs with pop sensibilities that had been honed through years of playing Top 40 covers.

'Eventually, The Beatles became too old-fashioned for us,' says Flür. 'We started to become more experimental and a little more way-out.'

While Kraftwerk were playing the art gallery and university beat, The Spirits Of Sound were appearing at the Düsseldorf Star Club (an affiliate of the famous Hamburg version). 'We knew that people liked to dance at the weekend,' remembers Flür. 'So there were three or four clubs who would hire us to play and people would dance in front of us. But we didn't make much money because we were always buying new equipment. We always wanted to improve what we had. When we wanted something very badly, if we didn't have enough money, there was a very good music store in Düsseldorf that would allow us to make a down-payment and take the equipment. Then we would pay the rest by instalments. But it took us a long time. For the first year I was in Kraftwerk, I was still making payments for equipment we had bought in The Spirits Of Sound!'

Though the two groups were involved in completely different scenes, Kraftwerk and The Spirits Of Sound were aware of each other. Hütter and Schneider were always keenly interested in places which would provide opportunities to meet girls so they were frequent visitors to the kind of clubs and dancehalls where The Spirits Of Sound played. They were impressed by the group's guitarist while, for their part, Flür's group were impressed by the fact that other musicians from Düsseldorf had got things together enough to make an album. 'That was a big thing in those days,' recalls Flür. 'We didn't much like their music – it was too strange – but Kraftwerk were a big thing all the same because they had made a record. That was what persuaded Michael to join with them when they asked him. He didn't like the music they were making but, because this was a group that had made a record, he felt that it was a step forward for him. I was pleased for him but I was still unhappy with Kraftwerk for breaking up our band!'

Flür also had other problems to contend with. He was now at the age when most young Germans did their National Service in the armed forces. 'It was very difficult to get out of,' he remembers. 'I had to fight with the government before I could release myself. It didn't cost anything to get out – well nothing but my nerves – but it was a difficult time. Ralf and Florian had to go through the same thing. For people like us, the whole idea of having to do something like that was completely against everything we believed in.'

In July 1973, Florian Schneider approached Flür and asked him to join

Kraftwerk. Flür refused at first, following the bad feeling over Michael Rother's departure from The Spirits Of Sound ('I was so angry about it, those young guys from a special scene with very rich parents! I thought, maybe they believe they can buy anyone, they can have anyone.'[6]) but he eventually relented and Schneider's second attempt at recruiting him was successful. It was the first step towards creating the group's classic line-up which would be completed with the arrival of Karl Bartos in 1975.

Flür remembers one of his first visits to Kling Klang, shortly after the recording sessions for the third Kraftwerk album had been completed: 'The studio was a big room in an old factory building with brick walls,' he explains. 'There were big home-made speakers, amplifiers and so on. Florian had his side, with his flutes and one of the very first Arp Odyssey synthesizers, while Ralf's side had Hammond and Farfisa organs and a Mini-Moog synthesizer.'[7]

By the time Flür joined, Hütter and Schneider had almost fully completed the third Kraftwerk album. It was to be called *Ralf & Florian* in recognition of the fact that the duo had written and produced everything on the record. The title also provided the first step in creating a recognisable identity. This new-found interest in the mechanics of image was, again, the result of their friendship with Emil Schult but it also drew from the theories of pop-art (Düsseldorf's modern art gallery had acquired an exceptional collection of pop-art, including significant works by Warhol and Rauschenberg) and the calculated irony of post-modernism which was to become something of a trademark for the group.

In keeping with these influences, they had also sourced a local artist who designed neon signs for the numerous cafes, bars and strip-joints in the area surrounding their studio. In the windows of these establishments, they'd see the name of the cafe or perhaps the figure of a naked woman sculpted in neon. This immediately struck a chord with several of their interests, including their growing interest in creating a recognisable identity, and with Schult's encouragement they commissioned two signs, one bearing Ralf's name, the other Florian's. Over the years they would pay several more visits to this same supplier.

To go with the LP, Schult designed what he described as a 'Musicomix' – basically a poster of comic cartoons and drawings by Schult and Schneider which included images of some of the people in the group's immediate circle such as Schneider's girlfriend Barbara

Niemöller and his sisters Tina and Claudia. 'When I met Emil and when he showed his comics to me,' recalled Florian some years later, 'I thought they looked like our music.'[8]

Barbara Niemöller also took the picture of Ralf and Florian in their studio which eventually appeared on the back cover of the album. The picture reveals exactly how basic their set-up still was. With its peeling, whitewashed brick walls and exposed pipework, the place looks more like a down-at-heel rehearsal room than a studio. The pair sit facing each other over their keyboards, though surprisingly it's Florian's equipment – including his flutes, his pedal-steel guitar and even an oscilloscope – which dominates. In the foreground are the newly-acquired neon signs while, in the background, clearly visible, are the distinctive gold-coloured speaker horns which Wolfgang Flür distinctly remembered from his first visits there. Acting as a focal point, in the centre of the picture, sits a lone traffic cone, a slight nod to the group's established trademark though it's one of the single stripe variety and not the double stripe version which Hütter had used for the group's previous album sleeves.

Both the title itself and the distinctive imagery on the sleeve of *Ralf & Florian* bore obvious traces of another avant-garde influence. In 1970, the British performance art duo Gilbert & George had appeared in Düsseldorf. Though their work included paintings and installations which referenced many of the developments in pop art, Situationism and post-modernism, Gilbert & George's most famous artwork was themselves. On the surface, their appearance was that of two very straight, square, quintessentially English, civil servants. This image was in direct contrast to the radicalism of their artistic strategies. They would play up their normality while, at the same time, creating art that was extremely unconventional and contentious. Their appearance in Düsseldorf had been introduced as *The Singing Sculpture* and consisted of two eight-hour performances of the song 'Underneath The Arches' made famous by the British music-hall duo Bud Flanagan and Chesney Allen.

Both Hütter and Schneider must have been intrigued by Gilbert & George's semi-ironic but unmistakably English art and, perhaps in view of their own cultural concerns, were inspired to use the essence of it to create something that was equally identifiably German. The front cover of the *Ralf & Florian* album featured a photograph that bore obvious traces of Gilbert & George's influence. Dressed in a very conservative suit and tie, Florian's appearance is most in keeping with their ironic traditionalism (only the large minim badge on his label provides any indication that he's not a bank clerk or a businessman), but Ralf too has made some concessions, by combing his hair behind his ears with a severe side parting. For its time, in terms of the long-haired, denim-clad aesthetic of their contemporaries in the music scene, the image was shockingly old-fashioned and square. But, if you could read the references and understand the joke, it was both humorously subversive and revolutionary.

It's interesting to speculate whether or not Kraftwerk and their friends on the Düsseldorf art scene appreciated the full resonance of Gilbert & George's performance in their hometown, however. 'Underneath The Arches' came from a long music-hall tradition that, by the time of the war, was in stark decline. The last of the real music-hall stars were The Crazy Gang, an irreverent group featuring Bud Flanagan and Chesney Allen, who performed songs, slapstick comedy and humorous sketches that were both wildly anarchic and hugely popular in the climate of pre-war Britain. There was a deeply patriotic but liberal edge to their comedy that appealed to many in the working and lower-middle classes, which made 'Underneath The Arches' – Flanagan and Allen's signature tune – one of Britain's most popular wartime songs. The fact that Gilbert & George chose to tour Germany performing it had obviously contentious overtones.

While arrangements were being made for the release of *Ralf & Florian*, the group were contacted by the producers of a late night, arts-based television show called *Aspecte*. They were interested in the possibility of Kraftwerk doing a live performance on the show. With an album to promote and keen to expand the group's profile, Hütter and Schneider eagerly accepted the offer and began rehearsals with Flür who, by this time, had also moved into the house at 9 Bergerallee.

Flür, however, wasn't impressed by the junior-sized set of drums the group had provided for him. 'The kit in the studio was terrible,' he explains, 'covered in dust and very unprofessional.' He decided instead to investigate the electronic percussion unit that had been used during the recording of *Ralf & Florian*. 'I decided to try it through an amplifier and straight away it sounded great. It sounded so great, it started me thinking about how good it would be if I could just play those sounds like normal drums.'

Having been brought up learning to make things with his own hands,

Flür retreated with the unit to his basement workshop in Bergerallee and began to work out a way of operating the rhythm box with a more conventional drumming style. At a local scrapyard he found some circular metal discs. 'Even now I still don't know what they were used for,' he says, 'but I quickly realised that I could use them as pads to play my own drum sounds.' Since he was a skilled carpenter, building a simple case wasn't a problem. With the metal discs mounted on the front and then connected to the circuits for each separate drum sound, he then wired up two thin steel rods – halfway between a knitting needle and a drum stick – which, when touched against the discs, closed the circuits and activated the sounds. The unit was completed just three days before the group travelled to Berlin to record their *Aspecte* appearance but Wolfgang Flür was now, officially the world's first electronic drummer.

The *Aspecte* show featured two of the tracks from the new *Ralf & Florian* album – 'Heimatklänge' and 'Tanzmusik' – together with a commentary from the presenter about the group's background, during which the LP cover was flashed up on screen. Despite their nervous performance, it was terrific publicity. As usual, Ralf sat to the left of the stage with his keyboards while Florian stood on the right self-consciously playing his flute into a microphone. In the middle, nonchalant and sporting a slightly incongruous moustache, sat Flür with the newly-fashioned electronic drum kit. With wires spewing out of the back and silver foil covering the casing, the unit looked half-finished and remarkably frail but it worked and Flür's perfect timing gave the late night German audience the first taste of the machine-like rhythms that would become an integral part of the Kraftwerk sound.

Flür's composure was curiously at odds with the obvious discomfort of his companions. Ralf looked painfully nervous and, towards the final section of 'Tanzmusik', played several glaring mistakes, worst of which was launching into the re-emerging melody in entirely the wrong key. Florian seemed marginally more relaxed, focusing determinedly on the microphone in front of him. But each time the cameras panned on to him as he put the flute to his mouth, he closed his eyes tightly and it was difficult not to be convinced that he was desperately wishing himself elsewhere.

Despite this, the release of the *Ralf & Florian* album in November 1973 proved that Kraftwerk were now making significant artistic progress. Together with Conny Plank, the sound they had forged was a unique combination of state-of-the-art instrumentation and traditional melodies. The adaptation of themes from German folk and classical music connected directly with the post-war generation's concerns about their cultural identity. By reclaiming these elements from the past, Hütter and Schneider were actively attempting to design music that related unmistakably to their national origins. This was partly a purely artistic strategy but it clearly had political overtones too.

'We woke up in the late '60s and realised that Germany had become an American colony,' explained Hütter. 'There was no German culture, no German music, nothing. It was like living in a vacuum. The young people were into the American way of living; cars, hamburgers and rock n' roll. Germany had lost its identity. We all felt very lost. To be able to feel any bonds at all, we had to go back to the Bauhaus school. It sounds strange but to be able to continue into the future we had to take a step back forty years. The Bauhaus idea was to mix art and technology. An artist is not an isolated creature that creates for the sake of creation, but as part of a functional community. In the same way we are a kind of musical workers. The spirit of Bauhaus in electronic sounds . . . Our roots were in the culture that was stopped by Hitler; the school of Bauhaus, German Expressionism. We didn't have many musical influences. One was Stockhausen, one of the pioneers of electronic music. We felt somehow that the age of composed music had passed and we strived for simpler music, something that could be played on the radio without having to be adjusted to current styles of music.'[9]

Hütter's feeling that Germany had become an American colony was especially prevalent in Düsseldorf which, around this time, still had a large number of British and American troops stationed at the nearby army base. Many local businesses specifically catered for the soldiers, with restaurants laying on English or American food. Similarly, cafes and bars stocked British and American beers and shops displaying signs printed in English were commonplace. Added to the inherent Anglo-American slant of pop culture, it's not difficult to appreciate why many young Germans such as Hütter and Schneider felt deeply passionate about the need to explore their own cultural identity.

The *Ralf & Florian* album signalled an important step forward for Kraftwerk both musically and in terms of the attention they were now beginning to pay to details such as crafting a distinct group image for themselves. It was also around this point that Hütter and Schneider began to approach their relationship with the music industry much more seriously. Initially, the group's business dealings had been conducted in a fairly haphazard way. The rights to the first Kraftwerk LP, for example, were sold to Philips (the record company which released the group's first four albums in Germany) for a figure of around $2000. Even by the standards of the early '70s, when the percentages offered by most record contracts were still notoriously mean, this was an embarrassingly bad deal.

On the Musicomix poster given away with the *Ralf & Florian* album was a credit for Kling Klang Verlag. This was the first ever reference to the group's new company which had been set up to take care of all aspects of their business. Increasingly, under Schult's influence, Hütter and Schneider were developing the idea of Kraftwerk as a broader artistic concept that could include a variety of activities. Instead of confining themselves only to recording, they began thinking in terms of an organisation that would include projects such as sleeve design, graphics, developing new equipment and Schult's painting and film-making. Over the next few years, this concept became increasingly refined.

'We do everything by ourselves, videos, sleeves and graphics,' Hütter pointed out, 'it's like a mosaic which leads to the productivity of Kraftwerk, but it doesn't represent one field only. In Germany, it is called *gesankt kunstwerk*. That's what Wagner was doing in his time with theatre and music . . . '[10]

Again, in terms of pop music, this was a strategy which was ahead of its time. Though it was subsequently adopted by a number of other artists, in 1973 the idea of a group directing a variety of creative avenues outside music was still revolutionary. This was, in effect, the beginning of Hütter and Schneider's drive to retain control over all aspects of the group's activities. Eventually it would result in the perfect combination of music and image that made Kraftwerk such a powerful conceptual force in the late '70s and beyond.

'We don't think of ourselves as musicians,' explained Hütter, 'but rather as people who create out of the different media or ways of expressing yourself, whether it is painting, poetry, music or even film. The ideal is to communicate to people.'[11]

In the years before punk expanded pop's horizons, this was an extraordinary statement. The climate of rock was completely dominated by artists who were eager to establish their credentials as musicians. It was a time when the music industry's most revered figures were guitar heroes or virtuoso drummers or keyboard players who were capable of adding a classical flourish whenever it was called for. In the music press, favourite terms like 'credibility' related not to street-awareness or originality but to years spent 'paying dues' and the bland worthiness of players who could find their way around the torturous complexities of progressive rock. Musicianship (in terms of technique, not talent) was pop's Holy Grail during these years. In the UK, for example, Eric Clapton was the excruciatingly dull subject of a common graffito which read 'EC Is God' – not because he was an exciting and original pop star who could write great songs, but because he could *play*. And here was Hütter – a classically-trained musician – subverting the whole notion by suggesting that 'we don't think of ourselves as musicians.'

Part of the mythology that surrounds Kraftwerk suggests that they are immune to the processes of pop. It's true that, through a series of inspired artistic strategies, they have managed to set themselves apart from it, but what's evident from their ability to play these kind of games is that Hütter and Schneider possess an acute understanding of the trends and ideologies which permeate the scene. At the centre of their drive to be more than just a pop group is their obvious affinity with the most radical and iconoclastic currents in music (Iggy & The Stooges, Stockhausen), art (Beuys, Warhol) and politics (liberal socialism). Equally, while it's conceivable that some people with their intellectual background might have considered pop music to be the most base and trivial form of cultural expression, they are very clearly arch pop fans with a deep insight into both its power and its attractions.

Hütter and Schneider would have been well aware of the pop psychodrama which was being played out across the English channel during the months when they were preparing for the release of *Ralf & Florian*. David Bowie had already been experimenting with the intersection between pop music, art and image for some time, but his 1972 LP *The Rise And Fall Of Ziggy Stardust And The Spiders From Mars* had catapulted him to international stardom. Prior to this release, Bowie – a shrewd opportunist who'd operated on the fringes of the mainstream since the early '60s – had been something of a one-hit wonder but his self-reinvention in the character of Ziggy hit the target with dead-aim accuracy.

Bowie's fascination with the mechanics of image mapped perfectly on to Kraftwerk's own increasing interest in developing a more recognisable identity. By skilful manipulation of his image, Bowie had transformed his career. But as the much-talked about Ziggy tour progressed, it became evident that the boundaries between the artist and the character were beginning to blur. For any keen student of pop, this was a fascinating phenomenon, but to Hütter and Schneider who understood exactly which sources Bowie had referenced in order to effect his transformation it was utterly compelling.

Like Kraftwerk, Bowie was operating in territory that was completely alien to the dull, blues-based worthiness of most mainstream rock. His influences were drawn from the avant-garde background of Beckenham's Arts Lab, the radical hippie scene of the late '60s and English music hall – all of which placed him outside the dominant trends of the music scene – and his records were informed as much by art and literature as by other music (though during his early career he cribbed shamelessly from a number of other performers progressing from Anthony Newley in the late '60s to Bob Dylan and The Rolling Stones and eventually Kraftwerk themselves). With Ziggy retired at the end of the 1973 tour, Bowie emerged as a new character – Aladdin Sane – but after losing himself once was this time careful to disassociate his private life from his stage persona. Instead he conjured up the image of the urban sophisticate for his day-to-day life, equally at home in a French château as in a London club, travelling across Europe by train (he cited a fear of flying as the reason, others suggested it was more like fear of a cocaine comedown at 6000 feet) and cultivating a quietly cosmopolitan air.

Hütter and Schneider charted the progress of all this in the music papers and found it captivating. Along with Schult's influence and their own heavily-artistic background, the Bowie phenomenon simply reinforced their increasing desire to create a powerful image for the group, behind which they could retreat at any time whenever they felt their privacy being threatened. They were also aware of how effective the synergy between music and image could be. Musically they had little in common with Bowie though they shared his passion for the more underground and alternative currents of the pop scene. In terms of conceptuals, however, they found themselves increasingly impressed by his work.

The long talks in the cafe round the corner from the studio or at home in the house at Bergerallee now rotated frequently around the subject of pop iconography. Fuelled by strong coffee, these debates might last for hours. Having been a student of Germany's foremost post-war artist Schult was both incredibly visually literate and up-to-date on current artistic theories. He understood how a good image could be made to communicate effectively. For their part, Hütter and Schneider already had a strong theoretical background in music and an equally strong interest in a number of other subjects ranging from the arts to science and politics. Wolfgang Flür also had a background in design. All of them were in love with pop music and discussions as to the relative merits of this or that would rage on with anyone else who happened to be around at the time.

The creative atmosphere around the group had never been stronger. Among their friends were fashion designers, painters, musicians, writers and performance artists, all of whom contributed to the free-wheeling debates late into the night. Schult had by this time set up a makeshift studio in the Bergerallee house, while Flür and Schneider had organised the basement into some kind of electronics workshop where they'd tinker with bits and pieces of equipment or refine items they'd already invented. Even when there were no parties going on, there was still a perpetual buzz of creative activity around the house.

At the weekends they'd drive out into the countryside, heading out along the autobahn until they arrived somewhere that appealed to them. Ralf, in particular, loved to drive. He found it relaxing he said. At night, they'd go out dancing or sometimes to a concert if there was anything particularly interesting going on. During the week, however, Kraftwerk's activities became more and more focused on their studio, developing a working routine that remained unchanged for years.

With the money Philips had paid for the *Ralf & Florian* album, the group also began investing in some new equipment for the studio, in an effort to make themselves even more self-sufficient. Around the same time, Conny Plank was in the process of moving his studio into a converted farm on the outskirts of Cologne. 'It was in the middle of nowhere,' remembers John Foxx. 'I came out of the studio one night when Conny was mixing just to get some fresh air. I walked for a bit and then suddenly realised I was totally lost because there were no street lights or anything and I couldn't see a thing.'

Better facilities in their own studio, however, meant that Kraftwerk could now do more of their recording in Düsseldorf. This allowed them time to refine and develop their music without the pressure of running up huge studio costs. They could improvise on a theme for hours, record the results and listen back to the tapes at their leisure, keeping only those parts that achieved, in Emil Schult's words, 'maximum expression' and rejecting any parts which weren't acceptable.

The group's confidence in their abilities was now higher than it had ever been. Surrounded by creative people, they had access to a pool of ideas and concepts that now helped them to develop at faster rate than ever before. The critical reaction to the *Ralf & Florian* album had already moved them ahead of many of their close contemporaries on the German scene and it must have seemed like everything was finally falling into place for the group. As they settled down to work on preparations for their next release, the future was looking very bright.

The quantum leap forward from their earlier LPs that *Ralf & Florian* had represented was now about to be repeated. But this time, it would gain Kraftwerk critical and commercial success on a scale that they had never imagined for themselves.

4

By early 1974, the various strands of Kraftwerk's artistic vision were beginning to come together. During their discussions about pop culture and image, one particular theme had recurred. In terms of pop iconography, Ralf and Florian agreed that a four-piece group was ideal. Having only three members presents particular problems, ranging from the obvious difficulties in translating heavily multi-tracked studio recordings into a live performance to the more specialist compositional complications presented when photographing or designing around a three-piece. 'They were very much looking for a whole group,' remembers Wolfgang Flür. Having decided on this point, they began to investigate the possibilities of recruiting a fourth member.

It was Florian Schneider who met up with the first likely candidate for the vacancy. Klaus Roeder was a guitar player and violinist around the local music scene, who had an interesting sideline actually making violins. Possibly it was this factor that attracted Schneider to him, since Kraftwerk were already involved in building or modifying their own instruments at this time. Roeder was something of an oddball character, often going barefoot and spending time alone in the country to be close to nature. It seemed a strange choice considering Kraftwerk were in the process of ridding themselves completely of the last vestiges of hippie culture.

Work began on preparations for the group's next LP soon after the release of *Ralf & Florian* in November, 1973. The cultural concerns which had led to them adapting melodies from German folk music (especially that of the North Rhine area) were still important and many of the improvised pieces they worked up during this period were inspired by the most successful moments of the previous release.

'The new songs are always born from the old ones,' confirms Hütter, 'like the new branch growing on top of the old one.'[1]

On the *Ralf & Florian* LP, the group had taken some tentative steps with their new synthesizers. But by the time work on the next album began, they were already beginning to master the subtleties and intricacies of these machines. This had an immediate impact on their music. Both Hütter and Schneider had always been interested in the textures and surfaces of sound, the synthesizers opened up a whole new playground of possibilities that continued to expand as they learnt more about them. Now their experimental drive had a new outlet, they could write more conventionally structured pieces and still retain the innovative aspects which appealed to them by focusing on individual sounds. Again, this was a move inspired by the theories of Stockhausen, but it became more relevant since they now had a very pop-conscious member – Wolfgang Flür – in their ranks, who was able to provide them with the kind of rhythmic structures that he'd learnt over a number of years playing hit singles in covers bands.

Unsurprisingly, Klaus Roeder didn't stay with the group for long. After contributing to some of the sessions for the new album (notably those which produced 'Mitternacht' and 'Morgenspaziergang') he elected to leave. 'He was very different to us,' explains Wolfgang Flür, 'but he wasn't with the group for very long. I think he was only around for a few months before he left. It didn't really suit him.'

From the intersection of all the late-night debates about German culture, art theory, pop music and the fresh possibilities offered by the new synthesizers, Ralf and Florian were gradually assembling firm ideas about where to go next. The arrival of Wolfgang Flür had coincided with their own growing interest in the strategies of pop. This had arisen out of their dissatisfaction with the abstract, meandering experimentalism of their first two albums; creatively, they felt they had exhausted the wilfully avant-garde sound of those records and were keen to explore a new challenge. The *Ralf & Florian* album had taken a giant step forward with a much more controlled sense of structure and melody but they were eager to go even further.

One unlikely, but significant, source of inspiration came from The Beach Boys. Hütter and Schneider were fascinated by their ability to encapsulate an entire slice of American life inside a three-minute single. 'Yes,' says Hütter, 'in their songs they managed to concentrate a maximum of fundamental ideas. In a hundred years from now, when people want to know what California was like in the '60s, they only have to listen to a single by The Beach Boys.'[2]

What intrigued Hütter and Schneider was the possibility of creating a German equivalent. By using their music to celebrate German culture they would simultaneously be re-appropriating it for their own generation. The most visible symbol of modern Germany at this time was the autobahn network. The autobahns were used as a blueprint for many of the road-building programmes around Europe in the late '60s and early '70s and were seen by many outsiders as a typical example of German efficiency. But for Germans, they were a reminder of a period that most of them would have preferred to forget since the autobahn network had been initiated by Hitler, not only as a means of providing better road links between towns and cities (enabling faster redeployment of troops) but as a way of providing jobs for Germany's unemployed. Most people elsewhere in Europe were unaware of this resonance. But for Hütter particularly, who was fond of driving, the autobahn was exactly the kind of cultural symbol his generation needed to strip of its past associations and celebrate instead.

Out of all of this, the idea for a new track began to coalesce. As usual, part of the group's inspiration came from a specific experience. 'We see films and we go out and get optical impressions,' explained Florian Schneider, 'so this often has an influence on our music and it becomes an acoustic film or acoustic poetry. That's the way that we try to express what we have seen and what we have heard . . . we were on tour and it happened that we just came off the autobahn after a long ride and when we came in to play we had this speed in our music. Our hearts were still beating fast so the whole rhythm became very fast.'[3]

As the idea began to take shape, the group embarked on several drives along the autobahn with a portable tape recorder and a microphone to record the sounds of the traffic. Originally the intention was to use these recordings as sound effects on the track but the wind noise and poor quality of the recordings led to the alternative approach of creating synthesized versions of the Doppler shifts and roaring engines they'd taped on location. Florian later boasted of his skill in duplicating the sounds of their environment: 'That's what you learn from working with electronics. You go to the source of the sounds and your ears are trained to analyse any sound. We hear a plane passing overhead and I know all of the phenomenon that go into the make-up of the sound, the phasings, the echoes. All these things that happen in nature . . . '[4]

The group had also acquired a custom-built 16-step analogue sequencer which had a profound impact on the development of the track. Along with Flür's metronomic drumming, this provided them with a firm rhythmic base for the music. They also used a trick they'd learnt from Conny Plank, tuning their echo unit to the timing of the track to give the bassline a rolling, cyclical feel.

Hütter and Schneider had already experimented with vocals on 'Ananas Symphonie' and were keen to use some kind of lyrical expression to help convey the track's meaning. They gave Emil Schult the task of writing the words. As the long improvising sessions continued they practised singing his words, creating a semi-ironic hookline that sounded remarkably similar to The Beach Boys.

The result was an astonishing twenty-two-minute epic that combined the group's experimental past with their emerging commercial sensibilities. This duality was perfectly expressed on the two versions of the track 'Kometenmelodie' that they completed for the new album. The first of these was a doomy avant-garde tone poem, full of strange dissonant synth sounds and no discernible rhythm while the second was an upbeat synth-pop prototype that translated the shapes of a classic rock n' roll groove into electronics.

By the time the group were ready to go into Conny Plank's studio in the early summer of 1974, most of the groundwork for the new album had already been completed. Wolfgang Flür didn't even bother to go to Cologne, since his drum parts were already on tape. But Plank was unconvinced by the group's new sound and tensions quickly became apparent. 'Conny didn't really like the very strict, regimented direction they were going in,' explains John Foxx. 'He preferred the more organic, free-form approach they'd had originally. He thought that sound was much more dynamic and appealing. He told me that the last few sessions he did with Kraftwerk became quite difficult because Conny was into this whole idea of what he called "organic electronics" and that wasn't really where the group were headed.'

Despite this, Plank completed a spectacular job on the LP. On 'Mitternacht' ('Midnight') he layered Roeder's violin with heavy echoes and built up a uniquely warm and atmospheric feel around the sparse, atonal arrangement. He used similar techniques on the gentle, pastoral electronics of 'Morgenspaziergang' ('Morning Walk') using slight echoes on the piano and flute to provide a warmer, fuller sound that was gently soothing in contrast to the piercing electronic squalls (Florian's approximation of birdsong) which introduce the track. But from 'Autobahn' – Kraftwerk's paean to the joys of the open road – he created a masterpiece. The complexity of the track, built up over months of improvisation and featuring several different melodic themes, was one obvious problem. Another was presented by the home-recorded feel of some of the material, keyboard melodies had leaked across into the vocal tracks and so on. Plank sat down with Hütter to carve some semblance of order from the mass of ideas, carefully balancing themes and counterpoints until the track conveyed the sense of movement that the group wanted to achieve. Then he set to work on building an astonishingly intricate web of echoes and reverbs around the instrumental parts, providing each individual sound with its own perfect separate space.

While Hütter and Schneider were in Cologne working with Plank, Emil Schult was back in the house at Bergerallee adding the final touches to a painting he'd begun during the first burst of enthusiasm for the 'Autobahn' track. The painting was an idealised countryside vista with a flaring sun and giant green hills. Running through the centre of the painting, from front to back, draped over the hills like a grey "ribbon" was the autobahn. It was an enormously romantic image, both nostalgic and forward-looking at the same time (which suited the intention of the track perfectly). With the addition of a sleek black Mercedes and a small white Volkswagen, this painting became the sleeve artwork for the new LP.

When the final mixing sessions for the album were completed, it was clear that both musically and conceptually Kraftwerk had taken a significant step forward. But, initially, at least, the *Autobahn* album failed to incite much comment. Soon after its release in November 1974, however, the group were contacted by an American concert promoter, Ira Blacker, who'd moved into management. Blacker had spotted potential in the burgeoning German rock scene and had already signed up a number of acts for US management deals. Now he was interested in adding Kraftwerk to his roster. Hütter and Schneider, keenly interested in expanding their horizons, readily agreed.

The timing couldn't have been better. From his offices in Hollywood, Blacker was able to exert pressure on the American wing of Phonogram (the parent company of Philips) to pick up their option on the album, pointing out that *Autobahn* was already selling well on import and attracting attention from some of the more progressive radio stations. Blacker's argument was convincing enough for Phonogram to arrange a release through their Vertigo subsidiary. He also fixed up a US publishing deal with the Gulf & Western subsidiary of Famous Music for the group.

It was a radio station in Chicago which gave the album's epic title track its first airplay. Both Chicago and Detroit are considered to be important test-beds for the entire American mid-west, so this was a very significant development. The head of Phonogram's Chicago office got to hear about this strange twenty-two-minute long track by a group from Germany being played on the radio and, sensing something special, immediately ordered his staff to edit together a short, radio-friendly version. Sure enough, the new single-length version began to pick up even more plays. The edited version of 'Autobahn' was rush released and was soon being played on radio stations throughout the country, climbing to #25 in the Billboard charts. As a consequence the album began selling well too and, though it peaked at #5, stayed in the charts for more than four months.

The success of the single in the US led to its release in Europe where it began a similar chart-bound trajectory. Blacker quickly began arranging a series of US concerts for the group to capitalise on their rapidly growing profile.

Kraftwerk had played some gigs in Germany during late 1974 where they had added Karl Bartos, a young classically-trained percussionist, to their line-up. Though Bartos had originally played around the local music scene in a covers band called The Jokers, hc was now studying at the Robert Schumann Conservatorium in Düsseldorf, hoping eventually to gain a permanent job with the Berlin Symphony Orchestra. Since Bartos was interested in both pop music and the avant-garde he fitted perfectly with Hütter and Schneider's vision of where the group was heading.

'When I started studying classical music in 1970, I had already spent a couple of years playing drums and guitars in bands doing all that pop music stuff,' remembers Bartos. 'Then, there came a time in my life, during my early 20s, when I thought that music should be my lifetime profession. So, being a typical German, I started studying music seriously because I wanted to be a professor or at least play in an orchestra. On top of that, I also had a background in jazz so I wasn't surprised at all when joining Kraftwerk. It was just a normal thing for me as I was already well into improvising whereas a lot of classical music people can only sight read.'[5]

Despite being a good deal younger than the others, Bartos was well-suited to Kraftwerk. His experiences as a member of The Jokers meant that he had a lot in common with Flür (in fact, during their early years with Kraftwerk, Bartos and Flür had a side project together called Sinus) while his classical education provided a good understanding of Hütter and Schneider's motivations.

'If you start playing drums on a classical level,' explains Bartos, 'you are confronted by all kinds of different compositions by people like John Cage and Karlheinz Stockhausen. Coming from the '50s and '60s they were already using techniques like miking big gongs and other percussion instruments to create unusual sounds. Sometimes I had to repeatedly play one instrument for ten seconds, constantly slowing down the beat or whatever – all these weird scores with strange graphics. I was pretty much used to it all so, knowing this, Kraftwerk had called my music professor, wanting a classically-trained percussionist to have a rather European, German, post-war approach, not an Anglo-American pop approach.'[6]

It was decided that Bartos should accompany the group on their US dates, despite the fact that he was still studying for his final exams at the Robert Schumann Conservatorium in Düsseldorf. The concerts had been arranged to run over a period of four weeks from the beginning of April 1975, finishing in plenty of time for Bartos to return home to sit his exams.

'When I first joined Kraftwerk,' he recalls, 'we had a nice dinner. Next I found myself playing mostly improvised music on VDR Radio in Cologne, where Stockhausen used to be based. The next big event was a concert at The Olympia in Paris and then we found ourselves performing on Broadway at the Beacon Theatre. It was really cool; I was young and didn't give a shit about it all.'[7]

The trip across the Atlantic was tremendously exciting for all of them. On one of their first evenings in America, Ira Blacker took them out to the renowned Rumpelmeyer's Restaurant and outlined his plans. As yet, no one quite knew what to expect. With *Autobahn* already climbing the charts, the predictions were healthily positive, but in the long-haired guitar-wielding climate of US rock the truth was that it was anyone's guess as to how audiences would react when confronted by four relatively immobile, straight-looking Germans standing behind keyboards without even the familiar comfort of a regular drum kit to put things in perspective

'The first time we were over there it was like being in outer space or something,' explains Flür. 'Everything is bigger and greater than here, even down to the ice creams and steaks. It was so strange, here we were just young guys from Düsseldorf and suddenly we found ourselves on Broadway . . . '

'That was one of the big adventures when I started off with Kraftwerk,' confirms Bartos. 'We were four guys having all the fun in the world, travelling around having a good time, all the time.'

The stage set-up comprised of most of the equipment from the group's studio – Ralf's Mini-Moog and Farfisa organ, Florian's flute and Arp Odyssey, the electronic drum pads (by now in a sturdier casing), the sequencer and, of course, the four neon signs. Despite the minimal stage show, the early dates went well, prompting Ira Blacker to add extra shows wherever they could be slotted in. Gradually the four-week tour became an eight-week tour and then finally stretched to three months as Kraftwerk played everywhere from New York to Little Rock, Arkansas.

'It all went so well,' remembers Flür. 'All the concerts were quite well-attended because "Autobahn" had already been a hit. We played large venues and small venues. We had some hillbilly audiences too. There would be fights and things and we would wonder what on earth was going on. In California we were on the *Midnight Special* television show with The Commodores. We had a lot of fun and experience. It really changed our minds.'

Most surprising of all, given Kraftwerk's reputation as the ice-men of rock, there were groupies too. 'There were lots of ladies,' he admits, demurely. 'Every evening. Sometimes it was difficult to hold back!'

There were some unexpected problems too. Used to dealing exclusively with guitar bands, the American sound crews had no idea of the kind of frequency range Kraftwerk's synthesizers were capable of outputting. 'We blew so many speakers,' confirms Flür. 'From week to week we had to hire another sound company because no one would put up with it . . . '

The ever-extending tour caused special problems for Karl Bartos particularly. Since he was due to sit his final exams at the Robert Schumann Conservatorium back in Düsseldorf, he had to fly back to Germany several times during the American trip. In what must have been an exhausting schedule, he'd arrive back in Düsseldorf, take his exam, and then fly back to America for the next gig. When he was due to sit the next exam, he had to repeat the whole process. He still passed with flying colours.

At a concert in Detroit, Hütter and Schneider met up with the legendary rock critic Lester Bangs who interviewed them for Creem. In the event, the story didn't run until September, by which time

Kraftwerk were back in Europe, but it was nevertheless a hugely important piece of press for the group. *Autobahn*, declared Bangs, 'is more than just a record, it is an *indictment*.' Significantly, Hütter was careful to point out the background.

'After the war, German entertainment was destroyed,' he explained. 'The German people were robbed of their culture, putting an American head on it. I think we are the first generation born after the war to shake this off and know where to feel American music and where to feel ourselves. We are the first German group to record in our own language, use our electronic background, and create a central European identity for ourselves. So you see another group like Tangerine Dream, although they are German they have an English name, so they create onstage an Anglo-American identity, which we completely deny. We want the whole world to know our background. We cannot deny we are from Germany, because the German mentality, which is more advanced, will always be part of our behaviour. We create out of the German language, the mother language, which is very mechanical, we use as the basic structure of our music. Also the machines, from the industries of Germany.'[8]

It's hard to believe that the notoriously contentious Bangs allowed Hütter to get away with comments such as 'the German mentality, which is more advanced . . .' without challenging him. But it's also difficult to believe that Hütter is being entirely serious. Throughout the interview he seems to be deliberately hamming it up, playing games with the stereotypical image of Germany. His comment about machinery from German industry being part of the basic structure of their music could have been taken one of two ways. Firstly, he could have been referring to the group's music-making equipment, although this is hardly likely since, at this point, the only German piece of kit they were using was the small 16-step sequencer. Alternatively, and more probably, he was talking about the rhythms of the heavy industry around the Rhine-Ruhr area as an inspiration for their music. Partly this idea comes from theories initially expounded by Luigi Russolo and, subsequently, by Stockhausen. But more recently – and Bangs would have been well aware of this – a similar tale had been spun by Iggy Pop to explain the steam-hammer rhythms of The Stooges (and perhaps appropriately the industry he was talking about comprised of the metal presses and fabrication yards of Detroit's auto plants).

With his typical aplomb, Bangs pointed out that 'because their

English is not so hot' Wolfgang Flür and Karl Bartos had been banished to their rooms while the interview took place. 'I have heard of members of bands playing on the same bills as Kraftwerk,' he added, by way of background detail, 'approaching these gentlemen with the words "So ya liked blowin' all our roadies . . . " The Germans smiled and clapped them on the shoulders: "*Ja, ja* . . . "' But perhaps Kraftwerk had the last laugh after all. Bangs was so obviously charmed to bits by the whole thing, that his piece – entitled *Kraftwerkfeature* – was a thoroughly compelling manifesto for the group's cause. As one of the most influential rock journalists in America, Lester Bangs gave Kraftwerk unforgettable PR.

Interestingly, Hütter and Schneider were already talking about the concept of 'the man-machine' even at this early stage, explaining to Bangs that Kraftwerk were not, after all, a group but, as the journalist notes, 'a you-guessed-it'.

'The *Menschmaschine* is our acoustic concept,' Florian pointed out, 'and Kraftwerk is power plant – if you plug in the electricity, then it starts to work. It's feedback. You can jam with an automatic machine, sometimes just you and it alone in the studio.'[9]

The American tour was Kraftwerk's first real experience of a concerted press campaign. Ira Blacker was a firm believer in the power of publicity and worked ceaselessly to ensure that the group gained maximum coverage. He persuaded newspapers and magazines such as *Variety*, the famous US entertainment industry publication to write pieces on the group while, in the UK, he master-minded an article on the Kraut-rock phenomenon in *Melody Maker*, providing his own quotes about the huge import sales the German groups were attracting. This emphasis on publicity continued throughout the American tour, providing Hütter and Schneider with some valuable experience of dealing with journalists. They learnt the ropes quickly. By the time they arrived in Detroit for the crucial interview with Lester Bangs they were becoming masters of the art, deliberately playing up to the deadly-serious, straight-laced stereotypical image of Germans that many Americans still retained from Hollywood war movies. Given their own well-developed sense of humour, they were probably rumbling with mirth on the inside as, poker-faced, they referred to their studio as a 'laboratory' while explaining to Bangs that they saw themselves more as scientists than musicians. They also played games with mainstream America's fear of the sinister aspects of machine-made music (then still a relatively unknown quantity in this guitar-oriented climate) dropping

Wolfgang Flür during the late '60s with the Spirits Of Sound in Düsseldorf
(*Wolfgang Flür Private Collection*)

The newly-configured three-piece Kraftwerk
on a visit to Hamburg in August 1973
(*Wolfgang Flür Private Collection*)

Kraftwerk playing live in the *Aspecte* TV show, note the home-made electronic drum kit
(*Wolfgang Flür Private Collection*)

Wolfgang, Ralf and Florian with manager Ira Blacker at Rumpelmeyer's restaurant in New York just before Kraftwerk's first American tour in April 1975. (*Wolfgang Flür Private Collection*)

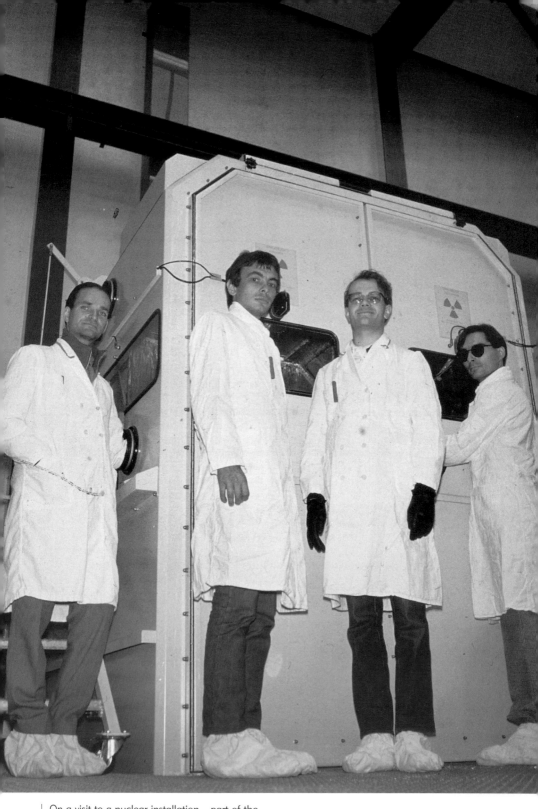

On a visit to a nuclear installation – part of the
promotion for the release of the *Radio-Activity* album
(*London Features*)

Another shot from the same session
(*London Features*)

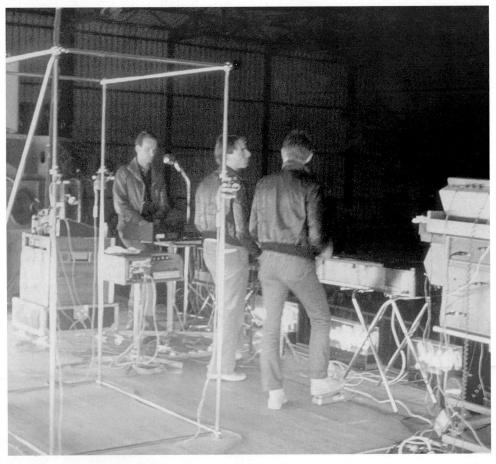

Onstage in the south of France, 1976. The vehicle carrying their stage clothes
had been held up in heavy traffic so, uncharacteristically, they had to do the
show in jeans and leather jackets (*Wolfgang Flür Private Collection*)

The cover shot from *Trans-Europe Express* before retouching and hand-tinting took place
(*Michael Ochs Archives*)

One of the promo shots from the
Trans-Europe Express session in 1977
(*Michael Ochs Archives*)

The robots onstage for the launch of *The Man Machine*, ironically Florian's doppelgänger is still holding a flute though the instrument didn't appear on this album (*Ebet Roberts*)

The robots investigate the Kling Klang equipment still posing in the standard – Ralf, Karl, Wolfgang, Florian – formation (*Glenn A. Baker*)

Karl Bartos and Wolfgang Flür onstage during the 1981 world tour (*London Features*)

Playing 'Pocket Calculator' during the 1981 world tour (*Redferns*)

Kraftwerk in their new V-shaped stage line-up conceived by
Wolfgang in order to make onstage communication more efficient
(*Ebet Roberts*)

On the 1981 tour –
Ralf Hütter, Karl Bartos,
Wolfgang Flür, Florian
Schneider. The 1981
stage set was designed
by Wolfgang Flür, note
the custom-built flight
case which houses
Ralf's keyboards
(*Ebet Roberts*)

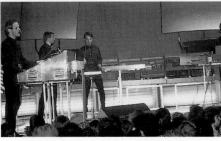

The Music Institute, Detroit. During the
mid-80s this is where Juan Atkins,
Derrick May and Kevin Saunderson took
Kraftwerk's sound into the future with
techno (*Tim Barr*)

Onstage at Tribal Gathering, Luton, England, 23rd May 1997
(*James Cameron*)

'The Man Machine' in action at Tribal Gathering
(*James Cameron*)

Emil Schult in his Düsseldorf studio at work on The Central Sun (*Wolfgang Flür Private Collection*)

Wolfgang Flür, February 1998, outside the house in Bergerallee which was Kraftwerk's home base from the beginning of the '70s until 1981 (*Tim Barr*)

heavy hints about possible brain-washing.

'We are manipulating the audience,' declared Ralf. 'That's what it's all about. When you play electronic music you have the control of the imagination of the people in the room and it can get to an extent where it's almost physical.'[10]

Bangs clearly relished the challenge of being faced with these witty and intellectual characters who had such a radical take on the aesthetics of pop imagery and played along accordingly, even flirting with the cultural residue of Nazism. At one point, he asked about the possibility of converting thoughts directly into music. 'Yes,' replied Ralf, 'this would be fantastic.' The final solution to the music problem, suggested Bangs. 'No, not the solution. The next step . . . '[11]

In contrast to the dull, clichéd rockspeak of most mainstream acts at the time, this was all radical stuff. Bangs explained his feelings that their music was rather anti-emotional. 'Emotion is a strange word,' countered Florian. 'There is cold emotion and other emotion, both equally valid. It's not body emotion, it's mental emotion. We like to ignore the audience while we play and take all our concentration into the music. We are very much interested in the origin of music, the source of music. The pure sound is something we would very much like to achieve.'[12] Again, this was a line lifted straight from Stockhausen's manifesto.

Towards the end of the interview, Bangs asked if they would pose for pictures the next day beside the Detroit freeway (America's version of the autobahn). No, they told him emphatically, we have our own pictures. Why? 'Because,' as Ralf explained, 'we are paranoid.'[13]

Hütter and Schneider's performance during the interview with Bangs was a master-stroke. In the grand, self-mythologising world of American rock, they had outmanoeuvred every other major act on the scene by projecting a revolutionary image which laid much of the groundwork for how they would be perceived from this point on. The *Creem* article was such a significant step forward that David Bowie subsequently modelled many of the interviews around his *Station To Station* album on similar themes, culminating in the 'Nazi salute' debacle that marred his return to London (in an open-top German limousine) during 1976.

As one of the most influential rock stars during this period, David Bowie's seal of approval was enormously important in broadening the group's audience. But he was obviously fascinated by Kraftwerk even to the extent of visiting them in Germany. 'When he came to see us in Düsseldorf in his Mercedes, he took the highway while listening to

"Autobahn" on the car stereo,' remembers Ralf Hütter. 'He said: it's exactly like that, everything is in your tune.'[14]

Bowie's own codicil to this story was equally entertaining. 'I like them very much,' he reported to *Melody Maker*. 'Florian in particular. Very dry . . . When I came over to Europe I got myself a Mercedes to drive around in, 'cause I still wasn't flying at that time, and Florian saw it. He said "What a wonderful car" and I said "Yes it used to belong to some Iranian prince, and he was assassinated and the car went on the market, and I got it for the tour". And Florian said "Ja, car always lasts longer". With him it all has that edge. His cold emotion/warm emotion. I respond to that.'[15]

Over the next few years, Bowie was to find a consistent source of inspiration in Kraftwerk's aesthetic, particularly on *Low*, the first album he recorded with Brian Eno in Berlin, and its follow-up *Heroes*. 'I think the biggest influence on that album was the work of Kraftwerk, prior to *Autobahn* . . .' says Bowie. 'I associated with it immediately because of my interest in what you could do with just random sound.'[16]

Despite the rigours of their heavy touring schedule, Hütter and Schneider were still finding time to write new music. At the show in Detroit, prior to their meeting with Lester Bangs, Kraftwerk had played an early version of the track 'Trans-Europe Express' which eventually emerged, in its final form, two years later. 'Ralf gets many of his ideas from travelling and being onstage,' explains Flür. 'We would often develop new songs on tour by playing them in front of audiences and refining them each time we played. Ralf likes to work this way.'

In Florida, Hütter had discovered an instrument which was to have a strong impact on the music that was developed during and after the American tour. The Vako Orchestron was a keyboard which could replay a variety of realistic sounds such as violin or vocal choir from plastic optical discs inserted into a slot in its casing. Though in essence it was a development from the Mellotron used by many of the big progressive rock acts in the early '70s, the Orchestron was still very much ahead of its time. Not many were made, but its distinctive sounds are strongly identifiable in tracks such as 'Radioactivity' and 'Trans-Europe Express' (which featured the Orchestron's violin sound in particular).

The American tour was significant in other ways too. Ironically, it was by travelling outside of Europe that the group were able to develop a stronger sense of their own cultural identity. 'It's a new conscience that we discovered during our trip to the American continent in '75,' explained Hütter. 'Everybody asked us how was life in Germany, in Paris. People wanted to know where was our culture at that point. People used to say that we were not rock n' roll, then thanks to these transatlantic trips we discovered our cultural identity as Europeans . . . distance allows us to see much more clearly. To get conscious of things, you must go out and watch. For us, the problem was to go outside of ourselves, of our existence limited by the same tours in Germany, to look at our own culture in a distance.'[17]

During the tour, Hütter and Schneider were also able to fulfil at least one long-held ambition by going to see The Beach Boys playing live. 'We have seen them in a big stadium,' confirmed Hütter. 'It was gorgeous, like a rebirth. There's a wonderful and very poignant song on their last album, "Once In My Life". I'd like to dare to say once in my life what Brian Wilson says in that song . . .' When the journalist Paul Alessandrini asked them about their passion for the group, Hütter explained that it came from 'the intelligence of their thoughts regarding American reality put on to records.'

'When we reached California and Hollywood,' added Florian, 'we were able to say: yes, it's exactly like that, like in the songs of The Beach Boys.'[18]

The tour of America represented an important watershed for Kraftwerk. It was an experience which provided them with the creative impetus for much of what was to follow. While many of their most creative ideas coalesced during the tour, it also helped consolidate many of the theories and concepts which they'd begun to explore back in Germany. Left to their own devices for much of the time, without recourse to their usual circle of friends (though Emil Schult, who'd studied in America during his teens, did join them during some of this period), the tour helped to forge a much stronger group identity. As had happened to The Beatles in Hamburg, Kraftwerk's experiences in America had a galvanising effect both on their music and their personalities.

The press campaign that Ira Blacker had so expertly stage-managed also helped confirm that, in terms of the group's image, Kraftwerk were heading in the right direction. Many of the ideas which eventually emerged during their trip to America had originally been talked about back in Düsseldorf, but the hyper-reality of the tour forced them to engage with these concepts on a much more practical level. The suits and short haircuts – adopted after Florian's lead – were the complete antithesis of music fashion, particularly in America where the coupling of art theory, heavy irony and avant-garde pop hadn't leaked much outside of New York. In addition, Kraftwerk's oft-quoted aphorism that 'our drummers don't sweat' was completely opposed to what Flür describes as the world of 'long-haired, sweating, rock musicians.' Add to that the fact of their strange, guitar-less stage show and, to many of the audiences who witnessed them on their frequent out-of-town shows on this tour, Kraftwerk must have seemed like they'd dropped from outer space. At the very least, for some of their audiences, this felt like a group who'd fallen out of the future.

By the time they returned to Germany, Kraftwerk had very definite ideas about where to go next. They spent a brief period in their studio working on the embryonic songs which they'd developed in America, but much of their time was taken up with the reorganisation of their business affairs. Having had extensive consultations with Ira Blacker, they tackled their recording contract first. Since their original commitment with Philips had now come to an end they began looking for a new deal. With a hit album and single under their belts, the group were in a strong bargaining position and were therefore able to make demands which many other groups simply wouldn't have entertained.

Hütter and Schneider were determined to wrest control of their affairs from the record company. With this in mind, Blacker helped them to develop the revolutionary terms of a deal which would allow them to retain ownership of all their recorded work, manage their own recording deadlines and gain a larger percentage of the profits. Though many companies were interested, Blacker eventually negotiated the deal with EMI (whose offices in Cologne were conveniently close to Düsseldorf) and their American partner Capitol. Their new recording contract was essentially a licensing agreement which transferred most of the control over the group's affairs to their company, Kling Klang Verlag. From now on, Kraftwerk would have a much greater degree of freedom than many of the world's most successful rock stars. It would take years before even the most astute artists would follow suit.

Their experiences on the American tour provided Kraftwerk with a boost in confidence in terms of their live show. Blacker booked dates in the UK for September. In between preparing for this tour and completing their business arrangements, the group began working on another album.

Oddly, some of the songs they'd begun developing in America – such as 'Showroom Dummies' and 'Trans-Europe Express' – were not part of the album recordings, though they were by now regularly included in the group's stage set along with tracks from *Autobahn*, *Ralf & Florian* and *Kraftwerk*. Despite the obvious strengths of these songs, it was felt that they didn't fit in with the firm concept of the new LP.

While work was progressing in the studio, Emil Schult was busy developing the slide show which Kraftwerk had unveiled in its early stages during some of their US dates. In contrast to the films which would accompany later shows, these early visuals were simply still images which were projected on to a screen behind the band, sometimes evoking the subject of the track and, at other times, seeming to be completely arbitrary. It was nevertheless obvious that the group were beginning to become increasingly aware of the power visual imagery could have in the context of their live act.

To coincide with the UK tour, Ira Blacker used his contacts to gain press coverage in *NME*, *Sounds* and *Melody Maker*, the UK's most influential music publications at the time. Though the article by Lester Bangs had only just been published in the US, it was clear that his prescient take on the Kraftwerk concept was already having an effect. The title of the *NME* piece on the group was direct and to the point, blurting out 'The Final Solution To The Music Problem?' across two pages (though the writer obviously didn't pick up on Bangs's perceptions of the group's strong anti-Nazi sentiments) while the *Sounds* headline declared 'We Not Only Try To Brainwash People . . . We Succeed.'

Significantly, for the *Sounds* interview, Ralf was riffing hard on another Stockhausen theme. 'When you play electronic music, you deal with noises and gradually you become more aware of the world of sounds,' explained Hütter. 'We want to communicate our awareness, so that when you leave our concert and maybe walk down a street, you can still hear concerts by listening to the noise of traffic, the footsteps of other people . . .'[19]

In various forms, this concept was to become a regular feature of Kraftwerk interviews. But while it touches on the ideas of Stockhausen (and prior to that, the writing of Futurism's leading theorist, Marinetti) this idea has an equally interesting antecedent in the work of Miles Davis. Though Davis played jazz, he was classically educated at the Juilliard School in New York and kept up-to-date with trends in the avant-garde particularly. In the late '50s, he pushed jazz forward into the modal era after an epiphanic moment on 52nd Street when the combination of busy traffic, street noise and conversational fragments coalesced into a kind of urban symphony. As for Hütter, 'the noise of traffic, the footsteps of other people' had a compelling rhythm for Davis, who subsequently determined to capture this bruisingly modern sound in his music. The results changed the direction of jazz irrevocably. As a former jazz student (he'd met Florian Schneider on a jazz improvisation course, after all) Hütter would have been aware of this too, his originality lay in translating the idea into pop.

The first hints that Kraftwerk weren't entirely convinced by modernity came in the *Melody Maker* piece which followed a week later. 'We are ambivalent about the impersonal nature of modern life,' declared Hütter.'On the one hand we are excited by the colossal scale and coldness of technology. On the other hand we can be repelled by it . . .'[20]

For those who could decode Kraftwerk's imagery, this probably came as no surprise. Elements of both stark futurism and gentle nostalgia had permeated both the artwork and the music of the group's previous two albums. On *Ralf & Florian*, the monochrome photograph on the front of the sleeve (a demure Hütter next to Schneider in his conservative suit and minim brooch) suggested a different mood altogether from the colourful, hi-tech image of the group's studio on the back cover. Similarly, Emil Schult's painting on the sleeve of *Autobahn* projects two opposing themes.

'That's correct,' confirms Schult. 'It combines a love of nature and a simpler time in the past together with a fascination for the future and technology.'

Similarly, the music itself fused the futuristic sounds of the synthesizer and the electronic percussion unit with melodies inspired by traditional German folk and classical music. Kraftwerk's vision of the future seems to locate itself alongside the old adage that 'you can only see forward as far as you can look back.' It's neither utopian or dystopian, but perhaps more convincingly, lies somewhere in between.

Back in Germany, the group had acquired another piece of new technology. 'We have a new thing which is a speech synthesizer,' Ralf explained to *Melody Maker*. 'It is really a kind of computer terminal, designed to speak rather than typewrite, and it has a typewriter keyboard on which you can put in any syllables phonetically and it will speak to them. We can feed the output of the terminal into any of our synthesizers and use it to programme them, so we can have the music talking or singing.'[21]

In 1975, this was incredibly radical. While, creatively at least, Kraftwerk had left their German contemporaries behind, the idea to use a computer to speak or sing on a piece of music was bizarre and certainly more reminiscent of the way-out strategies of Faust (who used road-drills on stage) or Can (think of Malcolm Mooney's atonal screaming excursions) than any remotely conventional Anglo-American group. Just the previous year, a *Melody Maker* journalist had walked out of an interview with Tangerine Dream because Edgar Froese suggested that, in ten years, everyone would be playing synthesizers. And now here were Kraftwerk, floating the idea of using a computer to help make their music. In the denim-clad, guitar-dominated world of the pre-punk music scene, this was almost too much to bear.

Despite the fact that posters advertising the forthcoming Kraftwerk album were on display at the UK concerts, the group chose not to preview any of the new material, concentrating instead on the tracks that had been featured on their American tour. Alongside unfinished versions of 'Showroom Dummies' and 'Trans-Europe Express', the sets did include one unidentifiable piece which bore some obvious resemblance to 'Klingklang' but this didn't appear on the new album (nor any subsequent release).

The shows in the UK were reasonably well-received, though the group's experiences in England were nowhere near as inspirational as those they'd had in America. But by now, Kraftwerk had everything they needed for their assault on the future – a complete line-up, a well-defined image and a sound that would eventually change the world. By October 1975, they were back in the studio working hard to complete the new album. This was the release that they presumed would consolidate, if not expand, all of their recent successes. Unfortunately, it was inevitable that, even in Kraftwerk's cool, clearly calculated gameplan, there would be some malfunctions. The near future, at least, didn't work out as expected.

5

The concept for the follow-up to *Autobahn* originated somewhere over the Atlantic, as the group returned home after the final dates of their first American tour. 'Ralf was sat next to me on the aeroplane,' remembers Wolfgang Flür, 'and he suddenly said he had an idea about radio activity. That was the first time I had heard him talking about it. If you think about all the private radio stations in America . . . that was the idea. It had nothing to do with radioactivity in the air, or power stations.'

As part of his intense promotion for the US tour, Ira Blacker had arranged for Kraftwerk to visit as many independently-owned radio stations as possible in each of the states they visited. Hütter and Schneider would arrive in town before the show and head to the offices of the nearest radio station to greet the DJs and perhaps do a brief interview as a way of publicising the gig while the others began setting up and preparing for the show. The huge network of local radio and college stations in the US was something completely new to the group since in Germany, at this time, the state still retained a complete monopoly over the airwaves. But, encouraged by Blacker's strong emphasis on publicity and the wide-scale success of *Autobahn*, the group were becoming increasingly interested in the processes of mass communication and eagerly went along with these radio promotions.

Radio also had some symbolic attachments for Kraftwerk. One of the earliest, and most famous, electronic music studios had been set up in Cologne under the auspices of the West German radio station NWDR during the early '50s. Stockhausen worked in this studio from 1953 onwards and many of his most famous works were broadcast for the first time by the station. One of NWDR's programmes, *Nachtmusik*, provided Hütter with his first exposure to avant-garde music. 'This is our background,' he points out, 'this is how we were inspired to form a purely electronic group. When it was dark and we had to go to bed, we would hear it under the pillow on a transistor radio.'[1]

It's worth remembering that Hütter and Schneider grew up in the years before television became dominant. For them, the radio theme had a strongly nostalgic quality as well as its recognisably modern, technological aspects. They were children of the radio age but, as with *Autobahn*, their choice of theme wasn't entirely innocent of other references. During the war, the radio had been the principle weapon in the propaganda war and it had been used by both sides as a means of manipulating public sentiments. Their eventual choice of a wartime radio set for the album's sleeve image played with this ambivalence. The set, which Schult tracked down for the group after a long search, was a limited range short-wave device that had been developed under the direction of Joseph Goebbels (head of the Nazi party's Ministry Of Public Enlightenment & Propaganda) to prevent users from tuning into broadcasts from outside Germany. This touched on another of the group's interests – the power which comes from the control of information (a theme which later resurfaced on the *Computer World* LP and the group's subsequent handling of their own public image).

Recording progressed fitfully after their return to Germany, interrupted by negotiations for a new record deal and preparations for the forthcoming live dates in England. Nevertheless, the firm conceptual theme provided a template that Kraftwerk adhered to throughout most of the recording sessions. With the large advance from EMI/Capitol and what was left of the profits from the American tour ('We made a lot of money and we spent a lot of money', remembers Flür) new equipment was installed in the group's studio, alleviating the need to travel to Cologne or elsewhere to complete recording. This meant that, for the first time since Hütter and Schneider began their professional career, Conny Plank would have no involvement on the new album.

The bulk of the recording was carried out under the rush of enthusiasm which followed the success of the US tour and the purchase of the new studio equipment. The Vako Orchestron which Hütter had bought in America was used heavily on several of the new tracks, its distinctive sound providing the backbone for 'Radioactivity', 'Radioland' and 'Airwaves' amongst others. As on *Autobahn*, Emil Schult was given the task of writing the lyrics, particularly since the group had decided to record some vocals in English and Schult's command of the language – he'd spent time studying in America – was better than either Hütter or Schneider's. But the forced pace of the recording was at odds with the group's preferred method of evolving new compositions gradually through improvisation and editing.

The decision to record in English was strange given many of the group's feelings about creating a specifically German form of contemporary music. But it's clear that their experiences in America must have had an impact, not only on their ability to speak the language but in more subtle ways. 'For me the language of pop has always been English,' notes Flür, though his background was much more rooted in contemporary Anglo-American music than Hütter and Schneider's had ever been. His influence may have been a factor but it's also likely that the impressions left by spending the best part of three months being exposed almost exclusively to American pop had a significant effect too. There's also little doubt that the sheer scale of the US market had some bearing on this. At that time, the American market was the biggest in the world and, having scored once with *Autobahn*, the group probably felt less inclined to limit their appeal by singing only in German and thus excluding the majority from the messages they wished to communicate. Ira Blacker was certainly keen for them to extend their commercial appeal and it's possible that the decision to combine both English and German lyrics was something of a compromise solution to keep both Blacker's commercial instincts and Kraftwerk's cultural interests satisfied. For subsequent releases, the group would record alternative versions in German and English.

Similarly, the hurried nature of the new album was partly down to the pressure of the group's other commitments, but it was also the result of the huge success of the previous LP. Ira Blacker was keen to keep the momentum going and, having tasted wider success, no doubt Hütter and Schneider were also keen to capitalise on their new-found high profile.

But though the vibrant synth-pop of 'Airwaves' recalled the upbeat shapes of 'Kometenmelodie 2' from *Autobahn*, in many ways the recordings for the new album were much more reminiscent of the group's early avant-garde work. Creatively, at least, the group were stepping back from the meticulous, crafted surfaces of *Autobahn* in favour of a more immediate approach but their instincts drew them towards a less satisfying alliance between the experimental and commercial sides of their music. Despite the fact that these recordings were the most heavily lyric-oriented of Kraftwerk's output so far, the tracks displayed few of the sublime pop sensibilities which were to follow. Hook-lines as accessible as those which had launched the 'Autobahn' track into the charts didn't seem to be an obvious priority.

To fit in with the radio concept, the group recorded 'Intermission' (a brief electronic melody of the kind that broadcasters used to insert in the gaps between radio programmes in years gone by) and 'News' (a collage of muffled announcements, tuning frequencies and bursts of morse code electronics). Though both of these pieces connected perfectly with the LP's theme and with the group's fascination for Stockhausen, in the kind of mainstream circles into which *Autobahn* had introduced them they were never going to be seen as anything other than wilfully obscure and irritatingly atonal interruptions to the music. It's possible that Hütter and Schneider felt that these deliberately experimental interludes would reconnect them to the more subversive strategies of the first two Kraftwerk albums but they must have been aware that they were gambling with the attentions of many of those in their new-found mass audience. The nature of these two tracks demonstrated just how deeply ingrained the influence of the avant-garde was. Permeating the fluctuating static noises and whistling electronics was a tradition which touched base, not only with Stockhausen, but with the environmental noise experiments of John Cage, Schaeffer's *musique concrete*, Fluxus and Luigi Russolo. Explaining the album's concept sometime later, Florian Schneider offered a revealing insight into the background of these sonic experiments.

'You can hear the predefined information as intended when tuning in the station on your radio,' he explained, 'and you only have to adjust a little bit, maybe on the short-wave band at night, and you will get the craziest sounds, Morse codes, pure sounds, this is crazy; Radio Cairo and so on . . . This idea, LP as radio . . .'[2]

This notion extended beyond the idea of the LP as a radio broadcast to the idea of Kraftwerk themselves as a radio station. 'We were always hugely fascinated by this,' confirms Hütter. 'We always wanted our own . . . we saw us, Kraftwerk, in the Kling Klang studio, as a radio station. But this is not legally possible in Germany. In America we met people from our generation who have their own radio station . . . and blast their very own thoughts into the ether . . . and we see ourselves as a private radio station.'[3] (This idea resurfaced some years later when the group set up their own achingly minimal web-site which featured little apart from a line drawing of a radio transmitter beaming signals out into the world. After a gap of more than two decades it seems like Hütter's vision of Kraftwerk as some kind of radio station still has a powerful hold on his imagination.)

Somewhere along the line, the concept of radio activity became tangled with the contemporary debate about nuclear power. Obviously this stemmed from the words themselves, connoting both Hütter's original concept and the properties more normally associated with nuclear materials, but it seems that this realisation only occurred towards the final stages of recording. All but a few of the new album's tracks were directly themed on the broadcasting idea, while the additions – including 'Geiger Counter' and 'Uranium' – related to the developing nuclear concept.

Two tracks, however, bridged both ideas. 'News' declared plans for the building of 50 atomic power stations in West Germany 'each one able to supply a city of millions with current' while 'The Voice Of Energy' was slightly more ambivalent. The track had been inspired by the work of the German avant-garde composer Meyer-Eppler (whose work had often been broadcast on the NWDR show *Nachtmusik*) an early, though often over-shadowed, pioneer of electronic music. Meyer-Eppler used electrical hums, primitive vocoders and treatments of found sounds as compositional tools but his 'Stimme Der Energie' bears close comparison with the Kraftwerk track which, in German, bears the same name. The same references to 'giant generator' and 'servant and master' appear in both, while other lyrics appear to paraphrase each other closely. Kraftwerk's 'The Voice Of Energy' was both an observable pun on the nuclear theme and a throwback to Hütter and Schneider's own 'golden age of radio' when, so their story goes, under the bedclothes they'd listen to avant-garde electronic music being transmitted from the radio station in nearby Cologne. For anyone who cared to pick up the clues it was a superbly esoteric – and possibly self-mythologising – in-joke. For anyone who didn't it still mapped perfectly on to the, by this time, twin themes of the LP.

During the group's UK shows later that year, 'The Voice Of Energy' appeared to have a companion piece which Ian Calder of the UK fanzine *Aktivität* suggests must have been called 'Die Sonne, Der Mond, Die Sterne' ('The Sun, The Moon, The Stars'). This track, similar in form and content to 'The Voice Of Energy' was a vocoderised tone poem which, during the group's 1976 concerts, segued into 'Ohm Sweet Ohm' (a surprisingly English pun for such an overtly German group) but was never included on the final album release. It subsequently re-emerged on the group's 1981 tour, though in the UK gigs which took place in September 1975, the track bridged the two distinct versions of 'Kometenmelodie' from *Autobahn*.

As had occurred with the previous LP, the album's dominant theme also provided its title. *Radio-Activity* (the hyphen provided a significant clue to the record's original conception) was already being advertised at the UK concerts in September, though it wasn't issued until December in Germany, followed soon after by the UK and American releases.

However, if Ira Blacker and the group themselves were expecting a similar commercial success to that of *Autobahn* they were about to be sorely disappointed. The album failed to scrape into either the UK or US charts (though it did manage a meagre 140th placing in the Billboard listings). So what went wrong? Partly it was the result of the frenetic activity either side of the recording sessions which prevented the group from reaching the creative peaks they'd achieved on the previous LP. Without the relatively long gestation period that both *Ralf & Florian* and *Autobahn* had enjoyed, the group fell back on the avant-garde strategies that they were still most comfortable with. And, for the first time, Kraftwerk were making an album under the kind of pressures that only the creators of hit records can understand. How do you repeat the success without repeating the formula? How can you recreate a magic that you only partially understood in the first place? It's a conundrum which, over the years, has been manifested most visibly in what rock journalists describe as 'that difficult second album syndrome' when artists discover that the only thing more difficult than scoring a hit, is scoring the next one.

In addition, the group had filled their studio with new gear just before embarking on the recording sessions – a notoriously risky plan of action. Just at the point when they should have been directing all their creative energies towards the music itself, they were trying to figure out unfamiliar equipment or being distracted by the allure of a new electronic toy. There was also the fact that, without Conny Plank's input, Ralf and Florian were taking on their first solo production project. Stripped of Plank's intricate tapestry of echoes and warm psychedelic overtones, the LP sounded much starker and colder than the warm, wrap-around sound-fields of *Autobahn*.

The most obvious point though is that the group simply slipped out of sync with the times. It would take another five years before the sound that Kraftwerk unveiled with *Radio-Activity* would be accepted commercially. By that time, the group had moved on again. But the group who were most visibly influenced by the album, Liverpool's Orchestral Manoeuvres In The Dark, enjoyed a string of hits from 1980 onwards with a number of records – 'Electricity', 'Souvenir' and 'Maid Of Orleans' among them – which owed their existence to the distinctive sound that Kraftwerk blueprinted on the *Radio-Activity* album.

Shortly before the album's release, the group had visited a nuclear plant in Holland where they'd had a number of promotional pictures taken. Though this decision suggested a clear move to make the nuclear theme explicit it also underlined the group's awkwardly ambivalent feelings towards the burgeoning nuclear debate. For a group so obviously interested in the processes of modernity, atomic power was certainly a potent symbol but their decision to associate themselves with it so graphically seemed particularly risky, especially in Germany where the Green Party headed a growing anti-nuclear lobby.

Given Schult's connections and the level of their interest in current affairs, it's unlikely that Kraftwerk were unaware of this. Between the end of his 1974 lecture tour in America and the Green Party's eventual entry into the West German parliament in 1983, Joseph Beuys was an important figure in the ecology debate (the Green Party used his 'Appeal For An Alternative' essay as a basis for their social and ecological manifesto) and certainly his prominence in the North Rhine-Westphalia area would have ensured these issues were covered by the media around Düsseldorf and Cologne. For Kraftwerk, however, the strategy was an artistic one, which may even have been inspired by the talks Beuys had given in America under the title 'Energy Plan For The Modern Man'. Having courted controversy by celebrating the autobahn network on their previous LP, perhaps they felt they could repeat this tactic by approaching nuclear power in the same way.

This was a miscalculation that would take some years to set right. Subsequently the group made a significant effort to make their position clear, later revising the track 'Radioactivity' (both the live version played during their 1981 world tour and all subsequent concerts and the version which appeared on *The Mix* in 1991) to include an overt anti-nuclear message. Some months after the Chernobyl disaster, Ralf was interviewed by the *NME* and lamented that 'since Chernobyl . . . you go into the supermarket and the product on the shelf doesn't say "milk" anymore, it says "includes radiation percentage".'[4] But even by the time of the anti-Sellafield 2 benefit at G-Mex in 1992, Kraftwerk's involvement was viewed with some suspicion by those who remembered their apparently pro-nuclear sympathies around the time of the *Radio-Activity* LP.

When the track 'Radioactivity' was released as a single early in 1976, it failed to arouse much excitement and had little impact on the charts in either the UK or the US. In France, however, things were markedly different. In contrast with the lukewarm response elsewhere, French audiences showed as much enthusiasm for the new material as their British and American counterparts had done for *Autobahn*. The group's French label manager Maxime Schmitt was utterly convinced by the album and lobbied hard on its behalf. He succeeded in persuading Jean-Loup Laffont from the radio station *Europe 1* who subsequently adopted 'Radioactivity' as the theme tune for his show. This additional promotion helped the single release to become one of the year's big hits in France, notching up sales of around a million copies. Consequently, the LP began selling well (gaining the group a gold disc for sales of over 100,000 copies) and Kraftwerk began making plans for some concerts to take advantage of their increasing profile over the border.

The group's experiences in America had taught them the value of making an impact in a live setting. They were very aware that their static appearance and well-tailored stage clothes – poles apart from either the flamboyant narcissism or the dowdy denim-clad dullness of other rock acts – was a distinct asset in this respect but they had already begun experimenting with other aspects of their performance, including the use of Emil Schult's slide show to add visual interest and reinforce the idea of their concerts as artistic events. For their French concerts, however, they were keen to expand this side of their live show. The solution came from their success in constructing the electronic drum kit which had made its debut on the *Aspecte* show just after the release of *Ralf & Florian*. Having devised one way of triggering their drum machine, Wolfgang Flür began dreaming up a more visually appealing method.

Flür was inspired by a relatively new technology which employed light beams and photosensitive receivers to send electrical impulses. Though it had previously been used by the military, this technology – which subsequently became a common feature of electronic security systems – was only just beginning to make its way into the open market, so its adoption by Kraftwerk was fairly revolutionary. Flür's idea was to construct a frame and place a series of lights and receivers around it which would enable him to use his body movements to trigger the drums. He built the prototype – a tubular steel cage about six and a half feet high – in his workshop in the basement of the house at Bergerallee.

'I would stand inside the frame and make movements with my hands almost like a traffic policeman,' he explains. 'Each time my arms cut through one of the light beams a drum would sound. By moving in the right way, a pattern could be created. In rehearsals it was very effective.'

The plan was to open the concerts with 'Radioactivity' which would be prefaced by Flür's remote-controlled percussion. To the audience it would seem as if Flür was playing an invisible drum kit suspended in mid-air which was likely to provide a stunning opening to the show. But, despite the success of the device during rehearsals it proved to be typically temperamental once the tour got underway. 'I would be standing alone on stage inside my drum cage making my policeman drum movements,' recalls Flür. 'But often the light beams weren't strong enough to push against the residual lights from around the stage so it didn't work very well. Sometimes I could have sunk into the ground when the beam would not work. I'd be standing there praying for it to work. Even when it did work, the headlines were always mad the next day.'

There were other problems too. For one sell-out show in the south of France, the group were forced to play the concert in jeans and T-shirts after a truck carrying some of their equipment and their stage clothes was held up in heavy traffic. Despite delaying the gig for as long as possible in case the truck turned up, the group eventually had to accede to the increasingly irate promoter's demands for them to get onstage and play. Reluctantly, and in a state of some embarrassment, the group did the show but vowed silently that they would never be caught out again. Kraftwerk never played another concert without their stage clothes.

The concerts focused on material from the new album including 'Radioactivity', 'Airwaves' and 'Ohm Sweet Ohm' together with a loosely improvised version of 'Tongebirge' from *Ralf & Florian* and a number of, as yet, unreleased tracks such as 'Europe Endless', 'Showroom Dummies' and 'Trans-Europe Express' which formed the basis of the album that would eventually appear the following year. Both 'Showroom Dummies' and 'Trans-Europe Express' were by now almost fully-developed since recording for the next album was already underway.

David Bowie was also continuing his public love affair with Kraftwerk. Initially he had asked the group to support him on the tour to promote his newly-released *Station To Station* album. That idea however had foundered due to conflicting schedules and, ironically, because of some conversations Bowie had once had with Ralf Hütter about the fundamentals of his own trajectory to pop stardom. Early in his career, he confided to Hütter, he'd made it a policy not to play as a support act for other groups. That way – so his thinking went – nobody would see him as anything other than a top-of-the-bill artist. To adopt the role of a support act, by definition, was an admission that you were somehow inferior to the headlining group and so Bowie had decided to refuse all such offers. It was a tactical move, he explained, but it had eventually paid off because it had set him apart from the normal pop hierarchy and freed him from any associations which could have diminished the impact of the image he was building up around himself. Hütter, always a strategic thinker, got the point straight away and saw how Kraftwerk might benefit from the same game-plan. Perhaps Bowie came to regret giving the advice when Hütter and Schneider turned down his offer to play support on the *Station To Station* tour but he remained convinced enough about the wisdom of these tactics to suggest the same plan of action to the fledgling Human League a few years later.

Instead, Bowie decided to dispense with a support act and simply played tapes of Kraftwerk's music before his performances. He went further by stripping down his stage set, eschewing the lavish productions which had characterised his previous stage shows in favour of a stark, minimalist set that was obviously inspired by Kraftwerk's live concerts. The connection was made explicit by an equally minimal, almost monochrome, lighting design that included a canopy of white strip-lights suspended above the stage (Kraftwerk had been using fluorescent lights in their stage set for some time by this point, though by 1978, Bowie would appropriate the idea completely and use them to construct a complete stage set for the *Lodger* tour). The whole effect was uncannily similar to the kind of '30s Expressionist cabaret feel evoked by Kraftwerk's own onstage set-up.

Bowie's personal appearance had also undergone a remarkable transformation since his first meetings with Kraftwerk. The ostentatious haircut which had become his trademark on the *Ziggy Stardust* tour (and which was given pride of place on the sleeves of the albums which had followed, *Aladdin Sane, Pin Ups* and *Diamond Dogs*) had been replaced by a shorter cut that referenced exactly the same pre-war nostalgia that informed Kraftwerk's image. He'd also taken to wearing suits. In a 1975 television appearance with Cher, it even looked like he'd borrowed one of Florian's favourite jackets for his performance.

In the mythology that's subsequently grown up around this time (among Bowie fans at least), it's often been mistakenly suggested that this look was borrowed wholesale from the New York soul scene. But it was Bowie's influence which established this look among the soul fraternity. Before his arrival on the scene, soul aficionados were decked out in the flash ersatz glamour that distinguished most fashion trends during the early '70s. The subtle, sophisticated, almost nostalgic look which followed was one that Bowie engineered. And he took the inspiration for it from Kraftwerk. In that 1975 television appearance with Cher, as the pair crooned their way through a duet of 'Can You Hear Me', Bowie looked as though he'd stepped straight into the studio after a day-trip with Ralf and Florian.

During 1975, Bowie was also involved in filming for his first major acting role in Nic Roeg's adaptation of a dystopian sci-fi novel by Walter Tevis called *The Man Who Fell To Earth*. Bowie played Thomas Jerome Newton, an alien on a mission to find water to save his dying, drought-ridden planet. Bowie sourced much of his own wardrobe for the role. During the film which was released the following year, as Newton becomes inducted into life on our world, so his dress sense evolves from the funky alien chic he sports during the movie's early scenes towards the look of a cosmopolitan European businessman. In his hat and long Crombie coat, the link between Bowie-as-Newton and Bowie-as-Florian became explicit. Photographs taken during Kraftwerk's American tour in 1975 (among them the picture which was eventually used on the cover of *Trans-Europe Express*) make it clear that Bowie was using Florian Schneider as a template for his own take on the stranger-in-a-strange-land riff.

By the time of the *Station To Station* tour, Bowie's fascination with Kraftwerk had extended to a fascination with Germany itself. For the concerts, Bowie had adapted a look – white shirt, slicked-back hair, black trousers and black waistcoat – from Joel Grey's oleaginous MC in the Bob Fosse film *Cabaret*. Set in '30s Berlin, *Cabaret* mapped the period just before German culture succumbed to the Nazis. Again, this was familiar Kraftwerk territory.

Some years later, Simon Witter interviewed Bowie and noted that he often had to think hard about the answers to the questions Witter was asking him. But when the journalist mentioned Kraftwerk, Bowie answered straight away. 'A band I would have loved to have been in,'[5] he declared without any hesitation.

Interestingly, during the autumn of 1976, Hütter admitted that there were plans for a collaborative project with Bowie. 'We should have worked together already,' he explained to Paul Alessandrini, 'but the success of the last album forced us to tour until October and our projects were postponed. But with Bowie, what makes us close to each other, it's mostly similar considerations about psychology . . . We are going to record with Bowie. He will come to Düsseldorf pretty soon for that. We still don't know what we are going to do together, it's mostly an encounter . . .'[6]

'We have always been interested by what Bowie is doing,' added Florian, 'especially in his last albums. He started from hard rock and he's now on the cusp of electro-acoustic music, while we went the opposite way from electronic music to rock music. So I think what will happen will be thrilling.'[7]

The collaboration, of course, never took place. Instead Kraftwerk withdrew into their own increasingly self-contained world which remained impenetrable even to the advances of Michael Jackson when he expressed a keen desire to collaborate with the group some years later. But Hütter remained grateful to Bowie for his support. 'Bowie was speaking devotedly about Kraftwerk in interviews,' he pointed out, 'and that had a great importance for us. He was a very important trend-setter at that time and his statements made press and public look at us no longer as an obscure experimental band but as a group making popular music in German. Bowie made us trendy, but our ideas were still the same.'[8]

What was changing was the musical climate. During the long hot summer of 1976, the punk scene was beginning to coalesce. By the time Kraftwerk began their brief English tour in Coventry on Friday 8th October 1976 – the same day that the Sex Pistols signed their ill-fated deal with EMI – the country's music papers were full of the new phenomenon. That week, both *Sounds* and *Melody Maker* ran lengthy features covering both the recent Punk Rock Festival at the 100 Club and some of the most crucial faces on the scene, including Siouxsie Sioux, Mark Perry and, naturally, the Pistols themselves.

It's interesting to speculate on what Hütter and Schneider made of this when they arrived in England. No doubt they would have related to punk's reference points – bands such as The Stooges and MC5 – and the scene's dismissive rejection of rock dinosaurs like Pink Floyd and Led Zeppelin. But they could also have been forgiven if they'd experienced a slight *frisson* of apprehension. After all, they'd only just climbed to a position where they had achieved some recognition and here were these mouthy, anarchic kids threatening to overturn things completely.

Though, superficially at least, the rhetoric of punk suggested little in the way of common ground between Kraftwerk with their affluent backgrounds, classical music education and sophisticated European manners (not to mention their obvious lack of speed-thrill guitars) and the new sound of the streets, there were a number of factors which conspired to make them one of the few already established acts (along with Bowie and Roxy Music) who were embraced by the movement. There was the important point that David Bowie had already given the group his seal of approval – many of those in punk's inner circle were long-term fans of Bowie, who at that time held an influential sway that's hard to imagine at this distance (and one which has had no real analogue since thanks to the distrust of the star system instilled by punk and its aftermath). There was also the fact that many of the scene's key players – Malcolm McLaren, Nils Stevenson, all three members of The Clash, Jamie Reid and many of those who'd orbited the legendary London SS – were former art school students which provided them with an over-riding appreciation of Kraftwerk's aesthetic concept. There was another link too. If, as John Foxx suggests, Kraftwerk had constructed a Marcel Duchamp version of rock n' roll for themselves then, similarly, so had punk (though perhaps some might argue that one was based on *The Bride Stripped Bare* . . . and the other on found objects like his disfigured *Mona Lisa, LHOOQ,* or the urinal which shocked the art establishment for decades). Furthermore there was Kraftwerk's obvious isolation in a music scene which, until now, had mostly been dominated by the long-haired, denim-clad tribes.

'In 1975 we were very lonely,' recalls Hütter. 'Everyone was on a Californian trip: hippies, The Eagles . . . Kraftwerk has been attacked many times, especially in England. They were against us because we represented the end of this guitar music, we were a threat for their Californian dream . . .'[9] These sentiments are uncannily close to those of punk and could just have easily been uttered by one of the Bromley contingent or maybe The Clash's Mick Jones ready to launch into one of his 'high above the Westway' riffs.

Another factor in Kraftwerk's favour was that their synthetic sound had a clear resonance with one of punk's key reference points, Stanley Kubrick's 1971 film *A Clockwork Orange*. Adapted from the book by

Anthony Burgess, Kubrick's movie was a visually dazzling and highly controversial (it was later withdrawn from British cinemas) cult classic which, thanks both to the brilliance of the original material and Jonathan Barry's stunning set designs, appealed to exactly the same constituency that gave rise to punk. Ostensibly the tale of an amoral, misfit boot-boy set sometime in the not-too-distant future, the original novel was a blackly humorous social satire that was both viciously accurate and, ultimately, terrifying. For the teenage thugs, Burgess invented a language (he lectured in literature and phonetics) called Nadsat, a terminally hip contraction of English, German, Russian and Slim Gaillard's proto-rap jive. He also invented a pop culture for them, full of bands with names like The Legend, Cyclops and Heaven Seventeen (a monicker later borrowed by Martyn Ware's post-Human League project). But, crucially, Burgess isolated his sinister anti-hero, Alex, from this pop culture, casting him instead as a Beethoven-loving aesthete with a taste for "ultra-violence" and spiked milk. Alex's withering distaste for the hollow disposability of the pop scene mapped perfectly on to the feelings of those who, during the early '70s, remained unconvinced by the turgid excesses of progressive rock or the tacky schmaltz of Mud and the Bay City Rollers.

All this provided Kubrick with the material for a film which, more than any other phenomenon outside of Altamont, wrenched the '70s away from the era of Woodstock and Haight-Ashbury. But Alex's fondness for Beethoven, Mozart and Wagner presented Kubrick with a technical problem. After all, how do you make a futuristic, fast-paced pop culture film with a classical soundtrack? Kubrick's solution was as elegant as it was simple. He enlisted the services of Walter Carlos, a classical composer and electronic pioneer who'd scored a huge hit with the 1968 album *Switched On Bach*, a synthesized version of some of Bach's most popular concertos which had become the best-selling classical record of all time.

Carlos took the angular, often unlistenable cacophony of Stockhausen and transformed it into a dizzyingly lush, melodic confection that was as commercially viable as, say, the work of Leonard Bernstein (whom Carlos had once assisted with a concert of electronic music). He'd assembled his first electronic music studio at the age of 17 and by the early '60s was recording pieces such as *Dialogues For Piano And Two Loudspeakers* or *Variations For Flute And Electronic Sound*. In 1966, Carlos met a young engineer, Robert Moog, and explained his idea for an electronic sound producer which would also be a valid musical instrument. The pair collaborated on developing this device which became the prototype Moog synthesizer. Carlos used this to create *Switched On Bach* and its follow-up *The Well-Tempered Synthesizer* which did much to popularise the new instrument. Carlos was also the perfect collaborator for Moog. His artistic demands pushed the instrument's development at a rapid pace though he was also capable of coming up with technical solutions whenever Moog got bogged down (he had a degree in physics and was technologically-gifted enough to have built himself a small computer at the age of fourteen).

Kubrick's decision to hire Walter Carlos was a master-stroke. The composer provided lavish synthesized versions of Beethoven's Ninth Symphony together with adaptations of Purcell and Rossini for the soundtrack. Along with his own works (particularly the film's main theme and an achingly other-worldly piece entitled *Timesteps*) this provided Kubrick with an astonishingly innovative and powerful soundtrack that perfectly matched his visual pyrotechnics.

A Clockwork Orange was perhaps the most original and controversial film of the '70s. It aroused fierce debate and almost universal condemnation in the media (which, like the tabloid coverage of acid house during the late '80s, simply served to popularise it even further) though the themes at the heart of Kubrick's movie – the ache of modernity, emotional isolation and the dehumanisation of society – became steadily more relevant as the decade wound on into economic crisis and mass unemployment. But it also became a pivotal part of punk's catalysation. By the long hot summer of 1976, its central themes would be paraphrased and extemporised around endlessly by the new music revolutionaries.

The film's compelling soundtrack lodged firmly in the minds of the would-be punk hopefuls, subconsciously linking the synthesizer with Kubrick's guerrilla shock tactics and the ideas which were to become a central part of punk's manifesto. So although the first generation of punk groups all relied heavily on guitars, Kraftwerk's synthetic sound had associations that, spiritually at least, connected them with the movement's onward rush. The fact that Kraftwerk didn't look or sound like any of the bands which punk aimed to displace (in all respects they could almost have been tailor-made for *A Clockwork Orange*) helped them to become one of the few groups that punk celebrated instead of condemned.

When Kraftwerk played at London's Roundhouse on Sunday 10th October 1976 (within a few weeks of The Ramones' British debut there) the audience contained a number of punk's key figures. As the group made their way through a set which sounded remarkably similar to the one they would unveil on their 1981 tour, few people realised that the most important players in pop music's development over the next two decades were, for the first and probably last time, all together in the same place.

The Roundhouse concert featured tracks such as 'Kometenmelodie 2', 'Europe Endless', 'Radioactivity' and, of course, 'Autobahn' but also included the group's vocoderised treatment of an extract from Goethe's *Faust* which they'd played during the previous year's tour. For this performance, three of the tracks from the *Radio-Activity* LP were stitched together with 'Die Sonne, Die Monde, Die Sterne' to create what Hütter announced as 'the symphony of the radio star' (an awkward reminder of the quasi-classical suites which were so beloved by the progressive rock acts who were about to meet their nemesis in the shape of punk). Interestingly, Florian had also abandoned his flute parts on 'Autobahn', which was perhaps just as well since the punk aristocracy may have accepted 'the symphony of the radio star' (there were, after all, several symphonies in *A Clockwork Orange*) but, in their new world order, a flute was definitely *de trop*.

The gig was well-received and, for an encore, the group played 'Showroom Dummies' which fitted perfectly with punk's prevailing mood of dislocation and desensitisation. Within a few weeks of Kraftwerk's appearance in London, the new scene was on the cusp of a mass-market breakthrough that would polarise the musical climate and, seemingly overnight, unravel the rich tapestry that rock had wrought for itself. Only those on the winning side would survive with their reputations intact. Luckily for Kraftwerk, they fell into this category (this was more due to circumstance than design, but the end result was the same). For the first time in their career – though not the last – Kraftwerk were about to experience an immense cultural shift that would radically alter the music scene in their favour. The world was about to change.

6

Punk's very own version of *kristallnacht* took place on Wednesday 1st December 1976 just as London was settling down to tea. The Sex Pistols had been drafted in at the last minute to fill a vacant slot on the early evening Thames Television show, *Today*. Hosted by Bill Grundy, *Today* was an innocuous local programme that combined minor celebrity chat with a fairly undemanding look at the day's current affairs – the kind of cheap n' cheerful programming that broadcasters used to plug the gap between the end of the main news and the beginning of the proper (i.e. expensive) evening schedule. Until that night, *Today* could hardly have been accused of being epoch-making stuff, but it was about to find itself in the eye of a storm.

Unprepared and expecting another group altogether (the original guests were supposed to have been another EMI signing, Queen) Grundy was reluctant to interview the Sex Pistols at all but was eventually forced to accede to pressure from the show's producer. Minorly irritated, Grundy was even more dismayed when he was introduced to the group and noted their scruffy, street-urchin appearance. But the Pistols had also brought some fans – including Siouxsie Sioux and Steve Severin – with them, both as a way of providing some moral support and adding some background colour to the event. Siouxsie, with bleached blond hair and a star painted over one eye, was eye-catching enough for Grundy to pay her at least some attention.

As the show went on air, Grundy's irritation increased when the Sex Pistols began reading the introduction from his autocue along with him. As the interview got underway, however, there was little to suggest anything out of the ordinary was about to happen. Initially, the group were behaving more or less like naughty schoolboys but when Grundy, sensing he was getting nowhere, turned his attention to Siouxsie and essayed some minor flirtation the band's guitar player Steve Jones jeered. 'You dirty sod,' he chided. 'You dirty old man.' Grundy's temper bit the dust. In what has become one of the most notorious exchanges in British broadcasting history, Grundy rounded on Jones. 'Well keep going, chief, keep going,' he prompted, testily. 'Go on, you've got another ten seconds. Say something outrageous.'

Jones duly obliged. 'You dirty bastard,' he retorted. Grundy, losing control rapidly, urged him to go on. 'You dirty fucker,' offered Jones, seeming almost embarrassed by being put on the spot in this way. This time Grundy responded with sarcasm. 'What a clever boy,' he sneered. In turn, the guitar player's reply was revealingly old-fashioned. 'You fucking rotter,' he smirked.

Though it now seems no more shocking than an exchange of schoolboy taunts, in the television climate of 1976 expletives weren't thought acceptable even for late-night viewing. The furore began, almost before the programme ended as the telephone lines at Thames Television were jammed with viewers calling to protest. Within a few hours, the story was being carried by the main evening newscasts. When Britain woke up the next day, it was to blanket coverage of what the *Daily Mirror* described on its front-page as a 'rock outrage' despite the fact that the broadcast had only been seen in London. In addition to the story, some of the newspapers ran features on the scene, along a similar template laid out by that of the *Mirror* itself. 'Who Are These Punks?' screamed the headline before declaring that 'they wear torn and ragged clothes held together by safety pins.' Other headlines mugged wildly – 'Four-Letter Punk Rock Group In TV Storm', 'The Filth And The Fury!', 'The Foul-Mouthed Yobs' – as other newspapers rushed to join in the almost universal condemnation of the Sex Pistols.

Not since The Beatles had a pop group so thoroughly commandeered the media. It was better publicity than even the most wildly optimistic of punks could have dreamed. Within a few hours on the morning of Thursday 2nd December, in cities, towns and villages all over the UK, schoolkids who hadn't even heard of punk rock or the Sex Pistols the day before were aligning themselves with the new scene. Suddenly established rock acts seemed very dull.

The publicity continued as a planned tour by the Sex Pistols to promote their 'Anarchy In The UK' single came under fire. Also appearing on the tour were The Clash, The Damned and The Heartbreakers which gave the media's response the appearance of an all-out attack, not only on the Sex Pistols, but on punk rock itself. EMI, the record label which Kraftwerk shared with the Pistols, was also under attack. 'If you were a punk, you suddenly found yourself a scapegoat, an outsider,' recalls Jon Savage in his seminal history of punk rock,

England's Dreaming. 'This realisation – part delicious, part terrifying – radicalised a small but significant part of a generation.'

Punk reshaped the music scene. By flouting and subverting the conventional rules of pop, it also broadened its horizons to encompass musical developments which might previously have been marginalised. The events of those first few days in December 1976, opened a doorway through which Kraftwerk would eventually step. It was the catalyst which would allow them to reorder the future.

As 1976 drifted into 1977, the furore continued unabated. But the first truly revolutionary record of the year didn't come from any of the groups in punk's inner circle. It came from David Bowie.

In an effort to rid himself of a serious cocaine addiction, Bowie had by this time abandoned America in favour of Germany. His decision to relocate there, rather than any other European country, was at least partly encouraged by his infatuation with Kraftwerk. Though the plan to collaborate had fallen through, Hütter and Schneider helped Bowie to find a place in Berlin. Once his living arrangements there had been sorted out, Bowie lost no time in contacting Brian Eno.

Since the period he'd enjoyed as a member of Roxy Music during the early '70s, Eno had become England's most prominent electronic futurist although as far back as the '60s he'd been involved in various bizarre experimental projects and performance groups such as Merchant Taylor's Simultaneous Cabinet and Maxwell Demon. Eno was heavily influenced by modernist composers such as John Cage, La Monte Young and Steve Reich whose techniques he borrowed liberally for his own highly individual take on music. He was also an early convert to the synthesizer. His appearances with Roxy on *Top Of The Pops*, demonically twisting knobs on his EMS Synthi, gave the British public their first ever glimpse of the possibility that someday the synthesizer might replace the guitar as pop's principal instrument. For Bowie, he was the closest thing there was to an English Kraftwerk. Unable to work with the Germans themselves, he took the next best route and enlisted Eno to work on his new LP.

Equipping themselves with a number of synthesizers (including Eno's EMS, an Arp and a Mini-Moog) the pair installed themselves in Hansa Studios near the Berlin Wall and began recording a series of tracks that were radically different from anything either artist had previously worked on. The new direction brought together a range of influences that touched on soul, punk and the proto-ambient material that Bowie had tentatively worked on for *The Man Who Fell To Earth* (Bowie's music never made it to the soundtrack, instead the film's musical director John Phillips recorded some of his own themes at CTS Studios in London and combined them with pieces by Stomu Yamashta, Jim Reeves and Artie Shaw to create the finished score) but by far the most obvious influence on the sound that emerged was the music of Kraftwerk.

Bowie recruited many of the musicians who'd worked on *Station To Station* to flesh out the ideas he and Eno had put together. But even the presence of guitarists Carlos Alomar and Ricky Gardener couldn't obscure the overwhelmingly synthetic nature of the new material. In fact, most of the guitar parts were processed so heavily that they ended up sounding like synths anyway. Each of the keyboard parts was placed high in the mix while Dennis Davis's drum sounds were phased and flanged to give them an electronic feel. The first side of the resulting album, *Low*, was a masterpiece that managed to locate Kraftwerk's aesthetic into a pop song context before the group themselves had properly discovered how to pull off the trick.

But it was on the second side of the album, made up of exclusively instrumental tracks such as 'Warzawa' and 'Weeping Wall', that Bowie's Kraftwerk fascination was most apparent. On 'Art Decade' he used a drum machine rhythm (or as Bowie himself described it 'pre-arranged percussion') under layers of synthetic strings, Eno's squawking Moog and densely woven reverbs to evoke the kind of timbres used on tracks such as 'Kristallo' (from *Ralf & Florian*) or even earlier pieces such as 'Klingklang' (from *Kraftwerk 2*). On 'Subterraneans', however, Bowie took Kraftwerk's sometimes ragged edges – the legacy of their days as improvisers on the performance art scene – and polished them into an achingly taut, pristine sound full of perfect synthetic surfaces and simplified, though devastatingly effective, melodies. This was to be a key step in Kraftwerk's own progress towards the perfect electronic pop they would arrive at with *The Man Machine* the following year.

Given what was happening in England at the time, Bowie's strategy was perfectly timed. *Low* didn't sound like a rock record. In fact, in the context of early 1977, it didn't sound much like anything else at all. On the burgeoning punk scene, the album's use of unconventional arrangements and radical sounds seemed to suggest that Bowie too was rejecting the rock establishment. And since many of the tracks on *Low*, such as 'Breaking Glass' and 'A New Career In A New Town', were under three minutes long, Bowie seemed also to be reflecting punk's emphasis on short, concise musical statements (a reaction against the long, bloated, self-indulgent epics of the hated progressive rock scene). Added to the record's themes of alienation and dislocation, this allied Bowie with punk in a way which few other artists managed and located him amongst the small, select group of acts who survived the scene's explosion with their reputations intact.

In terms of Kraftwerk's own career, *Low* was a significant release because it changed mainstream pop culture's perception of electronic music and helped to disconnect a number of associations that had built up around it. Bowie's album located itself alongside Walter Carlos and *A Clockwork Orange* at the opposite end of the spectrum from the cosmic rock of Tangerine Dream or the dull virtuoso exploits of Rick Wakeman and Keith Emerson (a fact Bowie made explicit by prefacing his concerts with excerpts from the film's soundtrack). But because of Bowie's unique influence at the time, *Low* also helped to establish the notion of the synthesizer as a tool for making radical and revolutionary pop among a wider audience, creating a sympathetic climate for Kraftwerk's subsequent releases and those of the synth pop groups who were inspired by them.

Low arrived too late for it to have any impact on the content of Kraftwerk's sixth LP *Trans-Europe Express* (although Bowie did get a mention on the title track). Instead, what it did do was establish the relevance of Kraftwerk's music within the context of punk. For the first time since *Autobahn*, Kraftwerk found themselves moving back towards the mainstream of pop culture. This wasn't because their art was becoming any less revolutionary. It happened because, for the first time since the '60s, the music scene itself was shifting towards a more radical – and much more interesting – position.

Unlike the hurried sessions that had given birth to *Radio-Activity*, the new LP had a relatively long gestation period which stretched as far back as the 1975 US tour. Tracks such as 'Trans-Europe Express' and 'Showroom Dummies' had been around in one form or another since then, while 'Europe Endless' had emerged during the French concerts during the previous year. 'We travelled across all Europe and, especially after a tour in the States, we became conscious that Europe is mostly parks and old hotels . . . promenades and avenues . . . real life,' explained Ralf when a journalist asked about the inspiration behind the song. 'It's real life, but in a world of postcards. Europe when back from the States, it's only a succession of postcards . . .'[1]

Most of the recording took place in Düsseldorf at the group's recently-named Kling Klang studio but Hütter and Schneider made the decision to mix the record in America. Partly this was due to their own growing fascination with the distinctive sound of American productions but it's likely that, after the relative failure of *Radio-Activity*, Ira Blacker was also keen to reestablish the group in the US and saw this as an ideal way to make the group's sound more accessible to the American market.

With recording finished, Hütter and Schneider flew to America during the summer of 1976 to complete the mixing at one of the most famous studios in Los Angeles, The Record Plant, with engineer Bill Halverson. But, on their return to Germany, the pair changed their minds about some of the US mixes and booked time in Hamburg's Rüssl Studio to rework some of the tracks. This process continued as plans for the album, and some of the tracks themselves, continued to evolve. Even as late as the UK concerts in October 1976, the central melody in 'Trans-Europe Express' was noticeably different from the version which appeared on the final album release. After the French concerts in November, Hütter confessed that 'we still have a lot of work to do because, since we've had the chance to play the new songs live, we know what doesn't work.'[2]

But there were also a few happy accidents, such as the track 'Franz Schubert' as Hütter later explained. 'He played himself,' he told Andrew Darlington of *The Hot Press*. 'I was switching on the sequencing machines and then it was playing. It was something else we'd been setting up before, something much speedier, the machines just happened to be tuned at that thing the next day and I played it. I changed the octaves and I thought it was Schubert playing, like he's saying hello because he's master of German melodies . . . So it's like Schubert just came in for a few minutes and said hello to the machine spirit.'[3]

Though Hütter predicted that the album would be ready by January 1977, in actual fact the process of refining the tracks – and the overall concept – took longer than expected. In November, he explained the idea behind the album to Paul Alessandrini. 'Our album evokes the European culture,' he declared. 'It is spiritually European and it's a new conscience that we discovered during our trip on the American continent in '75. Everybody asked us how was life in Germany, in Paris. People wanted to know where was our culture at that point. People used to say that we were not rock n' roll, then thanks to these transatlantic trips we discovered our cultural identity as Europeans . . . In the name of the album there will be, of course, the word "Europe" and the sleeve will be made from a set of mirrors reflecting our pictures. There is a song called 'Hall Of Mirrors' on the album – the story of what we did since the beginning, our psychological trip, in some ways the other side of the background.'[4]

For various reasons the mirror sleeve concept didn't work out. Instead, perhaps aware that their own distinctive appearance was one of their best assets, the decision was taken to use a portrait photograph that had been taken in the Maurice Seymour studios in New York during the group's American tour in 1975. Originally based in Chicago, Seymour was one of America's most respected show business photographers and had been taking pictures of celebrities since the '30s when much of his work focused on publicity stills for big band leaders and musicians. In keeping with the style of that era, Seymour's work concentrated on highly-flattering, soft focus shots that were often retouched and air-brushed to tidy up the imperfections of real life. One of the photographs from this session was used on the front cover of the European release while, for the UK and US versions, a similarly embellished colour photo from a session with Jacques Stara in Paris was used. Both photographs – along with those on the album's inner sleeve – provided an oddly formal and heavily nostalgic look which contrasted with the modern sheen of the music inside.

The sleeve for the new album was the first since *Ralf & Florian* to focus on the group as identifiable personalities, though it did so with a kind of curious irony. Their experiences with David Bowie – whose face appeared on the sleeve of every one of his album releases and who as a consequence was probably the most recognisable pop star in the world at this point – was partly responsible for this move (from this point on Kraftwerk never again made an album which didn't feature their images in one form or another) but the ironic twist was all their own. Possessing none of Bowie's narcissism, it seemed that Hütter and Schneider felt it necessary to cover their embarrassment by subverting the context in which their faces appeared. For *Trans-Europe Express*, they chose to use a deliberately ironic retro glamour look. The powerful images which followed – the camp Kandinsky of *The Man Machine*, the computer terminal graphic of *Computer World*, the three-dimensional modelling used on *Electric Cafe* and, finally, the deconstructed robots on *The Mix*

– were all born from this same sense that there's something faintly ridiculous about the cult of personality that's at the heart of pop culture.

A similar tongue-in-cheek attitude has also pervaded the group's promotional videos. Kraftwerk were early converts to the medium. In 1975, following their US tour, they filmed clips for both 'Autobahn' and, subsequently, 'Radioactivity' inside Kling Klang. At the time, this was still a fairly revolutionary step – few artists had experimented with video at this point (although the famous promo for Queen's 'Bohemian Rhapsody', for example, appeared at around the same time) – but the group were encouraged by Emil Schult who'd been involved in film-making as a student. 'Film and video have always been in my toolbox,' confirmed Schult.

For 'Trans-Europe Express' the group used an elaborate combination of still photography (much of it shot on location at Düsseldorf's main railway station), archive footage (rare film of the futuristic *Schienenzeppelin* train) and modelling (a miniature replica of the *Schienenzeppelin* train travelling through a model cityscape) along with film of them on a train journey between Düsseldorf and Duisburg. In the finished cut, there's a scene shot in the railway carriage of the Düsseldorf-Duisburg train which features all four members of the group chatting or reading newspapers. Ralf stares out of the window, trying as hard as he can to maintain the image of an enigmatic, faintly poetic, pop star for the camera until finally he can't bear it any longer and cracks up into laughter. Most other groups would have edited these frames out but instead Hütter and Schneider opted to leave them in, revealing not only a subtle ambivalence towards the nature of pop iconography but an obvious willingness to subvert it too.

This theme, which recurs repeatedly throughout Kraftwerk's work, provides an intriguing glimpse of Hütter and Schneider's relationship with pop culture. It's clear from much of their dialogue over the years that they're deeply in love with the fabric of pop but they also seem acutely aware of its failings and its ultimate absurdity. 'We do not conceive ourselves as rock n' roll stars . . .' Hütter had explained to *Rolling Stone* in 1975, 'we're just private people.'[5] A few months later Schneider reiterated the point. 'We go beyond all this individual feel,' he told Geoff Barton of *Sounds*. 'We are no superstar band. We are more like vehicles, a part of our *Menschmaschine*, our man-machine.'[6] In contrast to the ego-driven star system that dominated the music scene in the mid-'70s, this approach was brutally down-to-earth. It was also one that had much in common with the original mythology of punk (though the reality ended up being somewhat different). This part of the Kraftwerk aesthetic wasn't lost on those in punk's inner circle who championed them. But Hütter and Schneider's distrust of the star ethos had its roots in events that were far more profound than the self-indulgent posturings of a few overpaid rock icons. 'Germany had a very effective star system in the '30s and '40s,' they explained to *Melody Maker* journalist Christopher Petit, 'which was not only perfected by the media but by politics too. People know where it can go.'[7]

As the group worked on the final stages of *Trans-Europe Express*, the global music scene was going through a period of intense change driven by twin engines which, at the time, seemed like polar opposites but which, with the benefit of hindsight, now appear as related movements in the battle to displace the turgid mediocrity of rock. In England, punk was going overground. The first punk album, The Damned's *Damned, Damned, Damned* had surprised everyone by breaching the charts, despite the fact that it was released on an independent label. Suddenly every record company in the country was throwing money at the scene, sometimes in the direction of bands who existed more by reputation than in any real rehearsing/gigging/playing sense. The Clash had signed to CBS, possibly the most prestigious major record label after EMI (with whom the Sex Pistols had signed and, following the Grundy debacle, in turn been swiftly dropped after releasing just one single, the incendiary 'Anarchy In The UK') while A&M – in a move that was either remarkably brave or remarkably foolhardy – decided to take the risk and pick up the Pistols for a sizeable £75,000 advance. They lasted just six days before A&M pulled out but the message was clear, punk was now an official money spinner.

Across the Atlantic meanwhile, disco was beginning to make an impact. Disco had its roots in Philly soul, Motown and amped-up rhythm n' blues but even as late as 1975 it was still a largely localised scene in the bars and clubs of Manhattan. As with house music some years later, the disco phenomenon was originally built up around gay culture though it quickly traversed the sexual divide as the scene expanded. And as with house, disco based itself on a fundamental democracy that stretched far beyond punk's principle of access. 'In the discotheque the spotlight is on everybody,' noted Hütter and Schneider in a *Melody Maker* interview the following year. 'Unlike concerts where you only see the star of the show and everyone else is in the dark. In discos everybody can be a part of everybody else. There is something about this we very much like. Of course there is good disco and bad disco. But it is the exact opposite of our classical music background where you couldn't even . . . look in your programme . . . or breathe. Disco should be very loose. We consider it the new art form.'[8]

The first major step in disco's ascent had been taken as far back as 1970 when Francis Grosso took over as resident DJ in a converted New York church known as The Sanctuary. Along with Michael Capello and Steve D'Aquisto, Grosso was the first to pioneer many of the techniques that characterised disco (and each of the subsequent dancefloor revolutions) such as beat-mixing records together to create one continuous groove, emphasising the hypnotic qualities of the music's rhythm track and keeping the dancers locked on the floor for as long as possible. Grosso also developed the technique of playing two separate records simultaneously to create something entirely new. In his book *Disco*, Albert Goldman describes the way that Grosso 'would superimpose the drum break of "I'm A Man" over the orgasmic moans of Led Zeppelin's "Whole Lotta Love" to make a powerfully erotic mix.'

In 1975, as disco surged into its upswing, the resident DJ at Galaxy 21, Walter Gibbons, hired a young drummer who'd just arrived from France to play live in the club so that the rhythm on the records he was playing could be enhanced to provide a reinforced, bottom-heavy beat for the dancefloor. Gibbons was the first of the New York DJs to move into studio work – his extended mix of Double Exposure's '10%' became the world's first dance remix – but his drummer, François Kevorkian soon followed suit and, after first learning how to DJ, taught himself studio techniques well enough to become one of the disco era's most prolific and respected producers.

Meanwhile, further across town, David Mancuso was creating a sensation for disco's in-crowd at The Loft. Characterised by an extraordinarily sophisticated sound system and a liquor-free policy, The Loft generated a utopian, upbeat vibe which was as much a throwback to the peace and love ethos of the '60s as anything else. 'The Loft was like a fucking religion,' remembers François Kevorkian. 'I saw people crying on the dancefloor because they were so moved by the music and the atmosphere. It was incredible.'

On April 27th 1977, just a few weeks before the official release of *Trans-Europe Express*, the most visible symbol of disco's upwardly-mobile aspirations opened its doors for the first time. Studio 54 was the brainchild of Steve Rubell and Ian Schrager, two college friends who'd embarked on their first successful club venture with the Enchanted Garden in Queens. After the Enchanted Garden was closed (due to complaints from neighbours) Rubell and Schrager obtained backing to move to a disused theatre on West 54th Street in Manhattan which had most recently been used as a CBS television studio. Within days of its opening – or to be more accurate, within hours of the notorious birthday party for Bianca Jagger which followed just a few days after the opening night – Studio 54 was the most celebrated nightclub in town attracting guests such as Andy Warhol, Elizabeth Taylor and Calvin Klein. Disco had arrived in style.

Studio 54 was hedonism incarnate. If anybody needed reminding of this fact, the centre-piece of the club – a huge, crescent Man-In-The-Moon which at intervals would lower from the roof and, in a telling pantomime, raise a spoon to its nose and snort starbursts of sparkling light – made it explicit. The vast interior of the club, packed with beautiful people especially chosen by Rubell and doorman Marc Benecke, suggested a curiously nostalgic, if unprecedented, glamour. 'You would be looking around and the place would suddenly flip, turning from a drowned ballroom into an art deco airplane hangar,'9 remembers Anthony Haden-Guest. But the club's highly visible success also encouraged other promoters to lock on to the disco boom. Soon Studio 54 was joined by Xenon and New York, New York where François Kevorkian became the resident DJ.

'At New York, New York I was playing to thousands of people every week, all of whom were completely enamoured with the idea that disco was the hottest thing that had ever existed,' Kevorkian recalls. 'It was amazing. That was the year that both *Star Wars* and *Saturday Night Fever* came out and there was a real excitement about the music. You'd show up at the club and you'd start putting music on and people would start screaming. There was this energy going on which I've never ever seen since then amongst the straight, general population.'

Trans-Europe Express was released in May 1977 just as disco was moving to take over New York completely. The insistent metallic groove and cold European glamour of the title track mapped perfectly on to the disco crowd's aspirations and soon DJs all over Manhattan were spinning both 'Trans-Europe Express' and 'Metal On Metal' its stripped-down variant. Anthony Haden-Guest remembers one night during that summer, soon after Studio 54 was discovered to be operating without a liquor licence and had its bars shut down:

'First, we dined and then had mimosas in Regine's. A tranquil interlude this. Then on to Hurrah, which was coming to life because it was moving toward three in the morning, and it was filled with elongated blondes pumping air iron to Kraftwerk's 'Trans-Europe Express'. Thence to New York, New York where lights of laser red and cobalt blue were fingering the dancers. Thence on to the drought spot itself, Studio 54.'[10]

Along with Donna Summer's 'I Feel Love', 'Trans-Europe Express' became one of the biggest disco hits of the summer, prompting Kraftwerk's US record company Capitol to release a special 12" edition of the single (backed with 'Metal On Metal') for the disco market, together with a subsequent edited and remixed 12" for radio promotion. For Hütter and Schneider, who had always been fascinated by discotheques, this was proof that they were travelling in the right direction.

'Electronics is beyond nations and colours,' Hütter pointed out to *Billboard* later that year. 'It speaks a language everyone can understand. It expresses more than just stories the way most conventional songs do. With electronics, everything is possible. The only limit is with the composer.'[11]

Hütter's point was a prescient one. By the height of the summer, Kraftwerk's sound was stretching far from the expensive niteries of Manhattan to the project housing in Harlem and the Bronx where their pulsating beat reached the ears of a new creative generation. In terms of 1977's conception of musicianship, none of them would have been considered musicians in the conventional sense. But within a few years, they would use Kraftwerk's dense electronic groove as a template to turn the music scene inside out. As Hütter suggested 'in front of the loudspeakers everyone is equal.'[12]

A few months later, along with Maze and Tavares, Kraftwerk were the surprise guests at the Pop Music Disco Awards at the Beacon Theatre on September 22nd. Disco's power at this point was such that the show was taped by the Hughes Independent Television Network for subsequent broadcast. Having travelled to New York to collect the award for 'Trans-Europe Express', the group decided to check out some of the city's clubs including one memorable visit to The Loft when Hütter discovered for himself how DJs treated Kraftwerk's music in a club context.

'They took sections of "Metal On Metal" on *Trans-Europe Express* and, when I went in, it was going boom-crash-boom-crash,' he explains. 'So I thought "Oh, they're playing the new album" but it went on for ten minutes and I thought "What's happening? That track is only something like two or three minutes." Later, I went to ask the DJ and he had two copies of the record and he was mixing the two. Of course, it could go on for as long as people were dancing. This was real development, because in those days you fixed a certain time on the record – under twenty minutes a side – in order to get the print on to vinyl. It was a technological decision to say how long the song would last. We always used to play different timings live, but there we were in this after-hours club and it was ten minutes, twenty minutes of the recording because the vibe was there.'[13]

'We liked the fact that our music was used as dance music,' adds Wolfgang Flür. 'When we went to clubs and they played our songs sometimes we would dance as well.'

For the launch of the *Trans-Europe Express* album in France, EMI arranged a train journey for a select group of French music journalists. They travelled in vintage carriages which recalled the style of the original train itself and the pre-war period which informed so much of Kraftwerk's future/past vision. 'What we were very much considering was the simultaneity of past, present and future,' explains Hütter. 'I think visions and memories synchronise together and I think certain things from a little way back look more towards the future than things which are pseudo-modern today. The real modernism may be somewhere else, a different way to what we think is modern.'[14]

The round trip from Paris to Rheims made for a fairly memorable album launch. 'It was a good promo,' remembers Karl Bartos. 'Maxime Schmitt, who used to work for our French record company, hired a train and put all the French journalists on the train. On the way back they all were so drunk. It turned out really good. On the speakers of the train we had Trans-Europe Express. It was a really good idea.'[15]

France was already succumbing to punk rock, with home-grown groups like Stinky Toys leading the rush to emulate developments in England. But across the channel, punk was beginning to fracture under the weight of its own success. The speed with which the tiny scene had been forcibly expanded by the attentions of the mass market brought its own unique problems. As more and more people were attracted to punk, often by nothing more subtle than a lurid tabloid headline, the movement's original aims became diluted or exaggerated to the point of caricature. Many of those who'd formed the scene's exclusive inner circle – creative types who had little interest in following, or even being part of, the herd – were already becoming disillusioned and had begun searching for something else. By the autumn of 1977, a new phrase had entered their vocabulary and quickly began leaking into the music papers.

'New Musick' became the title of a piece run by *Sounds* over two consecutive weeks in November 1977. Even by then the description already had a recognisable application. And what's more, it already had an anthem. Kraftwerk's 'Showroom Dummies' mapped perfectly on to the feelings of a growing number of people looking for an escape route, not only from the crumbling social and economic fabric of British society, but from an increasing sense that punk had been hijacked by people who were more interested in its sensationalist possibilities rather than by anyone who really cared. Having been let down once by their emotions, the brighter sections of English youth began disconnecting themselves from punk and creating a soundtrack that more directly articulated their alienation. Along with Bowie's new synthetic direction, the front-runners of 'new musick' were Kraftwerk themselves.

Bowie's admiration for Kraftwerk was even more apparent on *Heroes*, the album he released just as the 'new musick' debate was coming to a head in November, 1977. Laden with entropic, Kraftwerk-inspired instrumentals such as 'Moss Garden' or 'Neuköln', the new album even featured a tribute to Florian called 'V2 Schneider' but it was the aching, reflective pieces like 'Sense Of Doubt' and 'Sons Of The Silent Age' that touched best on a mood also mapped out by the work of groups such as Cleveland's Pere Ubu, This Heat and a bunch of Mancunian misfits called Throbbing Gristle who experimented with tape loops, avant-garde noise and synthesizers (an uncanny reminder of early Kraftwerk in fact).

'New musick' also stretched out to meet both dub and disco, sowing the seeds for the rich and varied anti-rock seams of post-punk which would embrace a variety of groups from John Lydon's Public Image Limited to Scritti Politti, the bedsit bossanova of Everything But The Girl and even Vini Reilly's Durutti Column. In each of these diverse currents, concealed in a hundred and one different permutations were the strands of both punk and the cool, obsessive introspection of Kraftwerk, Eno, Bowie, Pere Ubu and others.

On November 26th, Kraftwerk made the front cover of *Sounds*. In keeping with the subject matter, the cover was austere, spartan, revolutionary even. It depicted Ralf and Florian, dressed soberly in dark colours (though Ralf's white shoes hinted at an underlying tendency for sartorial wildness) standing at the edge of the Rhine, just a few yards away from the house on Bergerallee. The only text printed on the cover was the paper's masthead, together with the date and the price. But emblazoned across the bottom of the cover picture was the legend 'New Musick – The Cold Wave' (a sly pun on the 'new wave' tag which had, by this time, replaced 'punk' as the preferred description for the rapidly expanding movement). It was a brave editorial move but one which perfectly summed up the musical climate's drift from punk's hot blooded – and often calculatedly dumb – scare tactics to a more subtle, but ultimately more forbidding, sense of detachment and alienation. This was the politics of isolationism, dislocation and emotional disconnection and, in its way, it posed a more serious threat to punk than anything the rock scene had so far managed to muster.

'The source of sound is what matters today,' declared Ralf. 'It's a new awareness of the sources of sound that we bring about in our music. What it is really made of – waveforms, vibrations. A higher sensibility to the vibrations inside and outside yourself. Sound waves are being used in psychiatry. There's a place in Austria where they are making mental patients play electronic music for therapy. It changes your life. It is a life style.'[16]

This wasn't so far away from the riff that Florian had played out to a horrified Geoff Barton two years earlier in *Sounds*. 'We not only try to brainwash people,' he pointed out, 'we succeed. We see the audience out there staring at us, we find we can control their minds for the hour during which we are on stage.' Barton asked whether this meant they could manipulate people. 'Partly,' replied a diffident Florian. 'Not manipulate them into actual physical action, just to keep them quiet to enable them to receive our music very deeply.' But, countered Barton, could you go a step further and inflict injury? 'Well, yes we could,' Ralf answered. 'When you are aware of the fact that music is brainwashing and manipulation, you realise that it can also go in the direction of damage. We have the power to push the knobs on our machines this way or that and cause damage.' At two in the morning, miles from home (the interview took place in a hotel after Kraftwerk's first English concert in Newcastle) this was almost more than Barton could bear. And then

Florian delivered the killer blow. 'It can be like doctors with patients,' he said sinisterly. 'They have the same sort of power. Their patients are very much in their hands, as our audience is in *our* hands.'[17]

The logic was a simple but effective inversion of punk's empowerment. But it was also cerebral in a way in which few rock interviews during 1975 were. Even as far back as the American tour some months previously, Kraftwerk had proved themselves adept at the media game though the interview with Geoff Barton did provide a few revealing insights. 'Part of our music is derived from the feeling of our language,' admitted Florian. 'Our method of speaking is interrupted, hard-edged if you want; a lot of consonants and noises.' Ralf elaborated on this theme. 'We use the language also as a musical instrument,' he noted. 'It's like when we sing. People say "it's too low, we cannot understand the singer". But we are not singers in the sense of Rod Stewart, we use our voices as another instrument. Language is just another pattern of rhythm, it is one part of our unified sound.'[18]

Though in retrospect much has been made of punk's social and musical revolution, its most creative and fertile period was relatively brief – just a few short months between late '76 and the end of 1977's summer. The movement's most important achievement lay, ultimately, in broadening the horizons of the music scene. What happened afterwards became, in some ways, almost as important as the event itself. During the final months of 1977, Radio One's most influential programme, *The John Peel Show*, became essential listening as Kraftwerk's 'Showroom Dummies' shared airtime with extracts from Wire's *Pink Flag*, Throbbing Gristle's 'United' and Suicide's synthetic dystopia.

What punk created was a situation in which Kraftwerk's music could be understood and referenced. So what if there were no guitar solos? So what if there weren't even any guitars? The framework that punk established said that such things didn't matter. There would still be guitar heroes of course, but they would no longer have a dominant role in pop's onward creative surge. These events placed Kraftwerk in a position where their influence would ultimately dictate the future of modern music.

7

In April 1978, Kraftwerk's seventh album, *The Man Machine*, was launched with two extravagant parties; one at the Allied Pictures Studio on Park Avenue in New York and one in Paris, at a club on the 56th floor of the recently opened Tour Montparnasse called Le Ciel De Paris. Invitations to the Paris launch (known as the 'Soiree Rouge') stipulated that guests should wear red, in keeping with the red and black, El Lissitzky-inspired cover of the album. The club itself had been decked out with predominantly red lighting and a projection screen on which a preview of the promotional video for 'The Robots' was shown at intervals throughout the party. There was also a screening of a favourite Kraftwerk movie, Fritz Lang's *Metropolis*.

'We were very much influenced by the futuristic silent films of Fritz Lang; *Metropolis* and *Dr Mabuse*,' explained Ralf Hütter a few months later. 'We feel that we are the sons of that type of science fiction cinema. We are the band of *Metropolis*. Back in the '20s, people were thinking technologically about the future in physics, film, radio, chemistry, mass transport . . . everything but music. We feel that our music is a continuation of this early futurism. When you go and see *Star Wars*, with all its science fiction gadgets, we feel embarrassed to listen to the music . . . 19th century strings! *That* music for *that* film!? Historically, we feel that if there was a music group in *Metropolis*, maybe Kraftwerk would have been that band.'[1]

The party was also used to unveil the Kraftwerk's latest additions, four mannequins which had been remodelled to resemble the members of the group by an artist in Munich. Initially, this idea had been developed around the theme of 'Showroom Dummies' – which was after all what these were – but the notion became extended to include 'The Robots' which was how the dummies were referred to almost universally until the arrival of Kraftwerk's real robots in 1991 (though for some years after *The Man Machine*, Ralf displayed an impressive knowledge of the intricacies of mannequin manufacture, pointing out that the best were the wax versions made in Italy).

Dressed in the red shirts and grey trousers that the group had worn in Gunter Fröhling's memorable album cover shots, the mannequins were the focal point of the party. This was intentional. Following the lengthy American tour in 1975, the group had fantasised about being relieved of their gruelling promotional and touring schedule by automatons who wouldn't get bored or tired by the routine. As Karl Bartos had complained, the schedule was an exhausting one, marked only by a series of interchangeable reference points, an endless round of 'aeroplane, hotel, soundcheck, hotel, gig, hotel, aeroplane . . .'[2] Wouldn't it be great, they supposed, if somebody else did all that for us and we could just stay in Düsseldorf and concentrate on our music? The most immediate result of these wild daydreams was this replica Kraftwerk. From this point on, the mannequins were increasingly used to replace the group for one of their most hated tasks – the promotional photo shoot.

But the idea of the doppelganger, or double, was also a powerful myth in Germany, the stuff of fairy tales and nightmares. Wolfgang Flür recounts fond memories of his grandmother telling strange, fantastical tales as he and his brothers listened in awe, shivering under the bedclothes. Some of these stories were drawn from the Brothers Grimm, others were folk tales handed down through generations but the theme of the doppelganger weaved through a number of them, an exhilarating and sometimes horrifying narrative about what might happen if someone else was created in your image. It's important to remember here that the members of Kraftwerk grew up in the era before television when these stories still had a significant role in developing the fabric of children's imaginations. For Ralf Hütter, whose childhood experiences of 'playing around the bombfields and destroyed houses'[3] were also mediated by such tales, this kind of mythology had a deep resonance (as it did for each of the group's members). But it's worth speculating on Wolfgang Flür's feelings when the subject of the doppelgangers was first broached. As an identical twin, he was more aware of the implications this suggested than any of the others.

Though the group themselves emerged for only a few minutes at the Soiree Rouge – dressed, contrarily, all in black – the album Kraftwerk launched at Le Ciel De Paris was a masterpiece. The tentative experimentation of their earlier releases, the brief glimpses of a compelling marriage between electronics and perfect pop were now fully realised. On tracks such as 'The Robots' and 'Spacelab', the dancefloor aesthetic of 'Trans-Europe Express' (which Hütter had now taken to describing as "body music") had been sharpened and refined with the complex rhythmic interplays and heavy syncopations of funk. Even the electronic drum sounds had been transformed from, say, the simple bursts of white noise that had suggested snare drums on Autobahn into lush sculpted percussives and deep hypnotic pulses that drew unmistakably on black dance music.

'At that time we were going out a lot to discos and we had discovered funk,' confirms Flür. 'We were getting into James Brown and analysing his records, wondering how does he make such good rhythms. We especially liked the grooves and we were jealous that they were so good for dancing. George Clinton we loved very much. We listened to a lot of music and rhythms and we tried to have something that was more like that. That was our work sometimes, to analyse rhythm tracks and drum sounds. We would then try to create our own versions. We'd listen to particular records and say "We have to have that!" On The Man Machine, we were always trying to develop this further. We would build up the music, take some rhythms out and add some new ones. This happened all the time. It was a constant process for us.'

The group's interest in black American dance music led them to recruit Leanard Jackson, one of Norman Whitfield's studio engineers, to help with the final mix. The decision to use Jackson was made after the group discovered his name on some of the records they had been listening to.

'So during the very cold winter of 1977, Ralf invited him into our studio,' explains Flür. 'But he came from California where it was very warm and he had big problems with the extreme coldness here in Germany. He was not in a good mood about it and had only little influence on the mix.'

As with Trans-Europe Express, the bulk of the recording work was carried out at Kling Klang. For the final mixing, however, they transferred to another Düsseldorf studio, owned by Joschko Rudas who, along with Jackson, was responsible for engineering this last stage of the album.

Significantly, the new release also introduced Karl Bartos as a talented and creative co-writer (along with Hütter he was responsible for the group's only chart-topping single, 'The Model', and was credited on all six tracks on The Man Machine album). But the album's pristine surfaces and achingly taut grooves also demonstrated that the group were by now perfectly attuned to their technology. 'We used custom-built, very big, analogue-style sequencers with 32 steps,' remembers Bartos. 'They were cool. We had something similar built for the drums; an 808-style concept where you could watch the LEDs going along and change the rhythm as it was playing.'[4]

Much of this equipment was supplied by Matten & Weichers in Bonn. 'They were the only company doing this stuff at the time,' explains Bartos. 'They were just students; they started in a cellar under a discotheque somewhere in Bonn. They sold the first Mini-Moog in Germany.'[5]

Ironically, many of the productions on *The Man Machine*, particularly the use of echo or delay to enhance the rhythms and sequences on tracks such as 'Spacelab' and 'The Model', owed a debt to the elaborate weave of reverbs and echoes that Conny Plank had used on the group's early albums. But by now Kraftwerk had a secret weapon in their studio. On 'The Robots', for example, the devastatingly funky bass sequence was processed using one of the world's first digital delay units to provide the clean, sharp echo that gave the part its unique rhythmic feel.

'When we were in Ontario in 1975 a man came to meet us from the Eventide company,' explains Wolfgang Flür. 'I remember it was very cold, yet this man had been waiting for us to arrive at the concert hall for quite some time. He had brought the very first Eventide digital delay with him and so he demonstrated it for us. It was very, very expensive – about 30,000 Deutschmarks – but, of course, Ralf and Florian bought it. They always had to have the newest tools!'

The Man Machine was also the group's most determinedly futuristic album to date – a kind of self-fulfilling prophecy that Kraftwerk were indeed the band from the future. The science fiction theme permeated all but two of the album tracks, though even those – 'The Model' and 'Neon Lights' – sounded like they'd dropped intact from the 21st century. Dream-state narratives about robots, outer space laboratories and the strange, Nietzschean concept of the title track merged with the group's own identity and tapped into a growing identification with the future (this was after all, the era of *Star Wars* and Clinton's *Mothership Connection*), though the track 'Metropolis' itself pointed to the roots of this inspiration.

The album suggested other resonances too. On both 'Spacelab' and 'Metropolis' the relentless pulsing sequences and amphetamine-disco feel recalled the work of Italian producer Giorgio Moroder. Like Hütter and Schneider, Moroder was already in his late-thirties by 1978 but was enjoying huge dancefloor success with one of his protégées, Donna Summer. Based in his Musicland Studios in Munich, Moroder had developed a style he described as 'computer disco', a driving synthetic amalgam that was built around throbbing 16th note sequencing and oscillating 4/4 beats. During the previous year, along with Kraftwerk's 'Trans-Europe Express', the Moroder-produced Donna Summer single 'I Feel Love' had been a permanent fixture on the dancefloors of Manhattan – he was also responsible for a project called Munich Machine around this time – followed by a single under his own name, 'From Here To Eternity', which made the link with Kraftwerk explicit. 'In Germany, some people asked me if it was our new record,' noted Hütter a few months later. 'I was quite surprised that I haven't heard it yet . . .'[6] (Ironically, despite his Italian roots, it was Moroder who was chosen to provide the soundtrack for the 1984 restored version of Fritz Lang's *Metropolis*, Kraftwerk were too busy working on a new LP.)

The Man Machine was an unrepentantly dancefloor-based record. On its release, a new phenomenon was played out in the towns and cities where those who were already bored or dismayed by punk's spiralling descent into cartoon rebellion transferred their allegiances to Kraftwerk's stunning articulation of the new musick aesthetic. The experience of Harri – now one of the UK's most respected house music DJs – was typical: 'I remember the day I bought that album. It was just so strange and new. I took it round to some friends and we stayed up all night dancing to it. We just played it over and over again. We'd never heard anything else that sounded quite like it. We were just completely enthralled.'

In the context of 1978's musical landscape, *The Man Machine* was an astonishingly radical record. While most groups were still experimenting with the framework of a sound that had remained fundamentally unchanged since the birth of rock n' roll, the new Kraftwerk LP provided a whole new blueprint. From the opening, Stockhausen-inspired bars of 'The Robots' to the closing sequences of 'The Man Machine' itself, it was clear that the group's desire to create a truly modern soundtrack had resulted in a revolutionary new form of pop. But it was one which some people had difficulty coming to terms with.

'Kraftwerk's sound is hard to comprehend,' Ralf pointed out, 'because it goes beyond musical categories. It doesn't fit into the guitar-hero culture. I think our music has more to do with science, science fiction or futurism than with traditional musicianship. Mainly we are turning knobs and using filters, oscillators, switches, faders and cables. When we are on stage, we are not jumping around and playing loud music. We are standing there, creating sound.'[7]

Conceptually, *The Man Machine* was Kraftwerk's strongest album so far. Since their meeting with Lester Bangs during the American tour, the concept had been developed and refined, though Ralf's claim that machines in some way 'mirrored' human personalities survived intact.

'The machines are part of us and we are part of the machines,' he declared. 'They play with us and we play with them. We are brothers. They are not our slaves. We work together, helping each other to create. People fear losing their humanity to technology. That's nonsense. A human being in contact with a machine becomes more of a human. There is so much to be discovered about human beings from machines. They mirror our personalities and we, in turn, mirror the image of the machine. Today's society is technologized, no matter how you might want to avoid that fact. If you dismiss technology as a toy, you're only acting out of fear. It's basically man's fear of being dominated or his desire to dominate that causes so much harm in regards to technology. Whereas, if you cultivate a symbiotic relationship with machines, everyone benefits. When you're working with machines, your most basic elements are revealed. There is no room for pretension. You get to the basic structure. That's why a man-machine union is so healthy.'[8]

In the months that followed the album's release, Ralf expanded on this theme, adding and subtracting details in a remarkably similar way to the group's compositional style. Many of his pronouncements provided an interesting insight into Kraftwerk's relationship with the studio technology that had helped them realise their creative vision. Partly this was the result of a unique confluence of circumstances. Even by 1978, the kind of equipment that the group had installed in Kling Klang was well ahead of its time. For musicians who'd grown up in an era of traditional musicianship (and Kraftwerk belonged to the last generation to have done so) the concept of sequencers which could play musical parts still retained an aura of magic. Confronted for the first time by a machine that was capable of performing as well as, if not better, than a real musician, many of those who became involved with this kind of technology during the '70s and early '80s were understandably taken by the idea that a sequencer was like having another member in the group (albeit an electronic one). It was a short step from this point to Florian's particular spin on the subject when asked, soon after the album's release, whether or not the man in the man-machine relationship was submissive to the machine.

'I don't think so,' he said. 'It's rather a more sophisticated relationship. There is an interaction. Interaction on both sides. The machine helps the man and the man admires the machine. [While pointing to the journalist's tape recorder] This is an extension of your brain. It helps you remember. It's the third man sitting at this table. As for ourselves, we love our machines. We have an erotic relationship with them.'[9]

Florian's declaration that 'we love our machines' was probably accurate, but it's clear that his final suggestion here was one of Kraftwerk's characteristic in-jokes. Ever since their heavy exposure to the press during their first American tour, both Hütter and Schneider had taken a particular pleasure in gently mocking outside perceptions of them by exaggerating certain aspects of their public image. Partly this was a way of alleviating the boredom of the interview routine but it was also an interesting way of bouncing a few outrageous concepts into the outside world. Sometimes this could go wrong, as journalists unaccustomed to their wry sense of humour, reported such remarks word-for-word – as when Ralf, hamming it up during an interview with the *NME* during the previous year, declared that 'my wife is my synthesizer'[10] – though such asides did provide a remarkably human insight into the group who were already being characterised as 'the icemen of rock' by some sections of the music press.

'We have a special type of black humour,' admits Hütter. 'We always wear black. It has to do with truth and certain aspects of the truth. Funny and serious at the same time. Revolutionary and funny.'[11]

On a promotional tour in America during the autumn of 1978, however, Ralf was expanding on Florian's description of Kraftwerk's relationship with technology. 'We call ourselves the man machine,' he told Richard Robinson from *Hit Parader*. 'Without the machines we couldn't play or record or anything. That's a fact we'd rather admit than try to deny it. We've established this kind of friendship with our musical machines and they really sometimes are very nice to us. They respond very sensitively – they bring out so much of ourselves, like a psycho-analytical thing also. We've made experiments with some of our friends who are not into music at all – they're maybe architects or something else – and we play music with them also on the synthesizer and you can hear the vibration of the person when you put them to the synthesizer. It's really like a psychoanalytical mirror type of thing.'[12]

The Man Machine concept was also an implicitly political one in which the Russian Constructivist sleeve imagery, the group's uniforms, their insistence on their role as 'musical workers' and their abhorrence of the star system coalesced into a kind of utopian urban communism. The connections with the sleeve artwork were obvious. The uniforms created both a brilliant visual identity and suggested that each member was no more than a replaceable cog in the Kraftwerk machine. Hütter frequently reinforced the idea that the group's activities were no less and no more important than the jobs of doctors, architects, civil servants or scientists and was equally scathing about what he called 'the bourgeois concept of the artist'[13], the notion that creative types were somehow serving a higher purpose than those who dedicated themselves to more practical purposes. This was, inarguably, communism as it had been in the days when the Constructivists had been paid by the Revolutionary Government to create new and stimulating kinds of art for the new age. This was communism ripped from a time before the Stalinist purges sullied the term forever and relocated into a space-age future.

In keeping with this philosophy, the group had traded their beloved vintage Mercedes cars for less ostentatious Volkswagens. This was partly due to a growing ecological awareness in Germany, thanks to the activities of the Green Party, but it was also the result of the group's view that such luxury cars didn't fit with their socialist perspective. In keeping with this, they had often described themselves not as rock stars but as music workers. The logic was simple. Workers didn't drive Mercedes. They drove Volkswagens.

'In the beginning, when we were younger, we loved our cars and we loved to drive,' remembers Flür. 'Florian was the biggest Mercedes fan. He infected us all with his passion for them. He bought a dark blue Mercedes 600, the model used by Adenauer, the German Chancellor, the same car. It had the full luxury interior, air-conditioning and everything. We used that for our first European tour. We always preferred the more classic models. I had a 220SE which I refurbished, I was very proud of it. I managed to find an original ivory steering wheel for it. To start with, Ralf was always more into Volkswagens but he bought a 280, the luxury model, which we used on our second European tour. But we never had new cars, they were always second-hand, although Florian had enough money to buy the cars that didn't need renovated.'

The Soviet connections suggested by the sleeve imagery grew out of a linguistic coincidence. 'We were intrigued that the Russian word "robotnik" means "worker" and so much related to our ideas,'[14] explained Hütter. This provides a different insight into 'The Robots' which, for the group themselves at least, had a double meaning that was lost on a large percentage of listeners. With the benefit of Hütter's explanation, the track becomes as much a celebration of Kraftwerk's work ethic as it is a celebration of emotional disconnection and the pleasures of a mechanical universe.

The Man Machine also included what has become one of Kraftwerk's best loved tracks, 'Neon Lights', an irresistible and achingly romantic paean to urban nightlife. But, perhaps the view from the doorway of the group's Kling Klang studio explains more about the inspiration behind the song. From the windows of the strip joints and table-dancing bars on the opposite side of the street, during the hours of darkness, there is a blaze of coloured light – the names of the clubs, the words 'sex' and 'girls' and sometimes even the figure of a naked woman all sculpted from red, blue and yellow neon. Since Kraftwerk invariably worked at night (not discounting the fact that they were all keen admirers of the female form) and had to pass by these windows on their way to and from the studio, this fact was unlikely to have escaped their attention. During the day, this part of Düsseldorf is quiet, dead even. It comes to life after dark, and does – during those hours at least – seem part of a 'city made of light.'

In England, the first real evidence of Kraftwerk's profound influence was already beginning to emerge in the sound of a number of radical new groups. Significantly, the first signs of this new movement began to emerge, not in London, but in industrial centres such as Sheffield and Liverpool.

By the summer of 1978, Sheffield was already home to a number of groups who drew their prime inspiration from Kraftwerk. Principle among them were Cabaret Voltaire, who had already achieved some notoriety around the local music scene. Formed in 1973 at Sheffield University by three friends – Stephen Mallinder, Richard Kirk and Chris Watson – the group were both heavily experimental and as self-consciously arty as their name suggested (they had after all borrowed it from Hugo Ball's provocative Dadaist ensemble). Originally Cabaret Voltaire were fixated on Bowie, tape loops and weird noise but by 1978 their sound had twisted into a fusion of Kraftwerk-inspired electronics, punk and Can, interspersed with radio wave interference and defiant artistic strategies. 'They used to do shows in pubs,' remembers one early fan, 'and halfway through the set they'd just walk off stage and out the door. Nobody quite knew what would happen next . . .'

Cabaret Voltaire inspired other local groups such as Vice Versa (later ABC Radical Dance Faction and, subsequently just ABC), who adopted a similar approach, even to the point of deserting gigs mid-way through their set. But there were others too, like Graph, who wore their Kraftwerk influence like a badge of honour and those, like The Mekons, Paul Bower's 2.3 and Gang Of Four, who – though their music didn't betray any obvious debt to the group – were committed fans.

The group who drew most from the Kraftwerk blueprint were the group who, on the face of it, seemed least likely to succeed. The Human League started life as a duo called Dead Daughters, formed by Martyn Ware and Ian Craig Marsh. After recruiting Adrian Wright to provide projections and occasional synth, the group hooked up with Phil Oakey to become The Future before changing their name once more to The Human League and becoming, at least for a while, the most fervent anti-rock band in Britain. The group's early stage shows, impossibly minimalist and entirely synthetic except for Oakey's deadpan vocals, were modelled down to the last detail on Kraftwerk's live performance, even down to Wright's slide projections which provided an apocalyptic twist on the original template.

'Kraftwerk had a huge impact on us,' remembers Phil Oakey. 'I was inducted into the group when Martyn Ware came round to my house carrying copies of "I Feel Love" and *Trans-Europe Express*. There was a real feeling that this was something we could do. It was as simple as that. At the time, Sheffield was a really arty city and the underground scene was very strong. We'd been through Can and Faust, but Kraftwerk became incredibly significant for us. They combined synths in a way we'd never heard before. It was so inspirational. Their concept was so pure. In fact, for me Kraftwerk are probably the strongest concept group ever.'

Released late in the autumn of 1978 on Bob Last's independent Fast Product label, The Human League's debut single, 'Being Boiled', was one of the first indicators that Kraftwerk's cool electronic symphonies were about to redirect the course of British pop. By the time the group's *Reproduction* LP was released the following year, the revolution was already underway.

Not far away, in Liverpool, an eight-piece group called The Id splintered, leaving two of the members, Andy McCluskey and Paul Humphries to pursue their own distinctive take on the new musick aesthetic. The pair settled on the name Orchestral Manoeuvres In The Dark, according to Humphries, as a way of distinguishing themselves from the numbers of third generation (and almost exclusively third-rate) punk bands springing up in the wake of the scene's entry into the mainstream. Both Humphries and McCluskey were long-time Kraftwerk fans. 'For me there has never been a group who has given such a unique motivation,' noted McCluskey. 'They are a perfect creation.'[15]

Taking their cue from the retro futurism of *Radio-Activity*, Orchestral Manoeuvres In The Dark alchemised with Kraftwerk's electronic pop aesthetic. More than any other Kraftwerk-inspired group they tapped directly into the vein of synthetic nostalgia suggested by tracks such as 'Airwaves', writing songs about electricity, atom bombs and even pioneering physicists such as Nikola Tesla. Over the next few years they were to carve themselves a successful commercial career from these raw materials. But in the beginning, at least, they perceived themselves – as did many others – as the sole champions of Kraftwerk's sound.

'You became convinced that you and a couple of your friends were the only people in the world who were listening to it,' says McCluskey. 'It was quite a surprise, and something of a disappointment to discover, once we started playing live, that there were other bands like Cabaret Voltaire and The Human League. You thought you were on your own, but all of a sudden there were other people in other cities who'd been listening to the same thing.'[16]

Wolfgang Flür remembers meeting the fledgling Orchestral Manoeuvres (then still part of The Id) after Kraftwerk's first show in Liverpool. 'The concert wasn't very well-attended,' he recalls. 'Paul McCartney was playing in the city that same night on the *Wings Over Britain* tour so most people went to see him instead. Still, I was very pleased. To be playing in Liverpool at the same time as Paul McCartney was something very special for me because I was such a fan of The Beatles. After the show, the tour manager came to tell us that there were some guys waiting outside to see us. They said they were in a group so we brought them in. They seemed so amazed by us, touching us almost as if to see if we were real. It was very strange for us. It turned out to be Andy and Paul who were later Orchestral Manoeuvres. They were saying "You have shown us the future, thank you. We were in a guitar band and we didn't know where to go with our music. You have shown us to throw away our guitars and buy synthesizers!" We were very touched by their enthusiasm and sincerity. Then, of course, a few years afterwards, they were in the charts.'

Orchestral Manoeuvres In The Dark weren't the only British synth pop outfit to have the pleasure of meeting their heroes. On tour in Germany, The Human League had a memorable encounter. 'They came to see us in Cologne and we just fell apart,' remembers Phil Oakey. 'We were scared to death of them. We thought they wouldn't appreciate anything about what we were doing. Here we were, this sort of *Coronation Street* Kraftwerk, and the real thing had come to see us. We were so nervous it was unbelievable. But we met them after the gig and they weren't at all like we expected them to be. They were very funny and very encouraging. They weren't aloof like we'd thought they would be. They seemed to take a real interest in what we were doing. But it was probably one of the most nerve-wracking gigs we ever played.'

A few years later, Ralf Hütter remembered the group's own feelings about this surge of Kraftwerk-inspired activity. 'The new pretenders of industrial music cheered us up, for we were questioning our own work sometimes,' he explained. 'But the music is different because we have a Teutonic rhythm, really Germanic.'[17]

The Man Machine also spilled out into a time which would be crucial to the development of clubbing as the new dominant force in European youth culture. At the time, this didn't have anything to do with disco (which, in the wake of *Saturday Night Fever*, had become increasingly sanitised) though disco would eventually become part of the equation. What it did involve was Bowie, synth pop and, of course, Kraftwerk.

Set up originally as a kind of open private party by former Rich Kids drummer Rusty Egan under the (then) catch-all term of a 'Bowie night', Tuesday nights at Billy's – a gay club in the centre of London – became a template for a revolution in the night-life pursuits of a generation. For three brief months towards the end of 1978, those who had disconnected from punk, those who were eager to escape from the grey dullness of recession-hit Britain and those who simply wanted to reach out and meet the future head-on gathered to lose themselves in an atmosphere which was both determinedly hedonistic and exclusive. The soundtrack was pulled entirely from the canon of new musick – Bowie's 'Secret Life

Of Arabia', the synthetic disco of *Low, Trans-Europe Express* and *The Man Machine*, Eno and Ultravox! – but the other ingredients, alcohol, stimulants and science fiction wardrobes, made these nights worth remembering.

Derek Ridgers recalled that Tuesdays at Billy's were 'like walking into a Hieronymus Bosch painting: furtive but lively and with a dedication that's never been equalled since.'[18] These weren't the beautiful people of Studio 54, but they had high hopes.

Billy's suggested a new ideology. Though there were similarities with disco – the democratic emphasis on the crowd as stars, the appreciation of the DJ's skills in creating mood and atmosphere and so on – there was also a fundamental difference. This was guerrilla clubbing. Billy's didn't have an entrepreneurial function. There were no money-men behind it, nor was Egan (who later joined the Kraftwerk-inspired group Visage) looking for a get-rich-quick scheme in the way that, say, Steve Rubell and Ian Schrager at Studio 54 had been. Instead it was purely about self-expression because the night wasn't set up to serve a scene but to create one.

What Egan did was turn up at a small-scale nightclub, hire it for a week-night when, traditionally, no real business was done and then remap it for that one night into a place where he and his friends might like to go. It was a club concept, not as a commercial venture, but as a kind of social activism. The music that was played wasn't lowest-common-denominator chart material aimed at pulling in as many punters as possible, it was simply the music that the small, tightly-knit crowd liked. Music that embraced their hopes, dreams and poses. And contrary to all leisure industry experience it had an impact far beyond its limited expectations.

Though the Tuesday get-togethers at Billy's lasted for only three months, they provided a model which revolutionised the night-life landscape. The influential clubs that followed – Blitz, the Dirtbox, the Wag, Gary Haisman's Raid on Tottenham Court Road where house music got its first airing in London, Shoom, Spectrum and all the others – were built on this same template. Clubbing became an interactive phenomenon that was suddenly no longer a money-making adjunct to the music industry but a form of urban expression. This changed pop culture immeasurably and, because those who were involved in such ventures were by definition pop literate, gave groups such as Kraftwerk who were outside the normal conventions of chart music and radio playlists, a sphere of influence over trend-setters and taste-makers which would alter the course of the youth cultural soundtrack.

It wasn't long after the Tuesdays at Billy's gained notoriety, of course, that the entrepreneurs moved in. 'Bowie' nights were held in clubs such as Pips in Manchester, the Rum Runner in Birmingham and others. But wherever such nights took place, Kraftwerk records were a crucial part of the mix. Eventually, the new synth-pop groups that they'd inspired began making records – The Human League, Orchestral Manoeuvres In The Dark, Basildon's Depeche Mode, Belgium's Telex – and these too became part of the sonic fabric. But what these nights helped to establish was a framework in which Kraftwerk and the developments they inspired could flourish. A framework where the synthetic musical language the group had created could be understood and extrapolated.

An almost parallel development was taking place in New York. As disco peaked and began its descent, different versions of the clubbing experience were mapped out, albeit to a different soundtrack. In Manhattan's dockland, Larry Levan took the helm at a converted truck garage to create a distinctly underground club phenomenon which weathered the storm of disco's downturn. The Paradise Garage was a huge concrete edifice, full of steeply sloping ramps, vast spaces and interiors decorated with vividly pornographic murals. It attracted a largely gay crowd, though, like Billy's, its door policy (members and guests only) helped to maintain a uniquely creative atmosphere that was more about expression and lifestyle than conspicuous consumption and passive complicity in the entertainment process. At The Paradise Garage, Levan and his colleague David Depino created a whirlwind mix of raw, hedonistic disco (a million miles away from the glossy, sanitised version that had become commercially popular), European imports and Kraftwerk's *motorik* groove. Again the ideology – as with Kraftwerk's dogged rejection of the star system – was resolutely democratic. In front of the loudspeakers, on the dancefloor at The Paradise Garage, everyone was, after all, equal despite the fact that Levan later became one of New York's most celebrated DJs.

Outside of Manhattan, in the South Bronx and Harlem, the ubiquitous block parties, High School jams and impromptu sound-clashes were throbbing to a new beat as the access principle was flexed again and again. Here too, Kraftwerk records became locked to the new developments. Like many others, Afrika Bambaataa, a one-time member of the Black Spades gang, and now a local DJ with a growing reputation had been knocked out by the strangeness of 'Trans-Europe Express' (though his reasons were entirely different from those who'd danced the night away to it shoulder-to-shoulder with Halston or Andy Warhol) and began incorporating it into his sets. In the merging of Kraftwerk's electronic aesthetic and Bambaataa's raw, rhythmic street-sound were the seeds of another development which, over the next few years, would germinate into a fully-blown music movement.

Back in Düsseldorf, however, Kraftwerk were already embarking on a major redevelopment of their Kling Klang studio. Partly this was inspired by technological advances and the acquisition of a number of new devices but it was also prompted by increasingly ambitious plans for their live performances. The group were eager to make their studio more mobile so that it could be easily transported from one venue to the next with the minimum of interruption to their recording schedule. Again this was guerrilla thinking, though it was clearly driven too by technical concerns. As the group's music depended on their studio technology to a large degree and as the amount of technology they employed expanded so the possibility of playing concerts with only a stripped-down version of their equipment diminished.

This decision made it obvious that Kraftwerk still retained a strong interest in live performance. Ralf Hütter later explained the reasons behind this to Jean-Eric Perrin of France's *Rock & Folk* magazine. 'We find some energy in the environment of people who come to see us and who make us play in another dimension and at a higher psychological level,' he pointed out, 'because of a certain tension, different from the studio and in which we are interested. At the studio there is no phone, we are locked.' By contrast, he suggested that touring provided something different. 'It's the travel side, the open side, a rather anarchic situation . . . we are open to any vibrations that could change our music. The fact of playing in front of an audience implies that our music is not a magnetic product anymore, it's a situation open to improvisation. And the sensibility of the devices we created leads us to a new sensibility.'[19]

The redevelopment of Kling Klang did, however, take much longer than anticipated. By the time the group re-emerged some years later, the music world was spinning on a new axis. And it was one of Kraftwerk's making.

8

It's unsurprising that when the 19th century mathematician Charles Babbage came up with the theory that eventually gave birth to the computer, he had little idea of the way it would impact on society. Neither he nor the British Intelligence Services team at Bletchley (who developed the forerunner to the modern computer during the 1940s in the race to crack the Nazis' notorious Enigma code) perceived the device as anything other than a specialised machine stuffed full of algorithms which could be used for high-end mathematical purposes. What is surprising, however, is that IBM, the company which transposed the notion of the mainframe computer from its original setting into the corporate world (and made billions in the process), had even less idea about the implications.

When IBM launched the PC in March 1982, the company as a whole remained unconvinced that there was even a market for desktop computers. At the time, IBM was the world's biggest corporation (both in terms of the number of its employees and its gross profits) and had been so for many years. Few people at the company saw any reason to shift their attentions from the core mainframe business which had made IBM the most successful corporation in history and focus on a machine that had limited profit potential when compared with the millions of dollars that could be made on the sale of a single mainframe. This level of success made most of those at IBM complacent. In fact, the PC was only brought to market thanks to the foresight of a handful of visionaries at IBM who waged a long campaign on the product's behalf.

The PC was developed in a small IBM outpost at Boca Raton by a project team that was – by IBM standards at least – tiny. The PC team was crammed with IBM mavericks, people as close as the company's culture would allow, to the fast-paced, guerrilla style of those at small, incredibly youthful companies such as Apple, Texas Instruments and Microsoft (to whom IBM eventually contracted out the PC's operating system in a deal which eventually turned Bill Gates into one of the world's richest men) but in order to get their product to market, the executives in charge of the project had to fight a long, intensely political, internal war that demonstrated again and again that IBM as a company had little interest, or belief, in the notion of the personal computer.

Yet the logic was simple. The number of companies who could afford a mainframe computer costing millions of dollars was limited. Every time an IBM salesman sold a mainframe to one of these companies, the potential market contracted even further. And the success of IBM's sales force meant that, by the late '70s, most of the organisations who were interested in having an IBM mainframe already had one. Cushioned from this fact by the millions of dollars pouring in from the leasing arrangements for these machines, IBM had no idea that the future of computers lay elsewhere. Accustomed to million dollar profit margins, the company's culture couldn't accommodate the idea of making a profit of just a few dollars on a machine for the domestic market, no matter how large that market was and no matter how big the potential volume of sales. This was a tactical error which caused an unprecedented turnaround in the fortunes of the most successful company in the history of America.

The last decade has proved that those at IBM who fought for the PC were right and those executives who thwarted them at every step were wrong. We now inhabit a world where the desktop computer interfaces with every aspect of our daily lives. But IBM's share of the computer market has been transformed from a near monopoly to a tiny percentage. The company's inability to foresee the future, despite the efforts of the PC project team at Boca Raton, has cost them billions of dollars in lost revenue and allowed other, more adaptable businesses to take advantage of the computer revolution. Perhaps IBM should have hired Kraftwerk as consultants.

In May 1981, while IBM's PC was still bogged down in the company's notoriously inflexible bureaucratic processes, Kraftwerk released the *Computer World* album. Even for a group who'd already proved themselves capable of making profound imaginative leaps, it was an extraordinarily prescient release. It would take several more years for the IBM/Apple/Microsoft drama to fully play itself out, but somewhere inside Kling Klang, Kraftwerk seemed to have access to a crystal ball.

Computer World updated the clean, clinical surfaces of *The Man Machine* into an impossibly sharp, bright sound that has rarely been equalled in pop music since. But it was also unique in terms of its theme. In 1980, Japan's Yellow Magic Orchestra had appeared to be chasing close behind Kraftwerk with the *X100 Multiplies* album and their 'Computer Game' single, a wildly futuristic fusion of electronic game bleeps and shockingly innovative musical strategies that harnessed both classicism and pop. But while YMO shared the veneer of modernism with Kraftwerk, the resemblances were superficial. On closer inspection, they were following the established rules of pop; pick a youth craze – in this case Space Invaders – and set it to music. Their use of synthesizers too (appropriately they used the Japanese-built Yamaha CS80) was closer to the pseudo-classical manoeuvres of Space or Jean-Michel Jarre than anything that had come out of Düsseldorf. By contrast, *Computer World* sewed perfect pop into crisp, polysyncopated electronic rhythms not as a way of replicating an existing soundtrack (as YMO and their fellow countryman Isao Tomita had done) but to create the kind of music that a computer world might have. They hit the target dead on. As computer technology has permeated every aspect of our daily lives, modern music has evolved and adapted itself to Kraftwerk's blueprint.

The world which Kraftwerk predicted in 1981 – a binary world of home computers, government databases, computer dating and virtual sex – was one which even IBM's impressive team of analysts couldn't envision. But it is the world in which we now live. No other group in the history of pop music, before or since, has come close to matching this feat.

Conceptually, *Computer World* was an incredibly strong album, even more so than *The Man Machine* which, until now, had marked the high-point of the group's drive to weave image, music and lyrics into one cohesive theme. The album release was preceded by a extraordinary single, 'Pocket Calculator', which demonstrated how far ahead of contemporary pop Kraftwerk had stretched themselves. Combining a deceptively simple melody (played, according to the group's mythology, on a Texas Instruments calculator they'd spotted whilst doing some Christmas shopping) with a fiercely complex – but again apparently simple – interplay of bleeps, basslines and counterpoints, 'Pocket Calculator' proved that Kraftwerk had not only assimilated the principles of funk but had rewired them completely to fit with their own aesthetic. It was a unique congress – James Brown meets Karlheinz Stockhausen – all wrapped up in an impossibly perfect pop exterior.

'Pocket Calculator' also proved that the lyrical developments of *The Man Machine* had evolved even further. Emil Schult, who'd been responsible for the 'she's a model and she's looking good' hookline on 'The Model', worked on the lyric with Ralf. Schult's lyrics betrayed a keen ear for the flip, catchphrase stylings of pop hipsterism, a legacy of the time he'd spent in America as an eighteen-year-old student (it is, after all, just a short step from Stateside street-jive like 'I'm the man with the plan' to 'I'm the operator with my pocket calculator') but the lyric on 'Pocket Calculator' showed how far Kraftwerk were willing to push the envelope of pop convention.

Normal pop lyrics work on a network of resonances and associations, a web of meaning that informs simple phrases such as 'I've got you under my skin' or 'I get by with a little help from my friends' (and in some less eloquent examples, transforming simple doggerel into something approaching intelligibility). They thrive on an axis of ambiguity that enables the listener to imprint some of his or her own personality on the words, thus encouraging an identification with the song. In extreme cases, as with Charles Manson's horrific misreading of songs by The Beatles, this axis of ambiguity can have tragic consequences. But it has been, nevertheless, a fundamental part of pop song mechanics since before the birth of rock n' roll.

By contrast, the lyrics of 'Pocket Calculator' are direct and unambiguous. Lines such as 'I am adding and subtracting' or 'I'm controlling and composing' admit no further interpretation, offer no resonances beyond the meaning of the words themselves. They mean exactly what they say. It's a precise and perfectly controlled use of language that runs directly counter to the pop establishment's deliberately loose and imprecise linguistic conventions. But it's also a perfect artistic strategy. If the words of the song cannot be mis-interpreted, cannot be read in any other way than they're meant to be read, everybody gets the same thing. This hermetic lyrical approach was just part of Kraftwerk's increasingly refined political and artistic position but it didn't prevent a warm humour from suffusing brilliantly crafted lines such as 'by pressing down a special key it plays a little melody' (a particular favourite of The Human League's Phil Oakey).

Underneath these pared-down lyrical signals, however, was music that was weirder and wilder than anything that pop culture had so far thrown up. The Bowling Green's Micko Westmoreland points out that this is one of the particular ironies that surrounds the group. 'In the '70s there were all these bands who dressed up in leopardskin or whatever and tried to look raunchy,' he says. 'But then there was Kraftwerk – who dressed almost like businessmen – making music that was far, far more exhilarating than any of those bands.'

As with *The Man Machine*, Karl Bartos had been heavily involved in the writing of the new album, taking over from Florian as Ralf's main co-writer on many of the tracks. But Schneider did have a hand in one of the album's most astonishing tracks. 'Numbers' was Kraftwerk's most abstract and compelling moment yet. Little more than an a melodic synth riff and a punishing electronic drum groove, in the context of 1981 it was nothing short of revolutionary.

Computer World was the album that provided the blueprint for Detroit techno. From the opening bars of the title track to the final cadences of 'It's More Fun To Compute' Kraftwerk created a template that was extrapolated into the future by a handful of black musicians and subsequently transmitted on to the dancefloors of the world by those they inspired. Jeff Mills remembers what happened when the new Kraftwerk LP first reached Detroit. 'When the Kraftwerk thing came, it wasn't just little kids that it influenced,' he says. 'It influenced all of America and it hit Detroit really bad. The first track that hit mainstream radio was "Pocket Calculator". You'd hear some rhythm n' blues tune and then you would hear Kraftwerk. It was crazy. Even today, if you were at a party in Detroit and they played "Numbers" it would pack the dancefloor. I swear to God it would. It was the rhythm I think. People in Detroit . . . we dance, you know. So it was the rhythm that got us. That and the fact that it was so different from anything else we had ever heard. We had developed a certain craving to find things that were completely different from what we'd heard before. So when Kraftwerk came, it was just at the right time. It was perfect timing . . . there was a certain attitude and a certain lifestyle which the whole Kraftwerk thing fitted right in with.'

In fact, Detroit was one of the first cities in America to pick up on the new album, largely thanks to the efforts of WBLS-FM, a black music station which gave the release its first US airplay. Warner Brothers, the group's new record label was quick to take advantage of this, organising promotions at a chain of record retailers called Detroit Audio (prizes included a trip to Las Vegas and, naturally a number of promotional pocket calculators) and arranging for the 'Pocket Calculator' single to be shipped in an attention-grabbing package of yellow vinyl sheathed in a clear plastic sleeve. It was this single that provided Carl Craig with his introduction to the group.

'I was twelve years old when I heard Kraftwerk for the first time,' he remembers. 'Like all kids in Detroit back then, I used to listen to Electrifying Mojo's radio show religiously. Then one night he played "Pocket Calculator" – it was mind-warping! I found out what it was and went down to the record store to buy the single. I remember that it had a clear sleeve with the band's faces on it and some Japanese type. I thought they were from Japan and I dreamed about what they might be like. Soon after, when the *Computer World* LP was released, I bought that too. Then "Numbers" and "Home Computer" took over my attention. In Detroit, *Computer World* was considered a masterpiece, a work of art . . . Maybe it was the complexity of the rhythms that made it so interesting but it worked. I think that it was so stiff it was funky.'

Talking about this marketing exercise, Bob Regehr, Warner's Vice President in charge of Artist Development and Publicity, provided the US music bible *Billboard* with some interesting quotes about the Kraftwerk phenomenon. 'At their studio in Düsseldorf, they have scientists come in to help them,' he explained, pointing out that this kind of thing was 'closer to *Close Encounters* than rock n' roll.'[1] Obviously getting carried away with this line of thinking, Regehr concluded the interview by telling the journalist that the group's road crew for their forthcoming tour would also be made up of scientists. It wasn't true of course, but it made for a great story.

The tour that Kraftwerk had planned for 1981 was to be their most extensive yet. It was also partly responsible for the three year gap between the release of *The Man Machine* and *Computer World*. The group spent this time redesigning the interior of Kling Klang so that it could be stripped-down and rebuilt onstage as necessary. 'That idea came basically from Ralf and Florian,' explains Karl Bartos. 'They wanted to have a kind of musical laboratory and make the consoles look very scientific. The idea was to put everything on wheels so it could easily be taken on the road; we could now perform and record anywhere in the world. The concept was really, really good, I think, but it was very time-consuming to put it all together and equipment then was a lot more expensive than it is now.'[2]

The practicalities of the new studio/stage design were taken care of by Wolfgang Flür who had originally trained as a furniture designer at the suggestion of his parents, eager to ensure that he had something to fall back on in case his musical career didn't work out. Along with some local craftsmen and the studio technicians, Joachim Dehmann and

Günter Spachtholz, Flür set about rebuilding Kling Klang.

'It took three years to develop it from the first plans,' remembers Flür. 'It was quite a minimal design. That was for practical reasons. The mass of electronic cables were always a problem. We developed everything on our own. For touring, we built up the stage set like an open "V" because it's better for communication. If you have four people on one row it is difficult to watch each other. With the "V" shape we could watch each other onstage.'

Pictures of the Kling Klang interior taken before and after this work indicate the scale of this transformation. In a photograph from February 1977, the studio looks only marginally different from the raw, rehearsal room that had been pictured on the rear sleeve of the *Ralf & Florian* LP. The plain brick walls are still much in evidence though the back wall is now lined with speaker cabinets. In the middle of the room, the group's growing collection of synthesizers are arranged in two rows facing each other.

By November 1978, the group had acquired other rooms in the building. These were adjacent to Kling Klang and provided them with an office, a small kitchen area and some extra storage space. Inside the studio, some of the familiar scaffolding-style rigging had already been installed and the room had been soundproofed with the distinctive foam tiles then in vogue.

Promotional pictures, released around the time of *Computer World*, show the completed studio looking more like the laboratory Hütter had always claimed it to be. The equipment is built flush into brushed metal gantries and consoles with monitor screens, sequencers and outboard gear racked alongside vocoders (both the Sennheiser model which Ralf claimed 'Mr Sennheiser built specially for us in the early '70s',[3] and an EMS), Karl's Korg PS-3300 synthesizer, tuners, mixers and meters. Along the front of each console, banks of fluorescent lights reinforce, the bright clinical feel of the room. The effect is curiously retro, as though the blueprint for the design had been taken from a Fritz Lang movie, but it is unmistakably Kraftwerk.

The new studio set-up had been designed so that it could be transferred to stage with the minimum of disruption. Each of the consoles was on wheels, and those synthesizers which hadn't been fixed into them had instead been built into permanent flight cases. In addition, the group had acquired four large video screens from Sony in Japan to screen the visuals which Emil Schult had been working on with

Günter Spachtholz. These had been transformed from the simple slide shows of earlier live performances, into mini-films which combined appropriate archive footage with graphics and excerpts from the group's promotional videos.

'It took a lot of work to make the Kling Klang studio transportable,' explained Ralf during the summer of 1981. 'All the parts are connected. It's a new conception of Kraftwerk; before it was studio plus live, now it's live studio. We play the studio onstage. We thought it could be done rather fast, but it became more and more radical. We had to change everything. It took three years non-stop to fine-tune everything. We worked on musical compositions simultaneously because we do everything ourselves. We are not musicians, we are rather scientists. Kraftwerk is not chords and numbers, but rather a realistic concept to transpose ideas to their maximum. Ideas came to us as we were working. The identity of *Computer World*, the mechanics of instruments and the psychological side of sound and music, are the two concepts that lead to the fact that we don't have Kraftwerk anymore, but Kraftwerk and Kling Klang together.'[4]

The *Computer World* tour which began on 19th May 1981 in Florence was Kraftwerk's most ambitious yet. More than 90 dates had been arranged all over the world including concerts in Europe, America, Japan, Australia and even India. But, as Hütter pointed out, even the three year preparation for this massive undertaking wasn't quite enough. 'The paint was literally just drying off as the items were packed,' he told Mike Beecher from the UK studio magazine *Electronics & Music Maker*, 'and just in case any problems were encountered, two engineers started off our tour through southern Europe.'[5]

The group's set for the tour remained fairly static with only minor changes between the opening show in Florence and the closing concert in Utrecht on 10th December. But it was notable for the fact that all traces of the group's first three LPs had been eradicated, including previous live favourites such as 'Ruckzuck' and 'Tanzmusik'. At London's Hammersmith Palais on 3rd July, for example, the gig included all the songs from the *Computer World* album, 'The Robots', 'Neon Lights' and 'The Model' (from *The Man Machine*), 'Hall Of Mirrors', 'Showroom Dummies' and 'Trans-Europe Express' (from *Trans-Europe Express*), 'The Voice Of Energy', 'Geiger Counter', 'Radioactivity' and 'Ohm Sweet Ohm' (from *Radio-Activity*) and, naturally 'Autobahn' which, at this point, was still their biggest commercial hit. Changes to the running order were complicated by the fact that, for the live shows, the group had decided to use four-track tape machines synchronised to their sequencers in order to flesh out the sound, though the group were able to improvise around the recorded sections as Ralf frequently pointed out. Revealingly, he was irritated when journalists failed to spot this fact.

Writing in *The Times*, Richard Williams reviewed the Hammersmith show, noting that it was 'so bravely and resolutely static that one might as well have stayed at home and played their records . . . the boosting of the bass frequencies to a level well above the capacity of a domestic hi-fi represents the only modification.'[6] Hütter saw the review during a visit to EMI's London office and bitterly denied the assertion. 'He says we play exactly as the records which is not so,'[7] he complained with some annoyance to *Hot Press* journalist Andrew Darlington. Subsequently he was careful to tell journalists more about the group's approach to representing their recorded material in a live situation. 'We change always,' he declared. 'We don't feel bound to the records. We take the concepts and go from there.'[8]

A few months later, perhaps mindful of the criticism Williams had made about Kraftwerk's 'resolutely static' performance, Hütter defended the group's unique style of presentation. 'So many people move or even jump around onstage these days,' he explained. 'It's important for our music that we do not do this – our rather static performance is also necessary for emphasising the robotic aspect of our music.'[9]

Despite the fact that Kraftwerk remained relatively immobile during the concerts, the concept of their new show was still wildly original. The idea of setting up a complete studio onstage had previously only existed in the realms of fantasy and certainly no other group had ever attempted (even if they might have daydreamed about it) such an undertaking. As an artistic strategy, it was pure modernism; they were, in effect, stripping back the layers of artifice that separated them from their audience and revealing the means of their production without the aid of a safety net or, as Hütter once put it, throwing open the walls of their studio. Walter Benjamin would have loved it.

Hütter's explanation for this strategy was a simple one and, as so many times before, was a remix of principles first explored by Stockhausen. 'We play the studio,' he pointed out, 'so we had to take the studio with us. We don't have any duplicates of any of our equipment; we have only what we are always working with. It's all in units that break down and go into different cases and the various components fit together. Some of the components we have are standard things like echo machines but more than half of the equipment is custom-built, built by us or with our regular engineers because we couldn't play the music we wanted on regular instruments. We have a couple of standard electronic keyboards and a small mixing board, and we have digital storage for relatively short-term information up to six seconds. With this, we can store sounds and have them played back rhythmically. Then we have our special electronic percussion systems which can be programmed for different electronic sounds. We have made up a couple of percussion sounds ourselves with special circuits. And then we have our singing computer, our synthetic speech machines.'[10]

In the early '80s (before the advent of affordable sampling) so much of this must have appeared like science fiction, particularly when Hütter was working overtime to make the group's recording set-up seem much more complex than it really was. Most of the group's equipment was actually standard issue, off-the-shelf kit although some items had been modified on the group's instructions. Only a few items, including Florian's electronic flute, Karl's Italian-built keyboard controller and, of course, the electronic drum triggers had in fact been specially made. But Hütter was deliberately reinforcing the image of Kraftwerk as sonic scientists who took an active part in designing and building their equipment (much in the same way as, more than a decade later, the Aphex Twin would do). It was, after all, a much better story than any other contemporary group could come up with.

Hütter was well aware of the fact that Kraftwerk were better story-value than almost any other act on the music scene and consistently played the angles for all he was worth. In an interview with Dave Rimmer of *Smash Hits*, the conversation turned to rumours that the group's mannequins would replace them on tour (in the event, the replicas only appeared onstage during 'The Robots'). Hütter's excuse was that they weren't ready in time. Sensing some fun, though, he told Rimmer that 'they are probably being activated for some new films, all kinds of things. In Italy, we did a simultaneous performance with ourselves and the dummies. They were sitting in the front row. We had to buy them tickets. They watched us perform.' And, Rimmer asked, 'what did they think of it?' 'Yes,' deadpanned Ralf, 'they were quite pleased with our performance.'[11]

Other stories involving the group's doppelgangers emerged from the offices of EMI, the Kraftwerk's UK record company. Since the dummies were now replacing the group for photo sessions, the company's press office were given responsibility for them. Having to travel around with a group of life-size dummies became one of the more onerous duties that had to be undertaken by members of the group's press team (it probably didn't escape their attention that this was not for the first time either). Most embarrassing were the trips that involved flights. Since they occupied a seat each, tickets would have to be arranged for the dummies and a bewildered EMI press officer would have to sit next to one or other of them throughout the flight, desperately trying to ignore the enquiring looks of other passengers. Someone, somewhere, it seemed, was enjoying an immensely elaborate private joke.

Much of the peripheral interest in *Computer World*, and the subsequent tour, focused on the three year gap between *The Man Machine* and the new album. In the climate of the late '70s and early '80s this was seen as an inordinate amount of time to take over one release, when many acts were in the habit of releasing one LP – sometimes two – in the space of a single year. Hütter's response explained much of what had been going on in Kling Klang during this time.

'We have been building the set for the last three years,' he explained, 'whilst composing the music and preparing the video graphics. Most of the instruments were obtained in previous years but they were wired in a more typical electronic music studio fashion. Besides looking rather messy, the earlier layout caused problems in transport and hours of rewiring for each performance. It actually takes two hours at most to install or dismantle the new set. We always bring our own German stage crew but, of course, other people often help in the local halls. To minimise component failure and rough handling we use industrial specification or heavy duty devices in the equipment.'[12]

Typically, Ralf was also able to spin the design of the stage set into the man-machine concept. 'The physical layout of the equipment,' he asserted, 'besides being functional, was also to imply the idea of the man-machine which we've always talked about – that the music does not become dominated by one or the other. For example, some people perform with their musical machines built up high around them in an impressive way. We prefer the low-profile image, bringing man and machine together in a friendly partnership of musical creation.'[13]

Taking the studio on tour with them was, however, something of a risky strategy as Ralf indicated when *Sounds* journalist John Gill asked if the studio onstage was a replica of the studio in Düsseldorf. 'No, it *is* Kling Klang,' answered Hütter. 'We have only this one, so if the truck driver isn't careful we would be out of operation!'[14]

On the lengthy tour there were, of course, a few close calls. It was inevitable on a venture of this scale – involving huge distances and concerts in a number of different continents – that some problems would occur with Kraftwerk's relatively sensitive electronic set-up. Mostly the equipment coped admirably, with only the anticipated complications of stabilising the tuning of the synthesizers after long periods of transit and changing temperatures, causing any lasting difficulties. But the equipment, and the group themselves, faced the most severe test of all during the visit to India.

Kraftwerk's UK booking agency Wasted Talent had arranged two concerts in Bombay for the group as part of a stop-over before the Australian leg of the tour began. The group travelled to India a week before the concerts in order to rest and sample the local culture but, to their dismay, they discovered that they had arrived in the middle of the monsoon season. 'It was raining the whole week,' remembers Wolfgang Flür. 'There were thunderstorms all the time, all the streets were flooded and there was so much water in the air we couldn't see more than five metres from our hotel windows.'

Periodically, the rain would stop and the sun came out. 'When that happened we would take a cab into the city to go shopping and look around,' says Wolfgang. 'But soon the rain would come again and we had to hurry to find a cab to take us back to the hotel. The rain was so heavy that the roads would flood very quickly. On the way back to the hotel, water would leak in and cover the floor of the taxi and we'd have to put our feet on the seats. Sometimes even the car's engine would be submerged and we'd get stuck. I remember one driver taking his trousers off and using them to dry the machinery so we could get going again. We had never ever seen anything like it.'

Within a few days, most of the group were ill. The constant dampness caused other problems too. 'We had a very good hotel on the coast, a little way outside of the city,' Wolfgang recalls. 'But even inside it was so hot and wet that we couldn't stand it. We kept our clothes in the wardrobe but it was so damp all the time that they were covered in mould. They changed the beds every day, but even then, when you slipped in under the covers, the bedclothes felt wet. We hated it. We were in such a bad mood, even between each other, and everyone was sick. There were hundreds of people living in the streets outside the hotel – they actually had tents pitched against the walls of the building – and there were little children outside in all the rain, crying or begging, just for a little money or some bread. It made us very sad. We had never seen such poverty. It made us feel very uncomfortable. We didn't feel well in our situation. We lived a very luxurious life in comparison.'

The contrast between Kraftwerk's hi-tech futurism and their new surroundings was almost too much to bear. For the world's most technologically advanced pop group it suddenly felt like they'd been stranded on a different planet. Even the rigours of touring hadn't prepared them for this experience. 'The situation was not very positive,' remembers Wolfgang. 'It did show us the life of India and we did see things which most tourists don't see because they don't come during the rainy season. But it was very confusing for us.'

The concerts were due to take place on the Saturday evening. That morning, the group were busy making meticulous plans for their departure. 'We had everything properly organised, every detail, because by then we just wanted to escape,' says Wolfgang. 'We were ill and we had no rest from the heat and the damp. We were really sick of the whole thing. We just wanted to get the concerts over with and leave as soon as we could.'

At the venue, however, there was a major problem. When the group arrived at the hall, they discovered a tabla orchestra giving an impromptu concert. 'It went on the whole day,' explains Wolfgang, 'from morning until evening non-stop. When one player got tired, another person would take his place. The musicians changed hour by hour, they seemed to be bringing on substitutes as in a football match. It went on and on. Eventually, late in the afternoon, we had to take our chance and set up our equipment. This was very difficult because the roof was leaking and there was rain coming through. Stabilising the synthesizers was very hard. And we had to do this in front of all the people who'd come to see the tabla gig. All these people with turbans on, they didn't know anything about us, but we must have seemed so strange and futuristic to them that they were fascinated to watch us. The owner of the concert hall couldn't get them to leave. It was unbelievable.'

Kraftwerk played their first (and second last) concert in India at six o' clock on a Saturday evening in front of a crowd made up of people who had bought tickets to see them and a large number of tabla enthusiasts who hadn't. Despite the unusual circumstances, the gig went as well as could be expected. 'The humidity was causing all kinds of problems with the equipment,' says Wolfgang, 'and we felt so uncomfortable. But the crowd went crazy – all these people who had never heard of Kraftwerk before. So it was an experience.'

The second and final show took place just a few hours later but the crowd who'd watched the first performance were obviously eager to sit through the whole thing again and, once more, refused to leave. 'It was unbelievable,' notes Wolfgang, 'the owner of the venue was driven crazy but they just wouldn't go. Then all the people who had tickets for the next concert were pushing in as well. Outside the hall there were big crowds of people all trying to get in too. It was chaos. But we were taking no chances. We thought only to get the concert behind us. We had bought our tickets for a flight to Australia the same night. Before we started to play for the second time, we made sure that we had some taxis and limousines, waiting outside to take us straight to the airport. We even had our suitcases with us backstage. And we made sure that the drivers kept the engines running because of the rain. We did not want anything to stop us, since the timing was very tight for our flight, so they had to keep the engines running for two hours, all through the concert. And for the last song we left just the sequences playing while we ran to the taxis with our suitcases.'

The group were booked on to a British Airways flight out of Bombay. 'We thought we were going to miss our flight and be trapped there,' remembers Wolfgang, 'because the traffic was so heavy. But we made it just at the last minute. When we got on to the plane, even though it was full of tourists and babies crying, we were so relieved that we praised them very much. Inside the plane it was dry and air-conditioned. It was not hot. It was not wet. It was clean and fresh. And they served good English tea. Thank goodness for Europeans! We were so glad that it was all over. It really was a horror trip.'

Back in Europe, meanwhile, the generation of groups who'd drawn their prime inspiration from Kraftwerk were making their first assault on the album charts which, just a few years previously, had traditionally been the principle terrain of grindingly dull rock-oriented groups such as Bread, Status Quo and Genesis. While the *Computer World* tour wound on, albums by Visage, Ultravox (now without John Foxx and their Neu! inspired exclamation mark) and Orchestral Manoeuvres In The Dark were launching the synthetic aesthetic into rock's heartland. By August

1981, The Human League and OMD were locked into the upper reaches of the singles charts as well.

This was the direct result of a train of events that had been set in motion at Rusty Egan's Bowie nights in Billy's. Thanks to the efforts of two new magazines, *i-D* and *The Face*, who had no ties to rock music, the Billy's crowd were now at the centre of a fully-fledged scene that was initially referred to as 'Blitz culture' – after the club which Egan and Steve Strange had set-up during the aftermath of Billy's – before the more risible 'new romantic' tag entered the media's vocabulary. The soundtrack for this scene took its cue from the playlist at Billy's and Blitz, a heavily synthetic and danceable mix of Bowie, Kraftwerk and the new synth-pop groups. Keyed-in to this new phenomenon, groups such as Depeche Mode, The Human League and Orchestral Manoeuvres In The Dark now had a platform and a context which enabled them to take on the charts and win.

In a sly, referential twist, Andy McCluskey and Paul Humphries had decided to call the first Orchestral Manoeuvres album *Organisation*. Only die-hard Kraftwerk fans would have picked up on the illuminating in-joke, but the album sold in unexpected numbers, reaching the Top Ten in November 1980. Three months later, Ultravox's *Vienna* LP began an eight-week run in the Top Five. It would have been premature to suggest that the guitar's dominance of pop culture was under threat, but the cracks were at least beginning to show. Synth-pop may not have been the creative peak of Kraftwerk's legacy, but it suggested that their influence was capable of opening up new avenues of expression. And, as Ralf Hütter once pointed out, 'it's more important to open up than to dominate.'[15]

The *Computer World* tour provided Kraftwerk with the opportunity to reach a huge global audience. But events during the tour also offered some revealing insights into the group's disarming refusal to play out the role expected of normal pop stars as when the French journalist Jean-Eric Perrin was accosted by one of the tour roadies while he was waiting to do a scheduled backstage interview. 'These guys certainly make the most artificial music,' confided the roadie, 'but they're the most human people I've ever met. They refused to take their dinner in their box and they asked for permission to eat with the whole crew. Don't forget to write this in your magazine, man: the most human people I've seen in the whole music business!'[16]

This is a common theme in the accounts of all those who have come into contact with Kraftwerk over the years. Despite the fact that, in terms of their influence over pop culture they are comparable only to The Beatles, the members of the group remain steadfastly down-to-earth. In this respect, they are the first truly modern pop stars. 'I don't want to be an idol to someone,' maintains Wolfgang Flür. 'I'm a normal private person . . . Everyone should be his own fan.'[17] In its way, this is a far more subversive and revolutionary position than anything the Sex Pistols ever suggested.

'We find especially in the music business that individuals are overblown until they explode,' noted Ralf shortly after the group's 1981 UK concerts. 'It's all bullshit. We don't need that. In Germany, we can walk down the streets and work like everybody else. We are just another profession, nothing special. We do our work like everybody else does, like doctors or taxi drivers, bus drivers or dentists.'[18]

Given this attitude, it was hardly surprising that the group's chart success in the UK during the summer of 1981 didn't exactly go to their heads. The first single from the *Computer World* album, 'Pocket Calculator', scraped into the Top 40 just a few weeks after its release. In July, EMI released a follow-up, 'Computer Love' which did marginally better. But, later in the year, as the *Computer World* tour drew to a close, some enterprising radio DJs flipped over the single and began playing the other side which featured 'The Model' from the previous LP. In the acutely fashion conscious climate of Blitz culture, the irony was almost too perfect but, nevertheless, the heavy airplay prompted EMI to re-release the single.

'The Model' finally clambered to the top of the UK singles chart on 6th February 1982, just under four years after its initial release on *The Man Machine* album. Admittedly the trail had been blazed by the two biggest hits of the synth-pop era, Soft Cell's 'Tainted Love' and The Human League's 'Don't You Want Me' but by this point Kraftwerk-inspired groups such as Depeche Mode, Orchestral Manoeuvres In The Dark and Ultravox were frequent visitors to the Top Ten.

EMI followed 'The Model' with a re-release of 'Showroom Dummies' which disappointingly peaked just outside the Top 20 while Depeche Mode's 'See You' continued climbing into the Top Ten. Hütter, however, showed no sign of chagrin that the pallid synth-pop copyists were outstripping their mentors in terms of commercial success. Instead he focused on the positive aspects of this new development.

'I don't see it as any kind of competition,' he mused. 'It's the overall sound that I like. When we go out dancing in Düsseldorf it gets played a lot. German electronics, English, French . . . Electronic music is now breaking through and that's good. There are more places we can go and dance!'[19]

9

Early in the spring of 1982, Kraftwerk's impact on the future of black dance music manifested itself in a studio on New York's upper west side. Appropriately, perhaps, the studio had the suitably futuristic name of Intergalactic but it also had a secret weapon in the form of an $80,000 Fairlight CMI, the world's first commercially available sampler. Mindful of this fact, Tommy Boy label boss Tom Silverman had booked a session there for Afrika Bambaataa. In charge of the session was Arthur Baker, a one-time Boston DJ who was already creating a reputation for himself on the rap scene.

From its early beginnings on the streets of Harlem and the Bronx, rap had already entered the mainstream with the Sugarhill Gang's 'Rappers Delight' and by 1981 even white groups such as the Tom Tom Club were jumping on the bandwagon. Many of these early rap hits, however, eschewed the raw, street-wise flavour of the original sound in favour of a more commercially-acceptable, watered-down variant. By early 1982, only seminal moments like Grandmaster Flash's 'Adventures On The Wheels Of Steel' had provided any real key to the actual foundations of the style. All that was about to change.

With Baker and Shep Pettibone producing, the twenty-two-year-old Bambaataa had scored a minor hit during the previous year with 'Jazzy Sensation' but he was also one of the Bronx's most influential and original DJs, sewing together wildly eclectic sets that spliced Kraftwerk (by a stroke of neat coincidence Bambaataa had called his first High School group The Organisation) with Babe Ruth and James Brown. Bambaataa first stumbled across Kraftwerk on a downtown record-buying mission during the summer of 1977.

'Basically, I was just a crazy record collector,' he says. 'I used to look for things with weird covers and that's how I discovered *Trans-Europe Express*. It was real music for the future, a whole deep-feeling vibe. I'd never heard this kind of funky electronic music before but I knew it was deep. From there, I got into all their other stuff. Even when I heard *Autobahn* for the first time, I heard that same funky vibe. At the time, a lot of our parties attracted progressive-minded people who came knowing they were going to hear something different. So I started playing *Trans-Europe Express* to a black, latino audience and they got into it. *Computer World* for me, though, was the ultimate Kraftwerk album. It was very popular with our crowd. Around the time that came out, we had kids from the new wave scene, the hip hop scene and the punk scene all coming to our parties. That's when you heard everything being played, a real cross-breed of music, and that whole *Computer World* vibe fitted right in with it. Then I started digging up other electronic artists and that's when I realised that there was no black group out there doing that electronic sound.'

'Planet Rock' emerged from Bambaataa's wild turntable collages, a hybrid mix of beats and melodies sourced from disparate records. The track's prime inspiration came from Kraftwerk, though, as Arthur Baker explains, mid-way through the recording session he and keyboard player/programmer John Robie began to have second thoughts. 'When we were getting "Planet Rock" together,' explains Baker, 'we had the idea to use the beat from Kraftwerk's "Numbers" and the melody from "Trans-Europe Express" and put a rap on top. We rented a Roland drum machine from a guy who's name we'd found in *Village Voice*. We paid him $25 and he came in, we told him what we wanted programmed and he did it. But once we'd put the melody down, John Robie and I started to think that maybe we shouldn't use it after all because it belonged to Kraftwerk. So we put a whole lot of different Clavinet melodies down. In the end, of course, we stuck with the Kraftwerk melody for "Planet Rock" but, a couple of months later, we dug out those Clavinet parts and they became "Play At Your Own Risk". Sixteen tracks out of the twenty-four on the multi-track were 'Planet Rock' and the other eight were "Play At Your Own Risk". That is absolutely true, 100%. You have to make the most out of what you've got!'

The sessions which produced 'Planet Rock' were done over two consecutive nights. By the end of the first night, they had completed the musical backing and Baker knew they were on to something big. 'I was married to Tina B. (who'd rapped on the Kryptic Crew's mix of "Jazzy Sensation") at the time,' says Baker, 'and I went home after that first session and told her that we'd just made musical history. I was convinced that this record was going to change music. And we hadn't even put the vocals on at that point.'

Baker's instinct was right on the money. The finished track became one of the biggest dance hits of 1982 and had a profound impact on the subsequent course of hip hop. But the most immediate impact of its fusion of rap and electronics was a new sub-genre. Electro's relationship with the original sound of the Bronx was a seemingly tenuous one but its combination of bruising drum machine grooves, pop sci-fi and fast-as-lightning rap quickly reached epidemic proportions. Soon after 'Planet Rock' was released, The Fearless Four's 'Rockin' It' emerged, combining a punishing electronic drum track with a synthesizer riff borrowed from 'The Man Machine' and repeated insistently throughout course of the record. 'Kraftwerk – that's our soul group,'[1] pointed out the group's Peso. The Kraftwerk blueprint was also strictly adhered to on tracks such as 'Egypt, Egypt' by Egyptian Lover, Warp 9's 'Light Years Away' and Man Parrish's 'Hip Hop Be Bop' but one of the most significant post-'Planet Rock' records didn't come out of New York at all. It came from an unknown two-man group in Detroit.

Calling themselves Cybotron (note the futuristic robot chic implicit in the name), Juan Atkins and Rick Davis were two students at Washtenaw Community College in Michigan who shared a love of George Clinton and Kraftwerk. One of the earliest tracks they'd written together was 'Cosmic Cars' which took the basic electronic funk grid of 'The Robots' and rewired it with a gritty muscularity to fit the urban landscape around them. Similarly, 'Clear', the duo's first single for the California-based Fantasy label was a radical crossmatching of Kraftwerk's 'Hall Of Mirrors' and 'Trans-Europe Express' which became a huge hit on the burgeoning electro scene. But, as with 'Planet Rock', somewhere inside Cybotron's mix – for those who cared to look – were the seeds of a brand new music.

Electro took its name from an obscure dancefloor single called 'Electrophonic Funk' by Shock, but it was a term which had already appeared in Ralf Hütter's conversation as early as 1981. 'We like the audience to dance and move to our music,' he explained to Mike Beecher of *Electronics & Music Maker*, 'especially as in recent years people tended towards a more concert-listener approach. Electro music is a much more suitable title than electronic music for the way music in general is going. The instruments of electro music help to liberate people's creativity, allowing individuals to use studio technology in their home for almost any sound they want.'[2]

This was punk's access principle translated into hi-tech. By the early '80s a number of developments, including the arrival of Japanese instrument manufacturers such as Roland, Korg and Yamaha, were revolutionising the world of music technology. In 1981, the launch of Teac's M-144 Portastudio – the first cassette-based multitrack recorder – finally made home recording an affordable possibility for less than half the price of the nearest equivalent. This was closely followed by Linn's LM-1 drum computer, the world's first programmable drum machine. The Linn was still prohibitively expensive, but soon other manufacturers such as Roland were following this technological leap and providing similar machines, like the TR-808 which became an electro staple, at a fraction of the cost. Throw in some affordable synthesizers and a cheap, monophonic sequencer from any of the Japanese manufacturers and suddenly it was possible to set up a cut-price Kling Klang in the comfort of your own home.

If Hütter was worried by these developments, it didn't show. Kraftwerk's ideology was firmly on the side of access, a kind of 'electronics for all' attitude that had remained with them since their days as students playing concerts in the art galleries and universities around Düsseldorf. The idea of a network of producers and studios outside the normal channels of the music industry was one that Hütter particularly found attractive. It appealed to Kraftwerk's vision of themselves as sonic guerillas, challenging conventions through the force of their own defiantly independent position. For Hütter, access was a political issue.

'We have always managed without the established music business,' he pointed out, 'without publishers, managers, producers, studios, owners, employees and workers. From the very beginning, we made do without certain things for the simple reason that we did not have them. We started an alternative production by producing ourselves. Our first albums we did practically with our own hands, like in pre-industrial times. Studios were really expensive in those days. We were students on small grants and made money by playing the odd gig. We went into a studio, played everything in a flash to waste as little time as possible and that was our record.'[3]

This wasn't strictly true, of course. Though Ira Blacker was no longer working with the group, Doreen D'Agostino had taken over as Kraftwerk's American agent, while London's Wasted Talent handled their affairs in Europe. The group had also employed a number of people including *Trans-Europe Express* engineer Peter Bollig and studio technicians Joachim Dehmann and Günter Spachtholz. And as Afrika

Bambaataa and Arthur Baker found out, Kraftwerk also had a New York-based publishing company, No Hassle Music Inc., who took a dim view of the obvious (and uncredited) borrowing from 'Trans-Europe Express' and 'Numbers' which made up most of the 'Planet Rock' single.

'The record was already out and was beginning to blow up when No Hassle contacted Tom Silverman at Tommy Boy Records,' remembers Baker. 'Back then, what we'd done was a relatively new thing. We didn't sample their music, we played it in by hand, but it was very obvious where the inspiration came from. We never denied that. Tom just had to make a deal with their publishers. I think Tom had to pay them $100,000 but what he did was just raise the price of the record. So one week, "Planet Rock" was selling for $4.98, the next week he put it up to $5.98 and the record was doing so well he made his money back after a couple of weeks. Actually, I ran into Kraftwerk a few years later in New York. We were in a belly-dancing club called The Harem but we didn't really say much to each other . . .'

By the time 'Planet Rock' tumbled out into the world, Kraftwerk were back in Kling Klang working on a new album. Initially, this release was to be called *Technicolor* but, as Wolfgang Flür points out the album title was changed again and again. Because *Technicolor* was a US trademark we found that we couldn't use it and so we had to think of a new title.

One of the first tracks to be completed for the new album was 'Tour De France' which harnessed the clinically funky sound of *Computer World* to the kind of classically romantic melodies which had been a feature of Kraftwerk's previous output around the time of *Trans-Europe Express*. The track was directly inspired by a new hobby the group had taken up following the 1981 tour. Perhaps taken with the fact that the sport suggested the perfect man-machine congress, Ralf and Florian had become interested in cycling though it was Hütter, as always, who took the lead. 'Ralf had found a new love,' explains Wolfgang Flür. 'He was in a group with some very fanatical cyclists so he was always in the countryside with his new toy, strengthening his muscles and body. I think he loved cycling more than his synthesizer during this time. For the rest of us it was quite a frustrating time.'

'Tour De France' was scheduled to be the first single from the new album which was, by now, called *Techno Pop*. Despite the distractions of Ralf's new hobby, work on the new album was progressing well enough for a tentative release date to be set and an EMI Electrola catalogue number (1C 064-65087) was assigned to it. Among the tracks already completed for the new album was 'Sex Object', which in its early stages seemed an oddly rock-based piece for such a confirmed anti-rock group.

In preparation for the release of the single, the group made two videos for 'Tour De France' both of which were based on the cycling theme. The first of these, was filmed in and around Düsseldorf and showed the four members of the group, dressed in stylish all-black cycling gear, riding their bikes in group formation around some of the local roads at a fairly leisurely pace. Since Ralf and Florian were by now very accomplished cyclists, their lack of speed was surprising, especially since the single was dedicated to the most intense and gruelling cycle race in the world. But the fact that Wolfgang had only learnt to ride a bike a few days before the video shoot meant that the group were forced to travel at a pace dictated by him if they wanted to be filmed in formation. Hence, instead of the characteristic Ralf, Karl, Wolfgang, Florian line-up, Kraftwerk found themselves cycling with Wolfgang at the head of their four-man *peloton*. 'If you look closely, you can see me shaking,' notes Flür. 'I hated cycling. After that day I never got on a bicycle ever again.'

Kraftwerk were back in their regular formation for the initial sleeve artwork of both the 'Tour De France' single and the *Techno Pop* album which showed the four group members cycling in line, each in identical poses hunched over the handlebars.

When the 'Tour De France' single was released in July 1983, advertisements for the new album were already appearing in the German music press, headlined by one of Ralf's favourite phrases '*Es wird immer weitergeh'n – Musik als Träger von Ideen*' ('It will always go further – music is the bringer of ideas'). But as 'Tour De France' began making its way up the charts, Kraftwerk suffered a serious crisis that upset the planned release of *Techno Pop*.

'Ralf had a bicycle accident and he almost died,' remembers Karl Bartos. 'He fractured his skull and was away for a year almost. He hadn't been wearing a helmet . . . The single came out but then this accident happened and it took us a year to continue.'[4]

Hütter lay in a coma for two days and, for several long hours at least, it seemed as though Kraftwerk's story might end in real tragedy. Ironically, 'Tour De France' was proving to be one of Kraftwerk's most commercially successful releases. The group's original video for the track, however, was rarely seen. Instead a new video, pieced together from archive footage of the Tour De France, was used to promote the single. The new video was certainly more dramatic and suited the kinetic groove of the track better, though the original 'home movie' version provided a more intriguing glimpse of the growing tensions within the group.

As a result of the accident and Ralf's lengthy recuperation, the *Techno Pop* album was put on hold and a number of scheduled tour dates were cancelled. When the group returned to recording, new developments in music technology and a number of radical new records, prompted them rework the entire album.

'We got a little bit lost in technology to be honest,' says Bartos. 'In the mid-'80s, suddenly all this digital equipment came around, sampling appeared and there was this fantastic record called "Beat Box" produced by Trevor Horn. His drum sound blew our minds. So we had to step back and think it all over; incorporate MIDI and sampling and a lot of other stuff.'[5]

By 1984, hip hop had become a big enough commercial proposition to attract the attentions of Hollywood. *Breakdance*, directed by Joel Silberg, was already in production and, appropriately, Kraftwerk's 'Tour De France' was one of the tracks selected for the film's soundtrack. To outsiders, the notion of a white European group being asked to contribute to a movie about black American street culture was mystifying. But for those inside the scene, Kraftwerk's inclusion in the soundtrack was one of the few authentic touches in an otherwise appalling movie.

'When I first came to New York and heard rap music in '78 or '79, I was working with Joe Bataan,' remembers Arthur Baker. 'He told me that they were talking over records in the Bronx. He was pretty enthusiastic about it so I went up to 114th Street in Spanish Harlem to find out what he was talking about. The first thing I heard was that beat from "Trans-Europe Express" and it went on forever. Kids were just editing it together using the pause buttons on their tape machines to give them a continuous beat to rap over. Back then there were so few records that had the groove. Kids would just buy whatever was funky and use it. Later, after *Computer World* came out, I was in a park in Long Island and they were doing the same thing with "Numbers". Those records were a crucial part of the way the scene developed.'

For Run DMC's Jam Master Jay, Kraftwerk were equally significant. On a two-hour MTV Party Zone special, broadcast during the spring of 1998, he talked about the progression from Kraftwerk to 'Planet Rock' to contemporary hip hop, prefacing a screening of the 'Trans-Europe Express' video by pointing out that 'these guys proved to me you don't have to be where I'm from to get the music. That beat came from Germany all the way to the 'hoods of New York City . . .'[6]

The version of 'Tour De France' which appeared in the final cut of *Breakdance* (or *Breakin'* as it was originally known in the US) was a specially-commissioned remix by François Kevorkian who by that time had become one of the world's most in-demand remixers. Kevorkian had also become heavily involved in the electro scene, working alongside Arthur Baker and John Robie on Planet Patrol's seminal 'Play At Your Own Risk' and with Afrika Bambaataa and John Lydon on Time Zone's 'Wild Style' hit. After discovering his name on several of their favourite records, Kraftwerk decided that he'd be the perfect choice to update 'Tour De France' for inclusion in the *Breakdance* soundtrack and, accordingly, contacted Kevorkian through their US lawyers.

'I just got the call one afternoon, asking me if I'd be interested,' remembers Kevorkian. 'Of course, I told them I was and so, a little while later, I got a call from the group themselves.'

Kevorkian points out that his remix was, in fact, 'a collaboration' since the group came to New York and worked with him in the studio on the project, providing their own ideas and suggestions throughout the mix. The resulting version was a sparkling electro-tinged rewrite of the original and its subsequent commercial success (aided by the extra promotion of the movie and a memorable promo video edited from one of the film's better sequences) marked the beginning of a long friendship between Kevorkian and the group.

Back in Düsseldorf, work on the new album was still progressing fitfully as Hütter returned to his fanatical cycling regime with renewed vigour. The group had already invested heavily in some new digital equipment for Kling Klang, including wildly expensive devices such as the PPG Wave and the NED Synclavier but, for the first time, they found themselves being technically out-paced by the innovations of others, particularly the London-based producer Trevor Horn. On records for Frankie Goes To Hollywood, Art Of Noise and, latterly, Grace Jones, Horn took pop production towards an unprecedented creative peak, engulfing the efforts of his protégés in an extravagantly lush veneer of technological sophistication. Ironically, Horn's approach was, theoretically at least, closer than anyone imagined to Kraftwerk's – particularly his interest in the minute details of sound generation and his view of the entire studio as a giant virtuoso instrument – though Hütter was frequently dismissive of the trend towards the use of music technology as an end in itself.

'We have found that people who are into technology do things with such over-sophisticated means as to destroy what they are trying to do,' he explained. It's like catching a butterfly: it flies, you spot it, catch it in a net, put it in chemicals, pin it up and keep it behind glass – but it isn't a butterfly anymore. We find this syndrome in the whole area of musical technology, especially in England. What happens is that the living, creative idea dies on record and becomes boring. You use forty-eight-track technology, all kinds of gadgets, but you play the record and there's nothing on it. Some singers are made out to be all Brylcreem and deodorants and you have everything on the record, only it comes over as forty-eight deodorants. Listening to American albums, you notice how much more spontaneous and live they sound. That is because they work in a much more casual way, in some old barn with second-hand equipment from a radio station. I've been to a place like that, somewhere in the south US, and the scene was kind of humming dragonflies outside and humming technology inside. We only work on sixteen-track, recording directly quite a lot – just press the button. We have simplified technology for our use to a point where all we do is press a red button and let it run. We don't want to make intellectual music, everything is as far removed from the drawing board as possible. Most of our ideas are spontaneous, they are, how shall I put it . . . accidental. They just come flying in.'[7]

Kraftwerk's preference for American studios had been firmly established as far back as *Trans-Europe Express* which had been mixed down at The Record Plant in Los Angeles. Since then, however, they had completed nearly all their subsequent releases in Kling Klang (the only exception being the 'Tour De France' remix which was done in New York). Having now spent several years working on the *Techno Pop* LP, Hütter perhaps felt that his perspective on the album might benefit from a change in surroundings and so he flew to New York with the master tapes to mix the album at The Power Station, a studio which was then in vogue with artists such as Bryan Ferry and Duran Duran.

Hütter's choice of The Power Station may well have been decided simply by the synonymity of the studio's name with that of the group but the studio had recently been responsible for one of the most technically accomplished releases of the mid-'80s, Scritti Politti's *Cupid*

& *Psyche '85*. Recorded and mixed by Howard Gray, the album sheathed the processes of technology – Fairlight samples, machine rhythms and other-worldly synthetic timbres – in delicately sensual reverbs and extraordinarily tight compression to create a sonic world that was every bit as technically compelling as the very best of Trevor Horn's work. Unlike, say, Frankie Goes To Hollywood's *Welcome To The Pleasure Dome* or The Art Of Noise's 'Moments In Love', however, *Cupid & Psyche '85* was a gorgeously subtle record that shimmered and seduced where Horn's production style ran headlong into excess. As evidenced by Miles Davis's subsequent cover version of 'Perfect Way', Scritti Politti's album also alchemised with the kind of clinically funky syncopations that Kraftwerk had transmuted from black dance music. Maybe, after all, 'A Little Knowlege' was a louche, post-modernist version of 'Neon Lights' but, for Kraftwerk to stay ahead in the face of pristine technological moments such as this, they needed to shift into a completely new gear.

Hütter's decision to mix the *Techno Pop* album at The Power Station, however, was a gamble that didn't pay off. A version of the album's title track, completed during these sessions provides some clues to the group's sound at this point. Over a crushing electronic beat (processed with gated reverbs to provide the characteristic mid-'80s 'big' drum sound), the familiar panting breath sounds from 'Tour De France' and a heavily vocoderised voice dominate the introduction, while the full arrangement interweaves melodies drawn from both the classical tradition and the folk songs of the Rhine. This was a return to at least some of the techniques used on *Autobahn* and *Trans-Europe Express*, though in the coda these melodies are counterpointed with a nylon guitar sound (recreated using Yamaha's new FM synthesis) playing repeated arpeggios in a style that was already over-familiar from the commercial peak of the synth-pop era. Set against the pristine surfaces of Scritti Politti or Trevor Horn's production of 'Slave To The Rhythm' by Grace Jones (which was contemporary enough to have already assimilated the funky new grooves of Washington's emerging Go-Go scene), this version of the track sounded hopelessly out-dated.

On his return to Düsseldorf, Hütter wasn't convinced either. 'Ralf felt insecure about it,' remembers Karl Bartos. 'He thought we should do the whole production again.'[8] Having worked on *Techno Pop* for more than three years, this wasn't exactly what anybody wanted to hear, but it's an indication of the depth of Kraftwerk's commitment to their music that, within a few months, Kraftwerk had stripped down the entire *Techno Pop* album and were already hard at work reshaping it.

By the beginning of 1986, the reversioned *Techno Pop* was already nearing completion. Tracks such as 'Sex Object' had evolved from their original synthetic rock-funk fusion into something altogether more radical. That particular track retained the beat from the original *Techno Pop* recording together with some of the melodic ideas (such as the synthetic twanging guitar and the slap bass sample), others, however, were altered so much as to be unrecognisable from their initial versions.

François Kevorkian's remix of 'Tour De France' had provided the kind of glittering sheen that the group were eager to achieve. As the new version of the album neared completion he was approached to provide the final mix on the project. Unable to find a suitable studio, Kevorkian rented a friend's loft and installed the equipment he needed in preparation for the group's arrival in New York.

By this time, Hütter had decided to retitle the LP. Though the 'Techno Pop' track was still an key element of the new album, Hütter had established a different concept to embrace the recordings and had settled on *Electric Cafe* as the title. In many ways this was an odd decision. In terms of mainstream conceptuals, *Techno Pop* was both more immediately understandable to a wide audience and more dynamic. Even sources close to the group and some of their most ardent fans have struggled to come up with a cogent explanation for the idea. And Hütter's own definition shed little light on the matter.

'We're dealing with everyday environmental situations,' noted Hütter, testily adding that 'music and behaviour describe us better than words. Otherwise, I'd have been in literature.'[9]

Kevorkian's final mix of the *Electric Cafe* album was a masterpiece of achingly modern surfaces and liquid reverbs though it failed to conceal the fact that this was Kraftwerk's most abstract LP yet. The opening suite of three conceptually interlinked tracks – 'Boing Boom Tschak', 'Techno Pop' and 'Musique Non-Stop' – extrapolated the sound of *Computer World* far into the future, puncturing Kevorkian's pristine sound-field with sharp digital tones, crystalline beats and a tangle of disembodied electronic voices.

Many of the vocal parts on *Electric Cafe* were generated by one of Florian's developments which the group described as the 'robo-voice', a kind of hyperspace speech synthesizer. 'The robo-voice is just a computer program,' explains Karl Bartos. 'It's software and a little bit of hardware that you put into the computer and you type in all these phonemes like "aah", "eeh", "uuu" and "tsch". It's like Lego; you put the phonemes together to form words. It's an incredibly time-consuming process but the end result is very dramatic because it is speaking. It's just the computer speaking. When I heard it for the first time, years ago, I was really astonished and surprised. It gave me a real kick. I don't know what it is – magic! It was originally created for helping blind people to read. The new Macintosh computer has got software like this. You can type stuff in and it reads it out loud.'[10]

Bartos himself performed the vocal on one of the album's two relatively conventional songs. 'The Telephone Call' was mined from the same seam of perfect electronic pop that had produced 'The Model' but it remained both strangely asexual and – for a group with Kraftwerk's grasp of the principles of funk – oddly devoid of a groove despite the fact that Fred Maher, Scritti Politti's fiercely talented rhythm programmer, was also involved in the final stages of the mixing process.

The album's release in November 1986 was preceded by a single, 'Musique Non-Stop', early in October. The single was accompanied by an extraordinary video made by Rebecca Allen, a designer at the Computer Graphics Laboratory of New York's Institute Of Technology.

'For the 'Musique Non-Stop' video, they sent me their mannequin heads and I went through this horribly elaborate process of putting them into the computer,' she remembers. 'Then I animated them and brought them to life. I did the video, the album cover and all the press photos. The guys wouldn't let any realistic images of themselves out – they'd only send out computer versions. The press hated that. But they were just regular guys. For its time, the video was radical. I mean, they *played* with us. People would see them and get afraid because they were these strict German types but the whole thing was a put on.'[11]

Allen's video won the 1987 Nicograph Award for artistic and technical excellence and was also nominated by the National Academy of Video Arts & Sciences for its special effects. The single, however, failed to make a similar impact and didn't trouble the charts at all. This was unsurprising since 'Musique Non-Stop' was arguably too far ahead of its time, but the musical climate was also shifting rapidly. A rougher, more viscerally thrilling amalgam was leaking into the music scene from the clubs of Chicago. House music had arrived.

House music drew on two distinct but related musical developments – disco and electronics – to create a heavy, machine-oriented rhythmic pulse for the dancefloor. By the mid-'80s, its grip on Chicago's club scene was intense. Focused principally on two clubs, The Power Plant and The Music Box, house had all the crucial elements of an emergent youth culture phenomenon – music, fashion, drugs – and a ethos which was both anti-establishment and deeply communal. 'It was a whole new world,' explains Rachael Cain, who remembers meeting seminal house producers like Marshall Jefferson and Jesse Saunders for the first time on the dancefloor at The Power Plant. 'There was such a sense of excitement in the air and a feeling of being in on something special. It was a very unique time in Chicago.'

The scene that coalesced around these two clubs had been developing at an exponential rate since the heady summer nights of 1977 when Manhattan's clubs had first thrilled to the *motorik* beat of Kraftwerk's 'Trans-Europe Express' and Giorgio Moroder's computer disco. Before then, Chicago's night-life was mapped by bars and clubs where the only soundtrack was provided by jukeboxes. All that changed in 1977 when a young New York DJ, Frankie Knuckles, was invited to help launch a new club called The Warehouse on the city's north side. Originally, the job had been offered to his friend, Larry Levan, but Levan preferred to stay in New York and suggested Knuckles in his place.

Levan and Knuckles had started their career as DJs together, earlier in the '70s, as assistants to another New York clubbing legend Nicky Siano at The Gallery where they'd helped to dress up the space, lay out the food and spike the drinks with LSD (when too many people picked up on the fact that the drinks contained an added extra, Knuckles and Levan simply adopted the more subtle alternative of spiking the fruit). The Gallery attracted a strong following on the city's underground gay scene and Siano's attention to detail made it an instant success. Siano taught Levan and Knuckles the basics of DJing and they both graduated on to other venues – Levan to The Continental Baths and Knuckles to Better Days on 49th Street. Six months later, the pair were reunited when Knuckles left Better Days to join Levan at The Continental Baths. When Levan left to set up a new club, The Soho Place at 452 Broadway, Knuckles continued alone until The Continental Baths was closed by bankruptcy in 1976. Deeply involved in his own new venture and knowing his friend needed a job, when Levan was approached by two entrepreneurs looking to set up a club in Chicago, he pointed them in the direction of Frankie Knuckles.

When Knuckles arrived in Chicago, he brought with him all of the techniques he'd learnt in New York and applied them with enthusiasm at The Warehouse. Shuttling between classic Philly soul cuts, gay disco anthems and funk, Knuckles provided the city's party people with an ecstatic communion of energetic rhythms and soaring vocals.

The Warehouse catered to a predominantly black, gay crowd but word of the new phenomenon quickly spread over town. Soon Knuckles had competition in the form of The Future, a club run by a precocious west side DJ called Lil' Louis which drew a more mixed crowd. Louis had been experimenting with pause-button edits on a cassette deck – restructuring pieces of music in imitation of the new dance remix style beginning to emerge from New York – and he began taking his cassette deck into the club, sewing his own densely repetitive, personal edits of tracks like First Choice's 'Let No Man Put Asunder' into the mix in a parallel development to the way kids in Long Island were splicing together their own heavily extended versions of 'Trans-Europe Express'.

At the beginning of the '80s, Louis moved to another club, Horizon West, where the mix stretched even further, fusing Kool & The Gang with Kraftwerk, Devo and Martin Circus, always emphasising a hammer-like beat and an over-lying strangeness which keyed into the arrival of Ecstasy on Chicago's party-scene. One regular visitor to Horizon West was an up-and-coming DJ called Ron Hardy who eventually disappeared off the scene for a while, after landing himself a disco gig in California.

Soon after Frankie Knuckles left The Warehouse in 1983 to set up at The Power Plant, Ron Hardy returned to Chicago to take over a new club on the city's south side. 'The Music Box was an experience like no other,' says Rachael Cain. 'People were pressed body to body in there – it was like sex on the dancefloor. Ron was mesmerising. His sets had elements of everything; a real melting pot of different styles.'

While Frankie Knuckles concentrated on a more polished experience, Ron Hardy took The Music Box on an inspired journey through rough-house disco, European electronica and fast edits spun in off tape. 'If Ron liked a song, he would jam it to death,' recalls Rachael. 'He'd play two copies, stretching out the drops and repeating sections until the tension was almost unbearable. Then he'd let it go and the crowd would go insane. He'd play certain tracks ten or twelve times a night if that's what it took – Ron was just something else!'

In the course of a single night, Hardy would move from tracks like 'Let No Man Put Asunder' to Afrika Bambaataa's 'Planet Rock',

Ministry's proto-industrial workouts and Kraftwerk. Marshall Jefferson, who later became one of Chicago's most celebrated house music producers, remembers The Music Box as a place of almost disorientating intensity where the darkness and the lights merged with the drugs (a mix of angel dust, Ecstasy, LSD and cannabis) and the music to create a revelatory psychedelic experience.

'I went down right about the time it first opened,' he says. 'I went with this girl from my job at The Post Office. She was talking about this club she went to called The Music Box. So I went down there. I didn't even like dance music y'know – my whole life coming up I was into rock n' roll. But I went down to this club and – aw man – the volume man! I never heard dance music played like that. It was so loud! It was so loud that, like, the kick drum would sound like it was going through my chest right? It was like *boom, boom* – like someone physically had their fist beating on my chest. It was like that. And it was *amazing*.'

So far, house music's soundtrack was a combination of pre-existing developments. Both Knuckles and Hardy were by this time spinning their own edits into the mix from reel-to-reel tapes but it was Knuckles who came up with the first secret weapon in the increasingly competitive rivalry between the two DJs. The name of this secret weapon was Jamie Principle.

Principle had been experimenting at home with a synthesizer and a Portastudio, sewing a diverse range of influences – Kraftwerk, Bowie, synth-pop and Prince – into his own synthetically minimalist tunes. When a mutual friend gave a tape of some of these tracks to Frankie Knuckles, the DJ discovered they mapped perfectly on to the dancefloor at The Power Plant. Since Principle hadn't made any records and Knuckles was the only one with a tape, The Power Plant now had its own custom-made music.

The edge didn't last long. Another Chicago DJ, Jesse Saunders put together his own version of an Italian bootleg and released it on his own Jes Say label. It sold out almost immediately as the house kids rushed to buy a record which translated the rush and energy of their club scene on to vinyl. Encouraged by this, soon other club kids were trying their hand at making music. One of them was Marshall Jefferson and he quickly became Ron Hardy's equivalent of Jamie Principle, providing The Music Box with unique, warping grooves that replicated the sharp, abstract intervals of Kraftwerk's records over a relentless drum machine rhythm.

The early sound of house grew out of circumstances provided by drugs and technology. Since they didn't have access to musicians, the club kids created their own groups from machines; cheap synthesizers, budget drum machines and sequencers which enabled them to create melodies, basslines and beats unaided. The narcotic make-up of the house scene dictated that certain musical effects – non-linear melodies, simple repetitive rhythms, uncluttered arrangements – worked better than others in the context of the clubs. The templates for this new kind of synthetic music existed in disco to an extent, but a closer equivalent was to be found in synth-pop, electro and Kraftwerk. The house trend for detuned and heavily processed vocal sounds (as on 'No Way Back' by Adonis, Sleazy D.'s 'I've Lost Control', 'Blackout' by Lil' Louis or Maurice's 'This Is Acid'), for example, seemed purpose-built for enhancing the psychoactive effects of the new club drugs but it had its roots in the vocoderised treatments and robo-voices of Kraftwerk.

The impact of house on the European music scene was initially trailed by a number of singles from the more commercial strata of the Chicago scene. But as Ecstasy began to filter into Europe in growing quantities, the velocity of house music's assault on the mainstream accelerated with unprecedented force. Records as strange and weird as magic, made in basements and bedrooms and makeshift studios in London, Milan, Brussels and Frankfurt started to emerge as the new aesthetic took hold. The dynamic of this change, duplicated in towns and cities all over Europe, was both extraordinary and revolutionary. As Matthew Collin points out in *Altered State*, his indispensable account of the British experience of Ecstasy culture and house music, this 'deployment of technologies – musical, chemical and computer – to deliver altered states of consciousness' has 'sent out shock waves that continue to reverberate culturally and politically, affecting music, fashion, the law, government policy and countless other areas of public and private life.'[12]

Dance culture provoked a paradigm shift in modern music, a shift towards an aesthetic that Kraftwerk had been exploring ever since Hütter and Schneider had left their drum machine playing and stepped offstage to join the dancers. Yet, ironically, they were one of the groups who – initially, at least – were hit hardest by the arrival of house music. Compared with the raw, adrenaline-inducing shapes of a record such as Fingers Inc.'s 'Washing Machine' – made in the front room of Larry Heard's Chicago apartment with just a synthesizer and a drum machine – the lush, extravagantly-crafted sonics of *Electric Cafe* sounded, at best, irrelevant.

Electric Cafe stalled in the lower reaches of the charts on both sides of the Atlantic and, as a result, tentative plans for a Kraftwerk tour in the spring of 1987 were quickly abandoned. But it was obvious that the group were still maintaining a keen interest in developments on the dancefloor when a second single from the album, 'The Telephone Call', was released with an additional house mix by François Kevorkian.

'I'm not a musicologist,' explained Hütter to David Toop of *The Face* early in 1987, 'but I think black music is very environmental. It's very integrated into lifestyle . . .'[13]

Where house music was concerned, these were prophetic words. Over the next few years, youth culture and the lifestyles it accommodated would be reordered by a virus that had begun with Kraftwerk. Temporarily, however, Kraftwerk were outside of the loop as the revolution they had initiated was amplified and expanded upon by a new generation of electronic producers.

10

House music brought with it a matrix of ideas and values which were strikingly similar to those that had lain subtly concealed behind the pure artistic concepts of Kraftwerk. This ideology was part of what made the new culture so irresistibly exciting in the climate of 1988. Many of the riffs were familiar from disco – as Ralf Hütter had pointed out, in front of the loudspeakers, everybody was, after all, equal – though others, particularly the principle of access, also had their roots in punk (many of those in Chicago's punk/industrial scene had filtered into house through a club called The Space Place where all three genres co-existed during the early '80s). Comprehension of this fact was initially obscured in the euphoric rush of dance culture's new frontier, but if house music chose to conceal its sources another genre, born further across the American mid-west, made the connections explicit.

Techno tumbled out of Detroit, almost fully-formed, in the spring of 1988 by way of a major label compilation. Virgin's *Techno! The New Dance Sound Of Detroit* included tracks by the genre's three principal innovators – Juan Atkins, Derrick May and Kevin Saunderson – alongside others such as Mike Banks and Blake Baxter who would become key players in the scene's relentless advance into the future. Records by some of these producers – obscure 12"s on labels with strangely emotionless names such as Metroplex and Transmat – had already appeared in Europe on import, their angular, densely abstract sound often being mistaken for some wild mutant strain of house. Derrick May was quick to point out the difference.

'It's a difference of respect,' he asserted. 'House still has its heart in '70s disco. We don't have any of that respect for the past, it's strictly future music. We have a much greater aptitude for experiment.'[1]

Techno was born, like so much of Detroit's music – The Stooges, MC5, Parliament – out of the industrial rhythms of the city's auto yards; the repetitive metallic crash of the steel presses and assembly lines. But at its centre was a fusion which May made explicit. 'The music is just like Detroit,' he pointed out. 'A complete mistake. It's like George

Clinton and Kraftwerk are stuck in an elevator with only a sequencer to keep them company.'²

Where the elevator was headed was anybody's guess but weird, dystopian records such as 'First Bass' by Separate Minds (with its warped hookline wrenched from a computer game soundtrack to create an eerie and fiercely radical rewrite of Kraftwerk's 'Pocket Calculator') or X-Ray's amped-up twist on a riff borrowed from 'The Man Machine' showed where it had been. Techno was the ultimate integration of Kraftwerk's glittering futurist aesthetic and the unforgiving realities of black American existence in Detroit's decaying, post-industrial inner city.

'Berry Gordy built the Motown sound on the same principles as the conveyor belt at the Ford plant,' noted Juan Atkins. 'Today the automobile plants use robots and computers to make their cars and I'm more interested in Ford's robots than Gordy's music.'³

Atkins had already drawn up the blueprint for techno's fusion of Kraftwerk and Clinton as part of Cybotron. But increasingly unconvinced by the group's direction he had defected to set up his own solo project as Model 500. When a number of record companies found his new music mystifying, Atkins decided to go it alone and set up his own Metroplex label. His first release, 1985's 'No UFO's' was originally recorded in Cybotron's studio but demonstrated the extent to which he was already shifting forwards, revving up the bpms, layering spiked morse code rhythms pulled straight from the Kraftwerk catalogue with wild, atonal synth noises and a loose approximation of a Bootsy Collins bassline. This was followed by 'Night Drive (Thru Babylon)' a menacing collage that took Kraftwerk's cool futurism and chilled it to sub-zero temperatures. Ironically, the third Metroplex record was a 12″ by Channel One entitled 'Technicolor' though, as if to eradicate any doubt about the roots of this new sound, on a later track, 'Electric Entourage', Atkins also quoted directly from Kraftwerk, sampling 'Musique Non-Stop' and cranking it up to terminal velocity.

Two school friends of Juan's younger brother, Derrick May and Kevin Saunderson, were fascinated by the new sound and they embarked on their own techno ventures pulling the sound in two separate directions – Saunderson towards a warmer soulfulness, May into icy abstraction – plotting out the grid of techno's development and the way it would be redefined and transmuted over the following years by a thousand different producers. This was a crucial component of techno's design; an inbuilt drive to develop and push forwards with each 12″ displaying an incremental step in the evolution of the genre. Over the next decade, the Kraftwerk/

Clinton prototype pioneered by Atkins was to be dismantled and reassembled in an unimaginable variety of styles and sub-genres.

Despite, or perhaps because of, its diversity, more than any other genre, it is techno which has remained most faithful to Kraftwerk's original blueprint. In records by acts such as Underground Resistance, Basic Channel, Orbital and Black Dog – or any one of a million others who have switched on their sequencers and imagined themselves into the future – the traces of Hütter and Schneider's wildly imaginative leaps can still be found.

'When I heard Kraftwerk for the first time,' explains Juan Atkins, 'it was like hearing the future. It was so amazing. It was like finding the answer to something I'd been looking for. It just froze me in my tracks. If I had to pick just one track that summed up everything techno was about – the ultimate techno track – it would be Kraftwerk's "Home Computer" because that track really did beam me into the future. It changed my life. Without that, none of us would be doing what we do today.'

But by the summer of 1988, when Detroit's most switched-on club-kids were cramming into The Music Institute to hear the wild cybernetic strategies of Atkins, Saunderson and May, Kraftwerk themselves had withdrawn into Kling Klang, reducing contact with the outside world to a bare minimum. Unlike previous years, there were no rumours of an impending album release, no reports of possible tour dates, no suggestions of any activity at all. Having programmed the virus that was about to redraw the map of modern music, the group had, to all intents and purposes, disappeared from view.

In reality, the reversals that had occurred during the making of the *Techno Pop* album and the muted reception afforded to the eventual release of *Electric Cafe* had taken a heavier toll on Kraftwerk than anyone could have imagined. Having worked for five years to produce just thirty-five minutes of music, both Karl Bartos and Wolfgang Flür were becoming increasingly disillusioned with their roles in the group.

Flür was the first to leave. 'Suddenly I couldn't stand it any more,' he remembers. I began to feel cold. It became boring for me. I had the need to reach out for something new. In the end, I wasn't actually doing what I wanted to do. My heart was no longer in it. I just came when I was ordered, did what I had to do and went home. Ralf was still into cycling but the rest of the band tended to suffer as we were coming second-best to his bicycle. I mean, it was fine for him, he looks really good now and I think he must be the fittest of all of us. It was good for him that he had something else in his life other than just music. But I was a little jealous as I wanted something else too. I resigned from Kraftwerk between 1987 and 1989. It wasn't a sudden decision. There wasn't any great drama about it. Nothing new was being recorded so I went to the studio less and less and eventually no more. I still met with Ralf and Florian for coffee occasionally but after spending so many years with the robots, I wanted to feel warm blood running through my veins again.'

Flür's decision was prompted partly by the prospect of spending another five years working on an LP that wouldn't contain any new music. In response to a suggestion by Bob Kratzner from the group's American record company that they prepare a *Greatest Hits*-type collection, Hütter and Schneider had come up with the idea that they would rework some of their best-known material in a more contemporary style for the next Kraftwerk album.

'Ralf wasn't keen on just putting a record out without getting his hands dirty,' explains Karl Bartos. 'Maybe he thought it was a funny business idea or something. It didn't really appeal to him, so he came up with the idea of making a remix record. Back then, this had never been done before which shows he was really thinking ahead, but I think if you made the original record you shouldn't do the remix yourself. Somebody else should have done it.'[4]

Despite his reservations, Bartos did work extensively on the new album but grew increasingly frustrated at the painfully slow pace of progress. 'Maybe technology got in the way,' he muses. 'It was a big advantage but also learning about it takes away a lot of energy. I remember a time in Kraftwerk where I just sat about for two and a half years reading manuals, programming a Yamaha DX7 synthesizer with two Atari computers and two different types of librarian software, changing envelopes or whatever and not making one new composition.'[5]

Though, to the outside world at least, Kraftwerk appeared more reclusive than ever during this period, the group were maintaining a keen interest in developments on the dancefloor. They made frequent visits to clubs such as Tresor in Berlin, Frankfurt's Dorian Gray and numerous others around the Cologne/Düsseldorf area while working on the project. This manifested itself in the new dancefloor treatments that were applied to tracks such as 'The Robots' and 'Pocket Calculator' which, ironically, borrowed heavily from the developments leaking in from both Chicago and Detroit.

'That was just a natural development of our music,' claimed Hütter. 'We've always had these drum machine tracks . . . It's just a matter of everything coming together.'[6]

What the new album – by this time known as *The Mix* – suggested was that Kraftwerk were now in the middle of an electronic feedback loop of their own making. Having inspired both genres, they were now selecting elements from house and techno that had been extrapolated from their own music and recycling them, knowing that these elements would, in turn, become part of a new matrix of inspiration. It was the perfect artistic strategy; an infinite loop of inspiration, deconstruction and reconstruction which fitted perfectly with the processes of this new generation of electronic producers.

But, as the group discovered, recreating some of the distinctive sounds of their old material wasn't as easy as they initially expected. This delayed the process while Fritz Hilpert, the Kling Klang engineer who was now deputising for Wolfgang Flür, transferred the original analogue recordings on to digital format.

'Everything is digitally stored and then computer-controlled,' explained Hütter. 'We used all of our back catalogue from the last twenty years, sampling the original analogue sounds from the sixteen-track master tapes. We chose those sounds we thought were unique or irreplaceable or perhaps just in good shape and then others we changed or altered . . .'[7]

One of the most problematic, but also one of the most successful, reworkings the group attempted was 'Autobahn' which was cut down to less than half of its original twenty-two-minute running time and rebuilt around a shuffling triplet groove. But for the track's stunning middle section, it proved impossible to recreate the synthetic car horn sounds which had been a feature of the original version.

'On *The Mix* they're sampled from the old *Autobahn* master tapes,' reveals Hütter. 'We were unable to recreate them because they utilised a special tuning; they're chords incorporating tritones to sound car horn-like. We were never able to recapture that analogue sound – I think it was done on a Moog or an Arp – so we just sampled the original noises and used them to create something called a *hupenkonzert*. It's a common German expression that means 'car horn concert' – in other words a traffic jam where everyone is angry and honking his horn. So I played a little *hupenkonzert* there. We used white noise to create the sound of the cars whooshing by. At one point when the lyrics go, in German, 'the road is a grey ribbon with white stripes and green edges' we wanted to evoke the image of the rubber tyre crossing those white stripes so we used a backwards burst of white noise.'[8]

Other tracks which benefited from this radical overhaul included 'Radioactivity' (this time with an explicit anti-nuclear message and a deeply funky techno groove) and 'Musique Non-Stop' which clearly showed the signs of a brush with the new chemical generation. Both 'The Man Machine' and 'Neon Lights' were also reworked but didn't make it on to the final release.

In February 1990, the group played a series of four secret concerts, beginning in Bologna on the 7th, with subsequent appearances in Padua, Florence and Genoa. This was the first time Kraftwerk had played live since the extensive 1981 tour but neither their record company nor the press were alerted. Instead, in keeping with the group's previous working practices, the concerts were used to test out material for the new album. Embryonic versions of the new arrangements for tracks such as 'Home Computer', 'Radioactivity' and 'Autobahn' were played at each of the concerts but it was clear – from the obvious differences between these and the versions which finally appeared on *The Mix* the following year – that further refinements and adjustments were made to each of these tracks after the group's return to Kling Klang. Only 'Computer Love' appeared to be in its final stages while others, including 'Numbers', were similar to the versions that had been played live on the 1981 tour. It was also clear from the numerous mistakes that punctuated these performances that the group had had little time to rehearse.

These were the last concerts which Karl Bartos was to play as a member of Kraftwerk. A few months after this brief tour of Italy, in August 1990, frustrated by the length of time it was taking to complete *The Mix* project, he too left the group.

'It took me a couple of years to leave,' he remembers, 'although I started thinking about it after *Electric Cafe*. The longer we worked on *The Mix*, the more I felt a little useless. I wanted to play around with new stuff but had to work on this boring project on a day-to-day basis. It was unbelievable. Nowadays I think the next best thing I did – after studying music and meeting my wife – was joining Kraftwerk then leaving. I really enjoyed being in there, but you know every band had it's limits. I mean, it's different with The Rolling Stones but every other band, as far as I'm concerned, has a certain amount of time and then they're through or they have to reinvent themselves like Bowie does constantly. He's the master of reinvention; again and again, but with a different angle, different music, different image, different people. It's the same in the so-called real arts. Some painters are constantly stuck in one style. Apparently they make money at it, like Lichtenstein, he just repeated one picture all his life. I remain good friends with Wolfgang. We meet usually once a week. Probably we're going to do something together, if the time is right and somebody wants to hear it . . .'[9]

Bartos had, however, worked extensively on *The Mix*. 'I did all the programming on that,' he points out. 'They didn't credit me on the record, though!'[10]

For Hütter and Schneider this presented something of a problem. Kraftwerk's imagery was synonymous with a four-piece group and this would have to be reflected in the artwork for the new album. They had already commissioned four new motorised robots to replace their original mannequins and the initial plan was to have photographs of these on the album sleeve (since pop culture is still fascinated by youth, this was a perfect strategy because, unlike Hütter and Schneider – who were by this time approaching their 50s – robots don't age). Without Bartos, however, it was obvious that they were either going to have to change this concept or find a new member. With time running out, they came up with the solution of duplicating Fritz Hilpert's robot to create the illusion of a four-man group.

The new robots were a strange combination of Terminator-style deconstructed machine chic and (perhaps as a sly reference to the mannequins that had originally served the purpose) dressmaker's dummies. But this time, they were actually motorised.

'They're keyboard-controlled,' explained Hütter. 'A German engineer – someone Florian knows – programmed them. Normally, this engineer works on office computers and things like that, but we convinced him to use his skills in another area. So the robots are programmed but we can reprogram them. We'll see how reliable they are and how much we can get them to improvise!'[11]

The fascination with robots has now become one of Kraftwerk's most enduring themes, lasting more than two decades. Hütter's account of this obsession was characteristically oblique.

'Because they are machines that are very close to man, both in appearance and behaviour,' he declared. 'All of our work addresses this close relationship between man and machines. That's why we wrote this song "The Robots". We don't feel alienated because we have worked for so many years on trying to establish some kind of a closer relationship with machinery, more of a holistic approach than just thinking of machines as external things, like weapons for aggression or whatever, but rather as extensions of ourselves. In turn, we get a lot of feedback from them and that's what fascinates us.'[12]

As if to drive home the point, the release of *The Mix* was preceded in May 1991 by a single of 'The Robots' in its new updated version. This was accompanied by a video featuring the minimalist robots 'dancing'; a routine which consisted of nothing more elaborate than swivelling their heads and flexing their skeletal arms. It wasn't exactly *Terminator 2* but, as Ralf dryly pointed out, 'we are not Disneyland: there are limits to our economic resources.'[13]

Both the single and the album sold well, re-establishing Kraftwerk as a commercial force. To coincide with the album release, a world tour was organised with American dates planned for September 1991. However, the tour didn't progress beyond Europe, finishing in Budapest later the same year. No official reason for this has ever been forthcoming but the concerts did provide a glimpse of the group's new recruits, Fritz Hilpert and Fernando Abrantes, who had been brought in to replace Wolfgang Flür and Karl Bartos.

'Actually, we've known them as electronic engineers for some years now,' explained Hütter just before the tour. 'They'll be doing percussion and machinery and Florian and I will be programming our robots and mixing.'[14]

Abrantes didn't last long. After the UK dates in July, 1991, he was replaced by another Kling Klang engineer, Henning Schmitz, who'd worked on *Electric Cafe*. Again, there was no real explanation for this curious switch. Frits Couwenberg of the Dutch electronic music society Stichting KLEM met with Hütter after Kraftwerk's concert in Utrecht and received a particularly evasive reply to his question about the group's shifting line-up.

'This is always changing,' said Hütter. 'We have always worked with various musicians and engineers . . . on computer programmes and ideas. Video projects for example and also other projects, computer speech and computer graphics. We don't always make music, we work with many different people who rely on other projects. Just like a film, relying on the projects which we do. For the summer tour, a friend of ours – Fernando – worked with us and now for the whole winter we are on tour.'[15]

Unabashed, Couwenberg pointed out how long it had taken to complete *The Mix* and wondered if it had been worth all the effort. 'To us it is,' bristled Hütter. 'This is our work. Sometimes things go quicker and other times projects go slower. It differs. That is something you can't define.'[16]

Interestingly, when Couwenberg indicated a desire to visit Kling Klang, Hütter's reply showed remarkable consistency, echoing his answers to similar questions on the 1981 tour, ten years previously. 'That was onstage,' he explained. 'Only the walls are in Düsseldorf. We work there intensively and all manner of things happen there. That is where we retire.'[17] So, asked Couwenberg, you'll start work there immediately after the tour? 'Yes,' replied Hütter, 'but also on tour. During the afternoon we sit in the studio onstage and work. Throughout, new things, the music continually changes. Through chance, through everything . . .'[18]

This was a revealing admission considering the achingly slow pace of the group's work rate over the previous decade. But it also emphasised the depth of Kraftwerk's commitment to their art even during the notoriously exhausting business of touring which many groups half the age of Hütter and Schneider find gruelling. This obsessive dedication to the group's working regime was something that Hütter had hinted at a decade earlier when he had admitted that 'our daily schedule lasts some eight to ten hours in the studio.'[19]

Wolfgang Flür remembers how the group's daily routine would involve meeting at the studio in the early evening and working into the small hours of the next morning. 'After years doing that,' he notes, 'it is such a relief to be able to work normal hours in the studio. Now I choose to start work in the morning and finish recording at eight or nine in the evening. For me it is a much more sociable way to work.'

Flür now has his own solo project, Yamo, which was unveiled in 1993 with the 'Little Child' benefit single for Bosnia. To date, the group has featured a fluid line-up of musicians including Andi Toma and Jan Werner of the Cologne-based techno outfit Mouse On Mars and – in a remarkable musical reunion spanning more than 30 years – former Beathovens bass-player Gerd Willms. Yamo's debut album, 1997's *Time*

Pie, marked a return to the more romantic melodies of Kraftwerk albums such as *Radio-Activity* and *Trans-Europe Express* coupled with quirky, techno-edged grooves and the lyrical appeal of Flür's psychedelic fairytales.

'In Kraftwerk we were very much concerned with connecting the past – which was to us the folk songs of our country – with the future,' says Flür. 'That was the whole meaning of our concept of *elektronisch Volksmusik*. It is a sense of nostalgia for the past and a sense of excitement about the future and it has something for everyone. The concept of *Time Pie* is similar. If you cut into the pie, you'll find layers which relate to different periods of my life. It is a pie which has been baked from all my experiences over the years.'

Karl Bartos also re-emerged during 1993 as Elektric Music with former Rheingold member Lothar Manteuffel. The group's debut album, *Esperanto*, still bore traces of Kraftwerk but with a tougher, more sample-based aesthetic. 'If Kraftwerk were, for example, the Starship *Enterprise* we'd be something out of *Blade Runner*,' observed Bartos, 'something a bit dirtier that shows the part of technology that's rotten. Kraftwerk maybe only shows the chrome surface and we pull it apart and show some animals crawling around inside . . .'[20]

Bartos also travelled to Manchester to work with Bernard Sumner and Johnny Marr on Electronic's *Raise The Pressure LP*. Bartos played keyboards and was also involved in much of the song-writing, including the track 'Imitation Of Life' which had originally been planned for the second Elektric Music album. Electronic subsequently went on to work with Arthur Baker while Bartos collaborated with OMD's Andy McCluskey on 'The Moon And The Sun' (from the *Universal* LP).

In 1998 a second album by Electric Music (note the subtle change of name), this time without Lothar Manteuffel, was released by the German SPV label. Though more distinctly guitar-oriented than its predecessor, *Electric Music*, did feature one song, 'The Young Urban Professional' which dated back to the recording sessions for *Electric Cafe*.

'I can remember saying to Ralf it's like I have this jumbo jet in the garden but it never takes off,' explains Bartos about his years with Kraftwerk. 'Now I'd rather go and have a little Messerschmitt or a Stuka and do it myself.'[21]

Emil Schult has been closely involved with both Yamo and Electric Music, designing sleeves, working on lyrics and providing general artistic input. During 1997, Schult also helped design and direct the video for Yamo's 'Stereomatic' single.

Schult's involvement with Kraftwerk declined significantly following the 1981 tour on which he accompanied the group. Though he was credited on *Electric Cafe*, he spent much of the '80s in the Bahamas where, he points out, 'I showed my paintings underwater.' On his return to Düsseldorf in 1992, Schult's painting style, which he describes, in typically Kraftwerkian fashion, as 'research into maximum expression' was gaining recognition in the art world. At time of writing, he is currently hard at work in his Düsseldorf atelier preparing a retrospective exhibition, though he claims that his relationship with Kraftwerk is 'not over yet.'

'Emil hasn't really got the credit he deserves from Kraftwerk,' notes Wolfgang Flür. 'From my viewpoint he was as important to our success as the four people you saw on stage. Emil did a lot of work on the lyrics of some of our most successful songs. His artwork on many covers and designs became famous as well as our music. And now I'm very glad he is helping me with Yamo.'

Hütter and Schneider, meanwhile, continue to operate in a clandestine manner despite the keen interest of the music media. Since 1991, their contact with the press has been minimal and even their record company seem to be no more informed about their activities than anyone else outside the group's inner circle.

'The importance of our secrecy was necessary for our privacy and work,' revealed Ralf in a rare interview. 'We never wanted to be the idols for other people. We only wanted to make our music and, of course, we hoped to reach the people with our messages and melodies.'[22]

It is now also unclear whether any new recordings will ever surface from Kling Klang regardless of the group's recent live activities. Perhaps, as David Toop pointed out in 1991, 'this profoundly influential band has been overtaken by the competition'[23] and therefore have become reluctant to risk their unparalleled reputation as pop music's prime innovators on the gamble of a new release. Certainly developments in Chicago, Detroit, London and New York – where Kraftwerk's future pop has splintered into a number of different trajectories – have made their task more difficult. Is it likely that Kraftwerk can now match (never mind supersede) the vibrant, glitteringly innovative strategies of, say, Carl Craig's *Landcruising*, Kenny Larkin's *Metaphor* or Global Communication's exquisitely-crafted *76:14* album? These are the records that now map out the new electronic frontier, records which have taken Kraftwerk's original aesthetic and extrapolated it far into the future.

Perhaps we're asking too much. Having already redesigned modern music, is it realistic to expect Hütter and Schneider to do it all over again? Kraftwerk are now no longer a pop group, they are a myth. And having passed into the realms of mythology, the more time that elapses between their releases, the greater the weight that will be attached to any new material which issues forth from Kling Klang. Our expectations of what that material should be, what it should sound like, can never be matched. For Kraftwerk to satisfy those expectations, they must achieve the impossible and create something that is both *of* its time and simultaneously ahead of its time. As yet, not even they have managed to do this. It took the world three years to catch up with 'The Model', even longer for *Computer World*. It's a fact that the records which change our future are never immediately recognised as such. Why should now be any different?

Ironically, Kraftwerk's present status has its closest analogy in the career of Derrick May. After recording some of the most seminal records in techno – 'Nude Photo', 'Strings Of Life', 'It Is What It Is' and 'Icon' among them – May has existed in a period of creative stasis since the early '90s, either unable or unwilling to complete any new music. Partly, May ascribes this inactivity to the fact that he no longer lives in the apartment on Detroit's Second Avenue where all of his most influential tracks were written (the unwitting testimony of this being that a confluence of some kind of supernatural or mystical force contributed to these gigantic imaginative leaps). But, according to his closest confidantes, the reality is that May is frozen in the spotlight glare of his own iconography. Having created these moments of staggering brilliance, May is aware that anything less than a work of genius will diminish the reputation he already has. To maintain this, the only thing he can do now, it seems, is do nothing.

Having created the framework for modern music's leap into the future, Kraftwerk are now in a similar position. Rumours of a new album in advance of their 1998 world tour have turned out to be, as usual with the group these days, just rumours. The irony is that, without a new album to promote, these concerts were potentially just as damaging to the group's status, reducing the performances to the pathos of a '70s pop star eking out the twilight of their career on the cabaret circuit. Kraftwerk's secret weapon, however, was to use these concerts as a platform to introduce a number of new compositions. As they have proved in the past, and as Hütter has suggested, Kraftwerk ' . . .find some energy in the environment of people who come to see us and who make us play in another dimension at a higher psychological level . . .'[24] Whether this will provide the impetus to escape the situation they now find themselves in remains to be seen.

Another obvious point is that, with the departure of Flür and Bartos, Kraftwerk's unique chemistry has altered immeasurably. The group that created *Trans-Europe Express*, *The Man Machine* and *Computer World* no longer exists. In its place is something different.

'The most successful Kraftwerk records were made by four special characters who complemented each other,' maintains Wolfgang Flür. 'We influenced and admired each other. The music was the result of a very special chemistry. It was something like The Beatles. It came from the closeness we had with one another. We all came from educated families. We were very tied. We would speak to one another every evening and would do things together also. We were interested in culture and what was happening in the theatres and at the movies, in music presentations and concerts. The space, the earth, and mankind. The main theme was our manhood interest.'

Of the new material debuted during Kraftwerk's 1997 and 1998 concerts, perhaps 'Lichthof' ('Yard Of Light') offers some clues to the direction any new release might take. Obviously located alongside the dancefloor developments of Detroit, Chicago, Berlin and Frankfurt, the track occupies the space most clearly defined by Germany's techno scene – somewhere between Basic Channel and the adrenalised kinetics of Cologne's Mike Ink – but there are still extant traces of the unique syncopational skill that has become a Kraftwerk trademark over the years. Is it life-alteringly good? Does it match, for example, the pristine electronic emotionalism of, say, Larry Heard's *Alien* album or the supercharged electro-funk of Underground Resistance? Not really. Can it be compared with the glorious, wide-eyed innovation of *The Man Machine* or even the *Computer World* album? Perhaps. But then those records are now almost 20 years old. The world has changed since then, reacted to a virus initially programmed by a group who have gone on to become pop culture's most influential, most mysterious and, ultimately, most astonishing force.

Kraftwerk could still surprise us. After all, this material is still in its formative stages and Kraftwerk's past history – 'Trans-Europe Express',

'Showroom Dummies', 'The Robots', 'Home Computer' – is littered with unpromising live material that was later reshaped into recordings of uncompromising power and brilliance. The group's talent for improvisation and innovation in equal measures suggests that, whatever happens, a new record may yet be worth the wait.

'Today, even the greatest sceptic must have realised that techno in all its forms, from hardcore to trance, house and jungle by way of gabba and ambient has established itself as the music of the '90s,' observes Karl Bartos. 'With all its advantages and drawbacks . . .'[25]

The inference is obvious. Techno has vindicated Kraftwerk's original vision but it has also imprisoned the group inside a creative dilemma from which there is no sure escape.

'They are under huge pressure,' confirms Wolfgang Flür. 'If Kraftwerk really want to astonish their audience they have to go further. But the longer it goes on, the more complicated it gets. So they do not try.'

In some ways, Ralf's analogy about the butterfly which is captured, catalogued and pinned behind glass ('Only it is no longer a butterfly') has a profound resonance for what has happened to Kraftwerk over the last ten years. As John McCready suggests, 'the communal techno penny has finally dropped . . . without their fearless pioneering in persuading the world of the value of technology as a radical, viable and musical concept, Afrika Bambaataa might still be looking for the perfect beat and thousands of electronic explorers might be stuck for a purist sonic ideal to aspire to.'[26]

While Kraftwerk still operated on the fringes of the music scene they were free to explore, innovate and manoeuvre at will. They had the freedom to experiment without fear of losing face if it all went wrong. From their bunker in Düsseldorf, these sonic guerrillas constructed a radical musical manifesto because they had nothing to lose. Nothing was expected of them and, in return, they catered to no expectations. That's why even today, the greatest Kraftwerk records still sound like future shock pressed into vinyl.

The scenario now is very different. Kraftwerk are the focus of serious attention and expectation. The musical framework they have created, the devotion they have inspired and the developments they have provoked, reverberate to a soundtrack of their making. And at the centre of it all, locked in the hi-tech ivory tower of Kling Klang, Ralf Hütter and Florian Schneider have become victims of their own success.

At least, that's one point of view. It's impossible to discount the fact that Hütter and Schneider are impeccable strategists who – even if their story were to stop now – have already produced what may turn out to be pop culture's greatest artistic achievement. They are that rarest of commodities these days: artists who are also thinkers. Kraftwerk is their work of art, their *Gesankt Kunstwerk*, and it is arguably on a level with the other great modernist works of the 20th century. Who's to compare? Has *Computer World* turned out to be any less influential than *Les Demoiselles d'Avignon*, say, or *The Large Glass* by Duchamp?

Hütter's response to the proliferation of Kraftwerk's electronic ideal is typically under-played. 'We trouble ourselves actually very little about the greater musical development,' he points out. 'We concentrate on our work. What the future will bring, that will have to show itself first.'[27]

The group's awareness of who they are and what they have achieved is still healthily balanced by a characteristically dry, under-stated humour. In 1993, Simon Edmonds, managing director of Terratec Promedia, was working with Penny & Giles, a company who design and manufacture achingly high quality studio equipment for the more affluent end of the market. 'We were developing the MM16 at the time,' remembers Edmonds. 'It was a seriously expensive, programmable MIDI controller. Within a few days of us finishing the machine, a review appeared in the studio press and I got a fax from Florian saying that "We must see this. It looks like it was designed for us." So I called him back and we set up a meeting. I went over to Kling Klang early in December with the production prototype. I had wondered why they were so enthusiastic, but when I saw their gear, I realised. The machine looked like it had been custom-built for them. They loved it and couldn't wait to play with it. Over the Christmas holidays, I kept getting calls from them asking if they could have it. My daughter, who was about nine years old at the time, would answer the phone thinking it was one of her school friends and then all I'd hear would be [affects bored, terminally unimpressed child's voice] "Dad! It's Florian again!"'

The group subsequently ordered three of the units and Edmonds travelled back to Düsseldorf to deliver them. 'They played me some of the music they were working on,' he recalls, 'and I was very impressed. Florian struck me as being very nice, very genuine, very unassuming. They take their music very seriously but they don't seem to have any ego. There was a Kraftwerk convention coming up in England and I

asked Florian why he didn't just go over to it and put in an appearance.
"Oh no," he said, "I don't understand that type of thing. We're just
musicians." It's a very matter of fact approach. Both Florian and Fritz
were very clued-up about the equipment side of things particularly.
They approach it all very professionally. They have set hours in the
studio, just like any other job and when their day is finished they get in
their Volkswagen Golfs and go home again. They do try to live very
ordinary lives beyond what's obviously very extraordinary music. One
amusing point, though, was when it came to discussing the price of the
equipment with Florian. "What about a discount?" he asked me. I used
my usual response in these situations. What about it? "Well," he said,
"we are Kraftwerk . . ."'

Maybe it's still too early to tell how this story will end. Maybe –
though it seems unlikely – Kraftwerk will eventually reach the stage, as
Hütter once predicted, where their technology will allow them to
release several singles a day. As yet, they haven't done that, although
several producers from Chicago and Detroit have come close to doing so.
But in the end it doesn't matter. As long as Kraftwerk's music survives,
whether it's on sale in record stores or downloadable from the Internet
or simply circulated on *samizdat* tapes and discs, they will continue to
be the virus running wild in the program, their vision refracted,
magnified and extended by those they have inspired.

And for Kraftwerk, as always, the inspiration will come from the
weird, wired world that surrounds them. 'The world around us is a
complete orchestra,' explains Hütter. 'The noises from cars, coffee
machines and vacuum cleaners, we can use for our music. That is like a
film. We are the scriptwriters who with their ears pick up everything
and bring in new pictures.'[28]

The enigma of Kraftwerk continues to be as mysterious and
clandestine as ever but, over the last decade at least, the reference points
which help to make sense of this unique phenomenon have multiplied.
Dance culture has embraced many of the group's most potent strategies
and their maverick vision has been vindicated by the frequency with
which it emerges in the soundtracks of a thousand Saturday night dancefloors around the globe, in the music that leaks out of our television
screens and tries to persuade us to buy everything from margarine to
motor cars, in the sound that beams out of shop doorways, supermarket
tannoys and transistor radios, in the bleeps and bass pulses that issue
from our cinema screens. Their sound *is* the sound of the modern world.

'We're not really interested in tearing you up with the scratches and cuts tonight,' Derrick May once announced on his *Street Beat* radio show. 'We're more interested in educating you for the future . . .' As a declaration of techno's intent, these two sentences are just about perfect but they also speak volumes about the inspiration dance culture has drawn from Kraftwerk. They could just as easily have come from Ralf Hütter or Florian Schneider.

Kraftwerk's career has survived the commodification of pop culture and beamed new impulses into the grid of reference and influence on which the medium thrives. Their records have been the catalyst for a radical new version of modern music, a change which has reordered the world around us and infiltrated every aspect of our interface with daily life. But, most of all, their machine symphonies have educated us about how the future should sound. No other group in the history of pop has managed this as successfully as they have, nor had their vision as firmly vindicated.

'Without a loudspeaker, no one could ever experience Kraftwerk,'[29] reminds Ralf Hütter. And his message is clear. After all, in front of the loudspeaker, everyone is equal.

Epilogue

It's a pre-millennial Saturday night in Düsseldorf. As darkness falls, the city's alluring elegance is replaced by something altogether different; a quickening pulsebeat of almost feral intensity. The cars no longer glide, they roar. On the boulevards and *allees* people step, almost imperceptibly, into a different rhythm. It feels dull and sharp all at the same time.

On Königsallee, the designer stores and fashion houses have fallen silent. Not far away, in the Kunstammlung Nordrhein-Westfalen, the Braques, Mondrians and Klees breathe their colour into empty space as Greek taxi drivers crunch gears and thread their Mercedes through the one-way streets.

Head back towards the Hauptbahnhof where the bars and cinemas are waking up, alive with the noise of laughter and life crammed into weekends. During the day, this part of the city sleeps, after dark it swells with night-time workers like a reservoir after rain. Occasionally a door opens and techno music spills out into the night-time air.

Drive for an hour, in any direction, and you'll reach the urban perimeter. More than twelve million people work within this radius, at any one of 5000 different business addresses. This workforce represents 50 nations. This city is the foreign trade centre of Germany. At night sometimes it seems as if this city is made of light.

Outside the Hauptbahnhof, Konrad Adenauer Platz is full of cars and people oblivious to the metallic hum of trains arriving and departing. In an otherwise unremarkable building, close to the railway tracks, two men are plotting a new version of the future. They are planning a new project and they want to call it *Technopolis*. It's something to do with global networks, about how we're all hooked up and wired in. This concept began life as a story about modems and ISDN and intranets, now it has moved on, stretched deep into the 21st century. Now, as it always has been, it's about the future. Hours from now, when he gets bored, one of these men will decide to go home and walk back to where he has parked his car on Konrad Adenauer Platz. The name reminds him of a Mercedes he used to have. The other will work on, dreaming of melodies and cadences that sound like the mechanical throb of the trains that pass nearby and the synaptic crackle of electricity.

Across the street, the darkness is punctured by liquid colour – acid yellow, pulsing red, purple and eye-wateringly intense blue – that seems to hang in the air like magic. A constant vibrating pulse leaks from the club doorway, tangles with the colour and sucks itself back downstairs.

At the bar is a beautiful Hungarian girl. Her name is Christina. She is twenty-two. She has been in Düsseldorf for just two weeks, will stay for two more. She likes Michael Jackson and dance music. She loves to dance, she says. Soon it is time. She steps provocatively on to a neon-lit catwalk and unpeels her dress. A dense, bruising groove rips out of the speakers, laced through with a warm, familiar melody. The record – a techno cover version of Kraftwerk's 'The Model' – is savagely apt. Naked, the girl strides down the catwalk in time with the hammer-heavy beat, a real-life embodiment of the song, seducing the darkness with preternatural ease. At the end of the catwalk, she stops, and seems to dream for a moment. From where she's standing, it's just a few short steps to the studio where this song was originally born. She doesn't know it, of course. The studio, like the group who made the record in the first place, is cloaked in secrecy. But if she did, she wouldn't care. What's important about this record, after all, is that it's good for dancing.

On the other side of the street, in the tiny room which serves as Kling Klang's office, a light goes on . . .

Discography

ALBUMS:

Organisation – *Tonefloat* (1970)
RCA LP SF8111
Tone Float, Milk Rock, Silver Forest, Rhythm Salad, Noitasinagro

Kraftwerk – *Kraftwerk 1* (1970)
Philips LP 6305058
Ruckzuck, Stratovarius, Megaherz, Vom Himmel Hoch

Kraftwerk – *Kraftwerk 2* (1971)
Philips LP 63051117
Klingklang, Atem, Strom, Spule 4, Wellenlange, Harmonika

Kraftwerk – *Ralf & Florian* (1973)
Philips LP 6305197
Elektrisches Roulette, Tongebirge, Kristallo, Heimatklänge, Tanzmusik, Ananas Symphonie

Kraftwerk – *Autobahn* (1974)
Philips LP – 6305231
Autobahn, Kometenmelodie 1, Kometenmelodie 2, Mitternacht, Morgenspaziergang

Kraftwerk – *Radio-Activity* (1976)
Capitol LP – E-ST11457
Geiger Counter, Radioactivity, Radioland, Airwaves, Intermission, News, The Voice Of Energy, Antenna, Radio Stars, Uranium, Transistor, Ohm Sweet Ohm

Kraftwerk – *Trans-Europe Express* (1977)
Capitol LP – E-ST11603

Europe Endless, Hall Of Mirrors, Showroom Dummies, Trans-Europe
Express, Metal On Metal, Franz Schubert, Endless Endless

Kraftwerk – *The Man Machine* (1978)
Capitol LP – E-ST11728
The Robots, Spacelab, Metropolis, The Model, Neon Lights, The Man
Machine

Kraftwerk – *Computer World* (1981)
EMI LP – EMC3370
Computer World, Pocket Calculator, Numbers, Computer World 2,
Computer Love, Home Computer, It's More Fun To Compute

Kraftwerk – *Electric Cafe* (1986)
EMI LP – EMD1001
Boing Boom Tschak, Techno Pop, Musique Non Stop, Telephone Call,
Sex Object, Electric Cafe

Kraftwerk – *The Mix* (1991)
EMI LP – EM1408
The Robots, Computer Love, Pocket Calculator, Dentaku, Autobahn,
Radioactivity, Trans-Europe Express, Abzug, Metal On Metal, Home
Computer, Music Non Stop

SINGLES:

Kouhoutek-Kometenmelodie (1974)
Philips 7" 6003356

Autobahn/Kometenmelodie 1 (1975)
Vertigo 7" 6147012

Comet Melody 2/Kristallo (1975)
Vertigo 7" 6147015

Radioactivity/Antenna (1976)
Capitol 7" CL15853

Trans-Europe Express (1977)
Capitol 7″ CL15917

Showroom Dummies/Europe Endless (1977)
Capitol 7″ CLX104

Showroom Dummies/Europe Endless (1977)
Capitol 12″ 12CLX104

The Robots/Spacelab (1978)
Capitol 7″ CL15981

Neon Lights/Trans-Europe Express/The Model (1978)
Capitol 7″ CL15998

Neon Lights/Trans-Europe Express/The Model (1978)
Capitol 12″ 12CL15998

Showroom Dummies/Spacelab/Europe Endless (1979)
Capitol 12″ 12 CL16098

Pocket Calculator/Dentaku (1981)
EMI 7″ EMI5175

Pocket Calculator/Numbers/Dentaku (1981)
EMI 12″ 12EMI5175

Computer Love/The Model (1981)
EMI 7″ EMI5207

Computer Love/The Model (1981)
EMI 12″ 12EMI5207

Kometenmelodie 2/Von Himmel Hoch (1981)
Vertigo 7″ VER3

Showroom Dummies/Numbers (Remix) (1982)
EMI 7″ EMI5272

Showroom Dummies/Numbers (Remix)/Pocket Calculator (1982)
EMI 12″ 12EMI5272

Tour De France/Tour De France (Instrumental) (1983)
EMI 7″ EMI5413

Tour De France/Tour De France/Tour De France (2e Etape) (1983)
EMI 12″ 12EMI5413

Computer Love/The Model (1984)
EMI 7″ G4516

Tour De France (François Kevorkian Remix)/Tour De France (1984)
EMI 7″ EMI5413

Tour De France (François Kevorkian Remix)/Tour De France (Version)
Tour De France (1984)
EMI 12″ EMI5413

Musique Non Stop/Musique Non Stop (Version) (1986)
EMI 7″ EMI5588

Musique Non Stop/Musique Non Stop (Version) (1986)
EMI 12″ 12EMI5588

The Telephone Call (Remix)/Der Telefon Anruft (Remix) (1987)
EMI 7″ EMI5602

The Telephone Call (Remix)/House Phone/Der Telefon Anruft (Remix)
(1987)
EMI 12″ 12EMI5602

The Robots/Robotronik (1991)
EMI 7″ EM192

Robotronik/The Robots (Edit)/The Robots (1991)
EMI 1″ 12EM192

Radioactivity (Kevorkian Remix)/Radioactivity (Orbit Remix) (1991)
EMI 7" EM201

Radioactivity (Kevorkian Remix)/Radioactivity (Kevorkian 7" Remix)/
Radioactivity (Orbit Remix) (1991)
EMI 12" EM201

BOOTLEGS:

Kraftwerk – *Bremen*
(Cologne Concert 1971)
Unknown, Ruckzuck, Vom Himmel Hoch, Unknown

Kraftwerk – *Kometenmelodie*
(WDR Broadcast, Cologne 1975)
Ruckzuck, Kometenmelodie 1, Kometenmelodie2, Autobahn

Kraftwerk – *Machine*
(Paris Concert 1976/Utrecht Concert 1981)
Kometenmelodie 1, Kometenmelodie2, Tongebirge, Numbers,
Computer World, Metropolis, The Model, Computer Love, Pocket
Calculator

Kraftwerk – *Security Device*
(Milan Concert 1981)
Numbers, Computer World, Computer Love, Home Computer, The
Model, Neon Lights, Geiger Counter, Radioactivity, Voice Of Energy,
Ohm Sweet Ohm, Autobahn, Trans-Europe Express, Hall Of Mirrors,
Showroom Dummies, Pocket Calculator, The Robots

Kraftwerk – *Hyper Cerebral Machine*
(Florence Concert 1981)
Numbers, Computer World, Computer Love, Home Computer, The
Model, Neon Lights, Geiger Counter, Radioactivity, Voice Of Energy,
Trans-Europe Express, Hall Of Mirrors, Showroom Dummies, Pocket
Calculator, The Robots

Kraftwerk – *Computer Tour*
(Bristol Concert 1981/ Utrecht Concert 1981)

Metropolis, The Model, Radioactivity, Computer Love, Autobahn, Numbers, Computer World, Home Computer, Neon Lights, Hall Of Mirrors, Showroom Dummies

Kraftwerk – *Numbers*
(Tokyo Concert 1981)
Numbers, Computer World, Computer Love, The Model, Neon Lights, Radioactivity, Ohm Sweet Ohm, Autobahn, Hall Of Mirrors, Showroom Dummies, Trans-Europe Express, Pocket Calculator, The Robots, It's More Fun To Compute

Kraftwerk – *Tbon Pabothnk*
(Munich Concert 1981)
Numbers, Computer World, Computer Love, Home Computer, The Model, Neon Lights, Geiger Counter, Radioactivity, Voice Of Energy, Ohm Sweet Ohm, Autobahn, Trans-Europe Express, Hall Of Mirrors, Showroom Dummies, Pocket Calculator, The Robots

Kraftwerk – *Enregistree Live A L'Olympia*
(Paris Concert 1981)
Computer World, Home Computer, Computer Love, The Model, Neon Lights, Radioactivity, Voice Of Energy, Ohm Sweet Ohm, Autobahn, Hall Of Mirrors, Showroom Dummies, Trans-Europe Express

Kraftwerk – *Computer Welt*
(London Concert 1981)
Numbers, Computer World, Computer Love, The Model, Neon Lights, Geiger Counter, Radioactivity, Voice Of Energy, Ohm Sweet Ohm, Autobahn, Trans-Europe Express, Pocket Calculator, The Robots, It's More Fun To Compute

Kraftwerk – *Central Passage*
(Florence Concert 1981)
Numbers, Computer World, Home Computer, It's More Fun To Compute, Computer Love, The Model, Neon Lights, Geiger Counter, Radioactivity, Ohm Sweet Ohm, Autobahn, Trans-Europe Express, Hall Of Mirrors, Showroom Dummies, Pocket Calculator, The Robots

Kraftwerk – *Return Of The Mensch Machine*
(Bologna Concert 1990)
Numbers, Computer World, Tour De France, The Model, Computer Love, Home Computer, Autobahn, Radioactivity, Trans-Europe Express, Pocket Calculator, The Robots, Musique Non Stop

Kraftwerk – *Save Your Software*
(Bologna Concert 1990)
Computer Love, Radioactivity, Tour De France, The Robots, Boing Boom Tschak, Musique Non Stop

Kraftwerk – *Heute Abend*
(Various Concerts 1990-1991)
Numbers, Computer World, It's More Fun To Compute, Computer Love, The Model, Tour De France, Radioactivity, Trans-Europe Express, Abzug, Metal On Metal, The Robots, Robotronik, Pocket Calculator, Musique Non Stop, The Model [soundcheck], Pocket Calculator [soundcheck], Numbers, Computer World, Autobahn

Kraftwerk – *Non Stop*
(Solna Concert 1991)
Numbers, Computer World, Home Computer, Computer Love, The Model, Tour De France, Autobahn [edit], Radioactivity, Trans-Europe Express, Metal On Metal, Abzug, The Robots, Pocket Calculator, Musique Non Stop

Kraftwerk – *Neue Kraft*
(Copenhagen Concert 1991)
Numbers, Computer World, It's More Fun To Compute, Computer Love, The Model, Tour De France, Autobahn, Radioactivity, Trans-Europe Express, The Robots, Pocket Calculator, Musique Non Stop

Kraftwerk – *Düsseldorf*
(Düsseldorf Concert 1991)
Numbers, Computer World, It's More Fun To Compute, Home Computer, Computer Love, The Model, Tour De France, Autobahn, Radioactivity, Trans-Europe Express, Metal On Metal, Abzug, The Robots, Robotronik, Pocket Calculator, Musique Non Stop, Music Factory Megamix, Razormaid Gridlock Mix, Razormaid Sex Object Mix, Techno Pop [demo]

Kraftwerk – *Dynamo Deutschland*
(Various Concerts 1981-1991)
Numbers, Computer World, It's More Fun To Compute, Home
Computer, Computer Love, The Model, Tour De France, Autobahn,
Radioactivity, Trans-Europe Express, Pocket Calculator, The Robots,
Musique Non Stop, Numbers, Computer World, Metropolis, The
Model, Computer Love, Pocket Calculator, Radioactivity, Neon Lights,
Hall Of Mirrors, Showroom Dummies, Mini Calculateur

A number of bootlegs – recorded mainly from the BBC radio broadcast of
the event – also exist of Kraftwerk's appearance at Tribal Gathering,
including *Lebendige Menschen* which adds recordings made at the
Ludwigsburg concert in 1991. Similarly, there are a number of illicit
recordings such as *Lichtgestalten* which document the group's 1997
concerts in Linz and Karlsruhe. Finally, there are already numerous
bootlegs in existence relating to various dates on Kraftwerk's 1998 world
tour. These releases are unofficial and sound quality is highly variable.

References

Chapter One
1 Interview with Toby Manning, *Jockey Slut*, December 1997
2 Interview with Toby Manning, *Jockey Slut*, December 1997
3 Interview with Stuart Cosgrove, *The Face*, May 1988
4 Interview with Philipp Roser, *Rheinische Post*, 30th October 1991
5 Interview with Toby Manning, *Jockey Slut*, December 1997

Chapter Two
1 Interview with Mike Beecher, *Electronics & Music Maker*, September 1981
2 Interview with David Toop, *The Face*, February 1987
3 Interview with David Toop, *The Face*, February 1987
4 Interview with Mike Beecher, *Electronics & Music Maker*, September 1981
5 Interview with Mike Beecher, *Electronics & Music Maker*, September 1981
6 Interview with Paul Alessandrini, *Rock & Folk*, November 1976
7 Interview with Steve Taylor, *The Face*, March 1982
8 Interview with Dave Rimmer, *Smash Hits*, February 1982
9 Interview with *Musik Express*, April 1971
10 Interview with *Musik Express*, April 1971
11 Interview with *Face-Out*, Issue 6,1980
12 *Aktivität*, Issue 4, August 1993
13 Interview with *Face-Out*, Issue 6,1980
14 Interview with *Face-Out*, Issue 6,1980
15 Interview with *Face-Out*, Issue 6,1980
16 Interview with Mike Beecher, *Electronics & Music Maker*, September 1981
17 Interview with *Musik Express*, April 1971
18 Interview with David Toop, *The Face*, February 1987
19 Interview with Steve Taylor, *The Face*, March 1982
20 Interview with Andy Gill, *Mojo*, April 1997

21 Interview with Paul Alessandrini, *Rock & Folk*, November 1976

Chapter Three
1 Interview with Steve Taylor, *The Face*, March 1982
2 Interview with Paul Alessandrini, *Rock & Folk*, November 1976
3 Interview with Jean François Bizot, *Actuel*, November 1991
4 Interview with Paul Alessandrini, *Rock & Folk*, November 1976
5 Interview with Steve Taylor, *The Face*, March 1982
6 Interview with Dave Thompson, *Goldmine*, February 1998
7 Interview with Andy Gill, *Mojo*, April 1997
8 Interview with Paul Alessandrini, *Rock & Folk*, November 1976
9 Interview with Michael Dee, *Media För Musiker*, October 1991
10 Interview with Paul Alessandrini, *Rock & Folk*, November 1981
11 Interview with Saul Smaizys, *Triad*, June 1975

Chapter Four
1 Interview with Paul Alessandrini, *Rock & Folk*, November 1976
2 Interview with Paul Alessandrini, *Rock & Folk*, November 1976
3 Interview with Saul Smaizys, *Triad*, June 1975
4 Interview with Saul Smaizys, *Triad*, June 1975
5 Interview with Jonathan Miller, February 1998
6 Interview with Jonathan Miller, February 1998
7 Interview with Jonathan Miller, February 1998
8 Interview with Lester Bangs, *Creem*, September1975
9 Interview with Lester Bangs, *Creem*, September1975
10 Interview with Lester Bangs, *Creem*, September1975
11 Interview with Lester Bangs, *Creem*, September1975
12 Interview with Lester Bangs, *Creem*, September1975
13 Interview with Lester Bangs, *Creem*, September1975
14 Interview with Paul Alessandrini, *Rock & Folk*, November 1976
15 Interview with *Melody Maker*, 18th February, 1978
16 Interview broadcast on *BBC Radio 1*, July 1996
17 Interview with Paul Alessandrini, *Rock & Folk*, November 1976
18 Interview with Paul Alessandrini, *Rock & Folk*, November 1976
19 Interview with Geoff Barton, *Sounds*, 20th September, 1975
20 Interview with Karl Dallas, *Melody Maker*, 27th September, 1975
21 Interview with Karl Dallas, *Melody Maker*, 27th September, 1975

Chapter Five

1 Interview with Ingeborg Schober, *Musik Express*, 1976
2 Interview with Ingeborg Schober, *Musik Express*, 1976
3 Interview with Ingeborg Schober, *Musik Express*, 1976
4 Interview with Dessa Fox, *NME*, 10th January 1987
5 Interview broadcast on *BBC Radio 1*, July 1996
6 Interview with Paul Alessandrini, *Rock & Folk*, November 1976
7 Interview with Paul Alessandrini, *Rock & Folk*, November 1976
8 Interview with Michael Dee, *Media För Musiker*, October 1991
9 Interview with *Rock & Folk*, November 1981

Chapter Six

1 Interview with Paul Alessandrini, *Rock & Folk*, November 1976
2 Interview with Paul Alessandrini, *Rock & Folk*, November 1976
3 Interview with Andrew Darlington, *The Hot Press*, 6th August 1981
4 Interview with Paul Alessandrini, *Rock & Folk*, November 1976
5 Interview with Ray Townley, *Rolling Stone*, July 1975
6 Interview with Geoff Barton, *Sounds*, 20th September 1975
7 Interview with Cristopher Petit, *Melody Maker*, 4th November 1978
8 Interview with Cristopher Petit, *Melody Maker*, 4th November 1978
9 Anthony Haden-Guest, *Studio 54 The Legend*, Te Neues Publishing, New York, 1997
10 Anthony Haden-Guest, *Studio 54 The Legend*, Te Neues Publishing, New York, 1997
11 Interview with Dick Nusser, *Billboard*, 22nd October, 1977
12 Interview with Cristopher Petit, *Melody Maker*, 4th November 1978
13 Interview with Mark Sinker, *Music Technology*, 1991
14 Interview with Mark Sinker, *Music Technology*, 1991
15 Interview broadcast on *BBC Radio 1*, July 1996
16 Interview with Hal Synthetic, Sounds, November 26th 1977
17 Interview with Geoff Barton, *Sounds*, 20th September, 1975
18 Interview with Geoff Barton, *Sounds*, 20th September, 1975

Chapter Seven

1 Interview in *Future* #5, 5th October 1978
2 Interview with Hans Pfitzinger, *Sounds*, June 1975
3 Interview with Andrew Darlington, *The Hot Press*, 6th August 1981
4 Interview with Jonathan Miller, February 1998
5 Interview with Jonathan Miller, February 1998

6 Interview with Yves Adrien, *Rock & Folk*, June 1978

7 Interview in *Future* #5, 5th October 1978

8 Interview in *Future* #5, 5th October 1978

9 Interview with Yves Adrien, *Rock & Folk*, June 1978

10 Interview with Joe Stevens, *NME*, 24th December, 1977

11 Interview with Andrew Darlington, *The Hot Press*, 6th August 1981

12 Interview with Richard Robinson, *Hit Parader*, October 1978

13 Interview with Cristopher Petit, *Melody Maker*, 4th November 1978

14 Interview with Mike Beecher, *Electronics & Music Maker*, September 1981

15 Interview with Willi Andersen, *Fachblatt Musik-Magazin*, November 1991

16 Interview broadcast on *BBC Radio 1*, July 1996

17 Interview with Jean-Eric Perrin, *Rock & Folk*, November 1981

18 Interview with David Johnson, *The Face*, February 1983

19 Interview with Jean-Eric Perrin, *Rock & Folk*, November 1981

Chapter Eight

1 Interview in *Billboard*, 4th July 1981

2 Interview with Jonathan Miller, February 1998

3 Interview with Jim Aikin, *Keyboard*, March 1982

4 Interview with Jean-Eric Perrin, *Rock & Folk*, November 1981

5 Interview with Mike Beecher, *Electronics & Music Maker*, September 1981

6 Richard Williams, *The Times*, 1st July 1981

7 Interview with Andrew Darlington, *The Hot Press*, 6th August 1981

8 Interview with Charles McCardell, *Trouser Press*, November 1981

9 Interview with Mike Beecher, *Electronics & Music Maker*, September 1981

10 Interview with Jim Aikin, *Keyboard*, March 1982

11 Interview with Dave Rimmer, *Smash Hits*, 17th February 1982

12 Interview with Mike Beecher, *Electronics & Music Maker*, September 1981

13 Interview with Mike Beecher, *Electronics & Music Maker*, September 1981

14 Interview with John Gill, *Sounds*, 27th June 1981

15 Interview with Jean-Eric Perrin, *Rock & Folk*, November 1981

16 Interview with Jean-Eric Perrin, *Rock & Folk*, November 1981

17 Interview with Paul Wilkinson, *Aktivität* Issue 7, September 1995

18 Interview with Andrew Darlington, *The Hot Press*, 6th August 1981
19 Interview with Dave Rimmer, *Smash Hits*, 17th February 1982

Chapter Nine
 1 David Toop, *The Rap Attack*, Pluto Press, London 1984
 2 Interview with Mike Beecher, *Electronics & Music Maker*, September 1981
 3 Interview with Wolfgang Bongertz, *International Musician*, March 1980
 4 Interview with Jonathan Miller, February 1998
 5 Interview with Jonathan Miller, February 1998
 6 MTV *Party Zone* Special, May 1998
 7 Interview with Wolfgang Bongertz, *International Musician*, March 1980
 8 Interview with Jonathan Miller, February 1998
 9 Interview with Brian Chin, *Billboard*, 10th January 1987
10 Interview with Jonathan Miller, February 1998
11 Interview in *Mondo 2000*, 1991
12 Matthew Collin, *Altered State*, Serpent's Tail, London 1997
13 Interview with David Toop, *The Face*, February 1987

Chapter Ten
 1 Interview with Stuart Cosgrove, *Techno! The New Dance Sound Of Detroit*, Virgin Records, 1988
 2 Interview with Stuart Cosgrove, *Techno! The New Dance Sound Of Detroit*, Virgin Records, 1988
 3 Interview with Stuart Cosgrove, *Techno! The New Dance Sound Of Detroit*, Virgin Records, 1988
 4 Interview with Jonathan Miller, February 1998
 5 Interview with Jonathan Miller, February 1998
 6 Interview with Mark Dery, *Keyboard*, October 1991
 7 Interview with Mark Dery, *Keyboard*, October 1991
 8 Interview with Mark Dery, *Keyboard*, October 1991
 9 Interview with Jonathan Miller, February 1998
10 Interview with Jonathan Miller, February 1998
11 Interview with Mark Dery, *Keyboard*, October 1991
12 Interview with Mark Dery, *Keyboard*, October 1991
13 Interview with Mark Dery, *Keyboard*, October 1991
14 Interview with Mark Dery, *Keyboard*, October 1991

15 Interview with Frits Couwenberg, *KLEM* #59 (reprinted in *Aktivität*, Issue 4, August 1993)

16 Interview with Frits Couwenberg, *KLEM* #59 (reprinted in *Aktivität*, Issue 4, August 1993)

17 Interview with Frits Couwenberg, *KLEM* #59 (reprinted in *Aktivität*, Issue 4, August 1993)

18 Interview with Frits Couwenberg, *KLEM* #59 (reprinted in *Aktivität*, Issue 4, August 1993)

19 Interview with Mike Beecher, *Electronics & Music Maker*, September 1981

20 Interview with Mark Jenkins, *Future Music*, September 1993

21 Interview with Jonathan Miller, February 1998

22 Interview broadcast on *BBC Radio 1*, July 1996

23 David Toop, *The Times*, 24th July, 1991

24 Interview with Jean-Eric Perrin, *Rock & Folk*, November 1981

25 Preface to *Techno Style*, Martin Pesch and Markus Weisbeck, Edition Olms Zürich, 1995

26 John McCready, *Jockey Slut*, April/May 1997

27 Interview with Willi Andersen, *Fachblatt Musik-Magazin*, November 1991

28 Interview with Willi Andersen, *Fachblatt Musik-Magazin*, November 1991

29 Interview with Willi Andersen, *Fachblatt Musik-Magazin*, November 1991